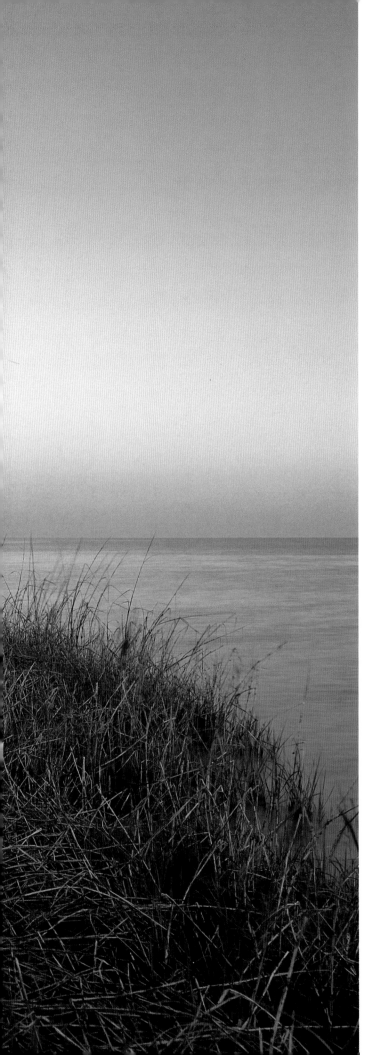

Lighthouses of the South

Your Guide to the Lighthouses of Virginia, North Carolina, South Carolina, Georgia, and Florida

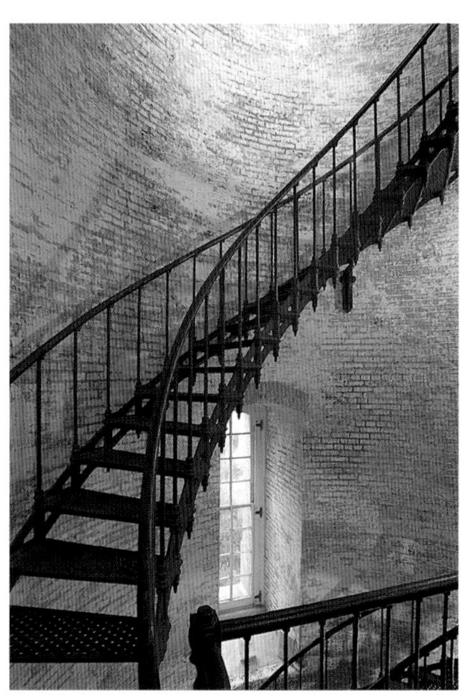

Text by Elinor De Wire
Photography by Daniel E. Dempster

A Pictorial Discovery Guide

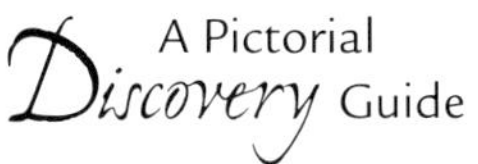

Voyageur Press

Edited by Kari Cornell
Designed by Maria Friedrich
Printed in China

04 05 06 07 08 5 4 3 2 1

Library of Congress Cataloging-in-Publication Data

De Wire, Elinor, 1953–
Lighthouses of the South : your guide to the lighthouses of Virginia, North Carolina, South Carolina, Georgia, and Florida / text by Elinor De Wire ; photographs by Daniel E. Dempster.
p. cm. — (A pictorial discovery guide)
Includes bibliographical references and index.
ISBN 0-89658-603-0 (hardcover)
1. Lighthouses—South Atlantic States. I. Title. II. Series.
VK1024.S52D429 2004
387.1'55'0975—dc22
2003015626

Distributed in Canada by Raincoast Books,
9050 Shaughnessy Street, Vancouver, B.C. V6P 6E5

Published by Voyageur Press, Inc.
123 North Second Street, P.O. Box 338
Stillwater, MN 55082 U.S.A.
651-430-2210, fax 651-430-2211
books@voyageurpress.com
www.voyageurpress.com

Frontispiece: *Like spokes on a giant wheel of light, the beams of Bodie Island Lighthouse pierce the misty North Carolina night. The beacon has marked Oregon Inlet on the Outer Banks since 1872.*

Title page: *As sunset ebbs over the Florida Panhandle, St. Marks Lighthouse prepares to greet the darkness that will soon descend. The 1842 tower is one of the oldest sentinels on the Gulf of Mexico.*

Title page, inset: *The cast-iron stairway of North Carolina's Currituck Beach Lighthouse curves elegantly upward along the inner wall of the 162-foot brick tower. Spiral stairs are the hallmark of tall lighthouses.*

Facing page: *A bright candy-stripe daymark against a backdrop of sand pines and palmetto scrub makes Sapelo Lighthouse easy to spot from sea. It has marked the sea road to Darien, Georgia, since 1820.*

Contents page: *Painted in alternating panels of black and white, the cast-iron Cape Henry Lighthouse has stood watch over the entrance to the Chesapeake Bay since 1882, when it replaced an earlier Colonial-era sentinel.*

Contents page, inset: *The view from inside the first-order lens of St. Augustine Lighthouse reveals a shimmering beehive of prisms and magnifying glass capable of transforming the light of a 100-watt bulb into beams visible twenty-seven miles at sea.*

Dedications

To the Tampa Bay Harbour Lights Collectors Club—a dedicated group of lighthouse preservationists for whom I have enormous affection.—ED

To my family and friends, who encourage and inspire me.—DED

Acknowledgments

The author wishes to thank the following individuals and organizations for their kind assistance in the preparation of this book. Dr. Robert Browning and the staff of the U.S. Coast Guard Archives, the Outer Banks Conservancy, the Outer Banks Lighthouse Society, Cullen Chambers and the Tybee Historical Society, Kathy Fleming and the folks at St. Augustine Lighthouse, Pat Morris and the crew of St. Simons Lighthouse, members of the Florida Lighthouse Association, Toby Brewer, Andrew Staub, and Connie Wiesehan of Anclote Keys Lighthouse, the Tarpon Springs Historical Society, Tom Taylor and the Reef Lights Foundation, Wayne Hawes and members of the Tampa Bay Harbour Lights Collectors Club, Bill Younger and the crew at Harbour Lights, Tim Harrison and Kathy Finnegan of the American Lighthouse Foundation, Wayne Wheeler of the U.S. Lighthouse Society, Cindy Herrick and the staff of the U.S. Coast Guard Academy Library, Paul O'Pecko and the staff of the Blunt White Library, the staff of the Mariners Museum, the staff and volunteers of Cape Hatteras National Seashore, Bob Trapani, Jeremy D'Entremont, Hib Casselberry, Paul Bradley, Derith Bennett, the "Lighthouse Nuts," the crew of the *Joshua Appleby*, and the men and women of the U.S. Coast Guard who keep southern waters safe. A special thank you goes to Kari Cornell for her patient and resourceful guidance during the editing process and to photographer Danny Dempster for collaborating with me on this project. His work speaks for itself, and I am honored to attach my words to his beautiful images. As always, I am grateful to my family for their continued love and support: Jonathan, my dear husband of thirty-one years and best friend, and Jessica, Kristin, Scott, and Rebecca, my wonderful children. —ED

Creating the images for this book wouldn't have been possible without the help of many people. First and foremost I want to thank my wife, Denise, and my children, Jason and Julia, for their patience and understanding. During the two years I spent photographing the lighthouses in this book I would often be on the road for weeks at a time. I want them to know how much I appreciate their patience and understanding.

I also need to thank the following people for all of their invaluable help on this project. Dennis Baker, Gary Wayne Brownley, and Captain A. J. Hurst of Mathews County, Virginia; Erik Lovestrand and Lisa Bailey of the Appalachicola Estuarine Research Reserve in Appalachicola, Florida; Captain Sandy Vermont of Georgetown, South Carolina; Wayne and Judi Hawes of Tampa, Florida; Toby Brewer of Dunedin, Florida; Pam and Ralphie Lefcourt of West Palm Beach, Florida; George Walker and Tracey Alexander of Sapelo Island, Georgia; John H. Johnson of Merritt Island, Florida; Earl Richards at the Old Point Comfort Lighthouse; Petty Officer First Class Christopher E. Tucker at the St. Johns lighthouses; Audrey B. Conner of Virginia Beach, Virginia; Joan Shinnick at St. Simons Island Lighthouse; Jane Oakley at the Bald Head (Cape Fear) Lighthouse; Captain Dennis Barbour who boated me out to the Cape Lookout Lighthouse; and Executive Petty Officer BM1 William K Schroeder II who allowed me to photograph the Oak Island lighthouse. I would also like to thank the entire staff at both St. Augustine and Ponce de Leon lighthouses. All employees went out of their way to be helpful as I shot photographs of both of these beautiful lights. I would also like to thank Kari Cornell for her guidance and advice and Elinor De Wire for her wonderful prose. –DED

When Ernest Hemingway visited Key West for the first time, he fell in love with its lighthouse. He returned years later and purchased a home across from the old brick tower. The beacon of the 1858 lighthouse shone in Hemmingway's bedroom each night, a balm for his bouts of depression. The sentinel was deactivated in 1969 and the compound is now a museum.

Photographic Notes

The images in this book were created using Nikon 35mm and Mamiya medium format equipment. I use Nikon F100 bodies in addition to Nikon lenses ranging from 17mm to 500mm. By adding a 1.4x teleconverter to my 500mm lens, I obtained the effective focal length of 700mm. I also used a Nikon 28mm perspective control lens to avoid the keystoning effect that normally occurs in architectural photography. When possible, I also used a Mamiya 645 Pro body and lenses ranging from 35mm to 420mm. Nearly all of the images were shot with the camera mounted on a Gitzo 320 Studex tripod with a Bogen 3039 head. I shot all of the images in this book with Fuji film. Almost all of the images were shot on Fuji Velvia transparency film, and I used Fuji Provia for the rest. The Velvia provided the rich, saturated color that I prefer in my landscapes. When I needed a lower contrast film or when people were dominant in the image, I switched to the Provia. Some of the lighthouses required a bit of a hike, so I carried medium format and 35mm bodies plus a wide assortment of lenses in a Tenba photo backpack. I also used other Tenba bags for additional equipment when I worked out of my vehicle.

Oldest operating light tower in North Carolina, Ocracoke Lighthouse was built in 1823, replacing an 1800 tower that had been destroyed by lightning. It remains on duty as the centerpiece of Ocracoke Island, famous for its pirate legends and wild ponies.

Contents

PROLOGUE

A Light Worth Saving

BETTER TO LIGHT A CANDLE THAN CURSE THE DARKNESS.
Chinese Proverb

Anclote Keys Lighthouse, framed by palmetto scrub, long-leaf pines, Brazilian pepper, and sabal palms, rises tall at the end of a long wooden boardwalk. The contrast of new walkway and old sentinel is quickly evident on this warm morning in late May 2002. Wayne Hawes, president of the Tampa Bay Harbour Lights Collectors Club (TBHLCC), stops to inspect the boardwalk and offer his appreciation for its sturdiness to the crew putting on the finishing touches. Hawes' group, a small contingent of collectors of fine lighthouse ceramics, is part of the "Relight the Light Committee." Their focus for several years has been raising money to restore, preserve, and interpret the century-old Anclote Keys Lighthouse.

Hawes pauses a moment to take in the ambience of South Florida at its most pristine, then snaps a few pictures:

"I've seen it dozens of times now and have hundreds of photos of it," he says. "But standing so tall and strong out here in the wilderness, even after all it's been through . . . well, it just gives me the shivers."

Emotion runs high among lighthouse preservationists, even for a shattered hulk like this one. Anclote Keys Light's rusted exterior, broken windows, and empty lantern speak of years of neglect. Its bent door, sledgehammer dents, and graffiti reflect rampant vandalism. A tree struggles to grow from a crack under the entrance step. The concrete pad beneath the tower is brittle and stained, and flecks of rusted metal dapple its surface. The walls of the 1894 brick oilhouse have collapsed, and many of its fallen bricks are missing, hauled away by some visitor-turned-thief. Only the foundations remain where two tidy nineteenth-century lightkeepers' homes once stood.

Accompanying Hawes is Toby Brewer, a longtime resident of the area and assistant park manager for the Gulf Islands Geo-Park, where the lighthouse stands. It was Brewer who brought the plight of the lighthouse to the attention of the TBHLCC and convinced them to adopt it as a group project.

"It has important things to say to us today, lessons to teach us about living simple and looking out for each other," Brewer believes.

Anclote Keys Lighthouse and its wild environs are a living piece of "old-time Florida," before time-shares, big hotels, theme parks, and tour boats. Its keepers were among the first residents of the area—rugged pioneers with the mettle to endure loneliness and deprivation and also to enjoy the pleasures of life on a semitropical island. Brewer feels a kinship with them:

"I like the quiet here, just the chatter of birds and insects and the rustle of wind in the trees and brush. Sometimes I climb the tower and look out over the water. It looks painted, it's so blue. It's exciting to walk in the keepers' footsteps, to think that they did these same things a hundred years ago. It would be great if this place could be restored so everyone could experience this, at least in a small way."

The vicarious experience is surely the better one. Life on the key was demanding when the lighthouse first went into service. The town of Tarpon Springs was a tiny rural

The disheveled and time-worn skeleton tower of the 1887 Anclote Keys Lighthouse awaits restoration on a lonely islet five miles off Tarpon Spring, Florida. A new boardwalk carries the promise of a brighter future, but efforts to refurbish the lighthouse must wait until additional money is raised.

community on the sparsely settled mainland, a five-mile boat row for the lightkeepers. Heat and mosquitoes plagued the lighthouse families; rattlesnakes and alligators were a constant worry with children on the island. Impoverished soil and intense heat made gardening a challenge. Fresh water had to be caught on the roofs of the houses during rainstorms and stored in a cistern. A supply ship was scheduled to visit every few months, but its rounds were seldom timely. Even as late as the 1950s, when Coast Guard crews were still living at the station, tending the light was considered difficult duty.

Seamen and merchants first suggested a lighthouse for Anclote Keys in the 1820s, due to its prominent position about halfway between Key West and Pensacola and its obvious boon to shipping headed into the burgeoning port of Tampa. Thirty-one other sites in the Florida Territory were deemed more important, however, and it was not until 1879 that plans began to move forward. In that year, state representative Samuel Hope, who had a home in the new town of Tarpon Springs at the mouth of the Anclote River, pressed Congress for funds for the lighthouse. It took six years before Congress responded with an adequate appropriation of $35,000. One-third of the funds went towards fabrication of the tubular design, begun in October 1886 at the Colwell Ironworks in New York City and delivered to Anclote Keys six months later.

The lighthouse tender *Arbutus*, a work ship in the employ of the U.S. Lighthouse Board, brought work crews to the key to assemble the lighthouse and build two houses for the lightkeepers. Crews completed the station in only three months, and on the night of September 15, 1887, the light was inaugurated by principle keeper James Gardner and his assistant Samuel Hope, Jr., son of the politician who had urged its construction. Gardner and Hope earned annual salaries of $600 and $400 respectively to tend the oil lamps, which were amplified by a third-order flashing lens manufactured in Paris. The lens's opulent prisms and brass framework had to be kept immaculately clean and, to properly revolve the lens, its small chariot wheels had to be kept well-oiled. A clockwork system, complete with weights suspended in the tower, kept the apparatus turning. The keepers alternated watches throughout the night and wound the weights every four hours.

Mosquitoes were the bane of Anclote's lightkeepers. Smudge pots smoldered to repel them, and cheesecloth was nailed over windows in hot weather to admit the breeze but not the bugs. Palmetto switches did double duty as swatters and fans when the most sweltering weather hit. "Mosquitoes very bad. Hot and sultry," Gardner wrote a month into his assignment. He disliked the duty and was gone within a year. A succession of men followed, including more relatives of Samuel Hope, no doubt politically placed. James Baggett arrived in 1888 as an assistant and took charge a year later. Only six days after his appointment as principle keeper, he sadly penned in the logbook: "October 6, 1889—Baby was taken sick at 5 p.m." The next day's entry read: "Baby boy died this morning at 2:30 o'clock. Keeper and wife went over [to the mainland] to bury him today." Clara Baggett gave birth to another baby in 1891, and the couple decided she would live ashore where a doctor was more accessible.

By this time, twenty-one-year-old Robert Meyer had arrived and would remain forty-four years—the longest tenure of Anclote's many keepers and one of the longest career records for the entire lighthouse service. Meyer witnessed many changes to the station and its surroundings. In 1891, the sponge industry blossomed nearby in Tarpon Springs, underscoring the importance of the lighthouse. That same year, Baggett resigned and Meyer was promoted to principle keeper. In addition, the Lighthouse Board changed the light to a kerosene lamp, making it necessary to construct a brick oilhouse on the island to store the incendiary fuel. Meyer brought his new bride to the lighthouse and began raising a family.

Modern-day keepers of the light, park ranger Toby Brewer (left) and Florida Lighthouse Association President Wayne Hawes visit the Anclote Keys Lighthouse often to monitor its condition. Unless restoration begins soon, the tower may irreparably deteriorate.

Though Anclote Keys Lighthouse is badly rusted and corroded, the star-shaped ornament above the entrance hints at the beacon's former beauty.

Years of neglect and vandalism have taken a toll on every part of the Anclote Keys Lighthouse. Graffiti mars its walls, shards of rust lie at its base, and the door to the central column of stairs has been torn off.

The Meyers raised pigs on the island; kept a small garden; caught fish, turtles, shrimp, and crabs in the waters around the key; and made jelly from the guavas that Cuban fishermen brought as gifts. Meyer's daughter Betty, born in 1914, recalled that the fishermen always sang as they sailed by Anclote Keys. She spent her days swimming, fishing, picnicking, collecting shells, catching butterflies, and monitoring the activities of a red snake that lived under the dock. The mangroves provided the perfect hiding place when imaginary pirates attacked, and a four-inch kerosene pipe that ran from the dock to the lighthouse became a balance beam of sorts for a young girl dreaming of becoming a dancer.

In 1903, the Lighthouse Board changed the light to an incandescent oil vapor beacon. Tourism was on the rise in Tarpon Springs, and the lighthouse had become a popular destination. Tourists would sometimes climb to the top of the towering lighthouse to admire the view. One such visitor from Tarpon Springs was enamored of the lighthouse and came to the station to see the newfangled apparatus. He underestimated the tower's height and died of heart failure after the climb. During pleasant weather, Meyer and his assistants could expect a daily parade of curious visitors. They dutifully donned dress uniforms and escorted groups to the top of the tower. To preserve privacy for their families, they built a public picnic area near the beach and dug a path to it from the dock. This addition reduced the number of strangers stopping by the lighthouse kitchen in expectation of a meal, a commonplace problem for lightkeepers at remote stations.

Keepers had to maintain careful watch over the stretch of ocean between the lighthouse and shore. Reports to the Lighthouse Inspector in Key West were replete with instances of rescues. The keepers pulled a man and a woman from the water after their boat capsized, and brought them to safety. After a hurricane left two sponge fishermen floating aimlessly for weeks in a damaged boat, keepers also towed them to safety. A summer rainstorm caused two vessels to founder, and keepers rescued all aboard and gave them shelter at the lighthouse until they could be taken ashore. The outcome of such mishaps wasn't always cheerful, however: in 1904 the keepers retrieved the bodies of five drowned sailors and took them to Tarpon Springs for burial.

In 1920, the lighthouse crew came under the scrutiny of Florida's federal prohibition officer, who accused the keepers of using the beacon to assist rumrunners. An investigation turned up no evidence, and the public blamed accusations on malcontent mainlanders who disliked the lightkeepers. By this time, Meyer was caring for a number of small navigation lights leading into the Anclote River, while his assistant Thomas Moody tended the Anclote Keys Light full-time.

Meyer retired in 1933 and handed the lighthouse keys to J. L. Pippin. Pippin was on duty when World War II began, along with three Coast Guardsmen assigned to watch for enemy submarines from the top of Anclote Keys Lighthouse. The "Coasties" lived in the assistant lightkeeper's house, which had been unoccupied since the beacon's automation in 1923. Young Coast Guard petty officer Andrew Staab, now living in Tarpon Springs, remembers the wartime atmosphere in 1943: "We stood watch, made out reports, played cards, ate, slept. We never saw any subs. It was pretty monotonous." There was little socializing with keeper Pippin or his wife: "They were odd . . . loners. I guess that's why they took the job," Staab recalled.

Pippin departed in 1943, but Coast Guard personnel remained at the station until 1952, primarily to keep a presence on the island during the postwar years. When they left, Anclote Keys Light was rigged to run automatically and began a steady structural decline. In 1984 the Coast Guard decided the light was too expensive to maintain, so they removed the beacon and darkness enshrouded the key. Arsonists set fire to the houses, and vandals shot out the lantern windows and defaced the tower. There was talk of razing the lighthouse. It was an eyesore and a liability.

The historic old sentinel stood a forlorn watch as a daymark until the early 1990s, when a Tarpon Springs businesswoman came to its rescue. "I couldn't believe anyone would let that piece of history be lost," Pat McSparren recalls. "We live in such a disposable society. This was something worth saving."

McSparren and her husband, who ran a local shop in Tarpon Springs, established the Relight the Light Committee and set about raising money. The effort gained moderate interest, then stalled and had nearly foundered when Toby Brewer gave his slide show about the lighthouse to the TBHLCC. Sighs erupted around the room and eyes misted as Brewer poignantly recounted the lighthouse's long history, and images of a rusted, forgotten old relic of Florida history appeared on the screen. Once called the "Angel of Mercy" by Tarpon Springs fishermen, the lighthouse needed the compassion and care of a modern world in order to survive.

Where some saw ruins, the McSparrens, Wayne Hawes, Toby Brewer, and their compatriots in the TBHLCC saw a lighthouse that deserved to be saved. They resolved to return it to its former glory as an active beacon and create a new role for it as a historic site. Like its namesake key, Anclote, which means "anchor" in Spanish, the people determined to salvage the light were moored by conviction and commitment. The tower itself is the tangible part of their rescue effort, but more important is what the light represents.

"There were people here long ago who did a job few of us would ever do today," says Wayne Hawes, looking up pensively through the rusted framework of the old lighthouse to the cerulean sky overhead. "They served in a way we can only imagine. There's something about that kind of obligation that touches me. I think it has something to say to all of us."

He sighs and wipes beads of perspiration from his forehead with the back of his hand. The sound of workers' hammers echoes in the distance as the walkway grows longer. By the end of the week, Hawes reckons it will be complete and will stretch all the way from the lighthouse to the pier. He rubs his hand over the railing. The smell and feel and look of its new wood make him smile.

"As soon as this is done, we'll start planning restoration of the lighthouse and trying to get the funding in place," he says.

It's truly a light worth saving.

During the tenure of keeper Robert Meyer, a brick walkway led from the dock to Anclote Keys Lighthouse, and two handsome wooden keepers' homes stood behind the tower. Meyer's daughter Betty was born at the station in 1914, a year after this U.S. Bureau of Lighthouses photo was taken. (Photograph courtesy of the U.S. Coast Guard Archives)

CHAPTER 1

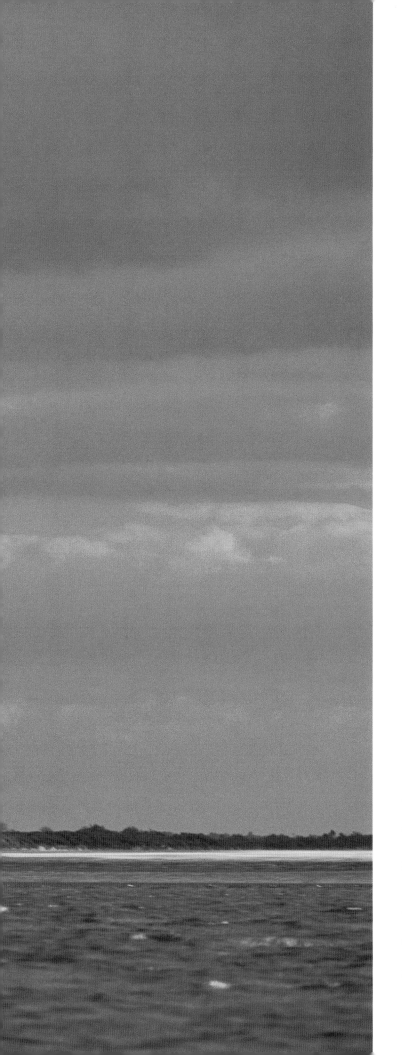

A Light in the Darkness

MANY CANDLES CAN BE KINDLED FROM ONE, WITHOUT DIMINISHING IT.
Talmud

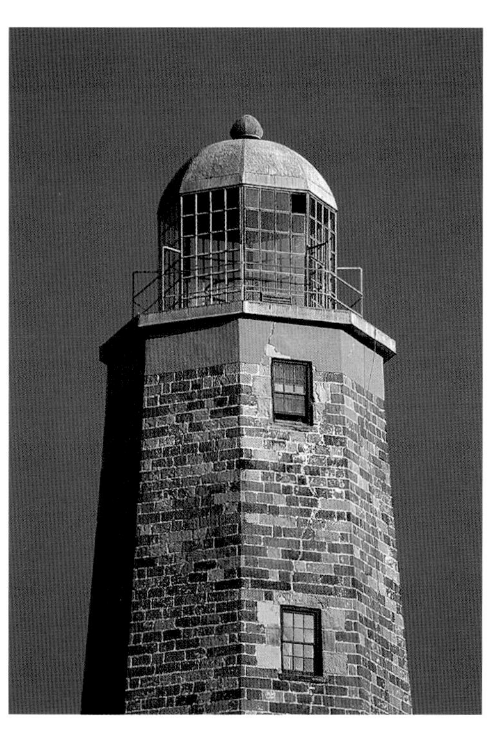

Left: *Like a ragged old soldier that refuses to give up his watch, the 1876 Morris Island Lighthouse stands a forlorn vigil over the entrance to Charleston Harbor. Erosion has reduced the once large island to a sandbar, and the lighthouse has been abandoned. Its predecessor, a stone tower built in 1767, was the first official lighthouse to shine over the South.*

Above: *A lighthouse for Cape Henry was proposed as early as the 1720s, but the tower was not completed until after the Revolutionary War. Had it been in service in 1781, it might have aided British ships trying to enter the Chesapeake Bay and thus changed the course of history.*

The first Westerners to encounter America's southern coast were delighted by its tawny beaches, barrier islands, and sandy estuaries, rife with valuable resources desperately needed in Europe. The many waterways accessing the interior promised an even greater bounty of riches. Yet to reach them, vessels faced myriad perils. The few maps available were unreliable, for this vast coastline was in constant flux, washing away one shoal only to replace it with another, redrawing its outline year by year.

The great arm of the Outer Banks, stretching like an impenetrable barrier from the Chesapeake Bay to South Carolina, proved so dangerous that it would eventually earn the ominous title "Graveyard of the Atlantic." The mouth of the Savannah River was riddled with shallows, leading Spanish explorers to dub it *Bahia de los Bahas*—Bay of Shoals. Cape Canaveral was equally daunting as the northbound Gulf Stream slipped past it and pushed ships shoreward. At Florida's southern tip, coral reefs lay submerged in turquoise shallows, ready to rip open the belly of any unwary ship.

The Spanish established the garrison of San Marcos at Apalachicola Bay in the late sixteenth century and ordered a "watch tower beacon" built at the mouth of the Apalachee River about 1678. Two soldiers and several Apalachee Indians tended the beacon, lighting it only as needed to guide ships and repel pirates. It was surely a crude affair, for when the French explorer Charlevoix sailed past in 1722, he wrote of seeing "fires on the continent . . . *balizes* or seamarks, which the Spaniards directed us to follow." These probably were bonfires or wooden poles supporting fire baskets, but only a few years later, the Spanish built a stone tower on the west side of the river entrance and, if a light shone from it, it was the first sentinel in the South. During a U.S. government survey of West Florida in 1799, cartographer Andrew Ellicott provided the only documented account concerning this lighthouse when upon seeing it in ruins he noted, "On the top there appears to be a light-house, but from the condition of the bay, being so shoal and full of oyster banks . . . it appears to have been unnecessary."

Sailing by the stars and the seat of their pants, shiploads of optimistic settlers began arriving in America beginning in the early 1600s. Despite the rigors of a trans-Atlantic voyage and the danger of making landfall on an unknown coast, more than a century passed before a lighthouse was built in the colonies. In 1716, the port of Boston held a lottery to raise money for a sentinel. A small stone tower with a chandelier of tallow candles in

Graveyard of Ships

Full fathom five thy father lies,
Of his bones are coral made.
William Shakespeare (1564–1616)
The Tempest

The Outer Banks of North Carolina have an ominous reputation. Nearly 5,000 documented shipwrecks have occurred along this long stretch of barrier shore in the past 500 years. Some lie buried deep in the sand, while others have been exhumed by wind and water, like skeletons arisen from their graves.

On the Outer Banks, the slightest change in weather or smallest error in navigation can result in catastrophe. The Gulf Stream, pushing northward at a clip of up to five knots, hugs the shoreline at Cape Hatteras. Its companion, the Labrador Current, lies just east of it, moving south at nearly an equal pace. The currents create two distinct directions of sea traffic that are easily disrupted by freak thunderstorms, powerful hurricanes, and the mists that arise as a result of the disparate temperatures of water.

For most of recorded history, the Outer Banks have existed as three distinct islands—Bodie, Hatteras, and Ocracoke—which enclose Pamlico Sound and shift endlessly to open and close channels and reveal a number of sea-washed surprises. Each island has its own lighthouse marking specific navigational perils and entry points into the quieter sounds and important rivers of the Carolina coast. The beacons were beneficent additions to this unfriendly shore, additions which saved many lives and property, but not everyone was pleased with their helpful beams.

One of the earliest occupations on the Outer Banks was wrecking, the practice of salvaging shipwrecks. It was a lucrative business that still operates today, although with much less activity and profit than in the days of sail. Although wreckers traditionally perform a critical service for seaman and their insurance companies, one wrecker in particular has come down through history with a nefarious reputation that not only tarnished the good name of others in the business, but bequeathed a nefarious title as well.

Nags Head, a well-known tourist town on Bodie Island, took its name from the cruel habit of this unscrupulous wrecker. Because the wrecker could only profit from such tragedies on the darkest of nights, he despised moonlit nights when ships could see to safely navigate around deadly shoals and sandbanks. This earned him the nickname "mooncusser." On moonless nights, he displayed a false light to lure ships onto perils so he could profit from the tragedy. The bogus light, called a "Judas Lantern," was hung from the neck of an old horse. The blameless nag was paraded up and down the beach with the lantern swinging to and fro. If a ship's captain spied the light, he assumed it was another ship, rocking safely at anchor, and steered for it. The result was a wreck, which the mooncusser quickly boarded and claimed. The beach where he did this foul deed came to be called Nags Head.

Even after lighthouses went on duty, shipwrecks continued. In the 1870s, the U.S. Lifesaving Service was established, which built lifesaving stations at intervals along the Outer Banks to provide assistance to the shipwrecked. Each station had a crew of surfmen who trained in lifesaving methods daily and patrolled the beaches day and night, watching for ships in distress. They worked alongside the lighthouse keepers, whose job was to prevent calamities, but when these occurred, the lifesavers came to the rescue.

Sometimes lifesavers used a surfboat to row out to a wreck and rescue survivors. When the seas were too rough, they shot a lifeline to the vessel and rigged up a curious vehicle called a lifecar. Lifesavers used the device, which was like a submarine attached to a line, to pull survivors through the surf. The ride through the tumultuous waves often was rocky, but castaways remained dry inside the little metal car and made it safely ashore.

With the advent of modern navigation systems, fewer shipwrecks have occurred off the Outer Banks; less than a dozen have been recorded in the past twenty years. But it remains one of the nation's most dangerous coasts. All of its old lighthouses are still active, as well as a new one on the Frying Pan Shoals, attesting to the need to keep this shore well-lighted. Maritime historians and old sailors enjoy an amicable dispute about the location of the nation's most terrible shipwreck coast. Some claim the entrance to the Columbia River between Oregon and Washington is the worst. Others vote for the backside beach of Cape Cod, New Jersey's Long Beach Island, the south shore of Long Island, and the Florida Reef. In the end, the Outer Banks get the most votes, holding firmly to the title "Graveyard of Ships."

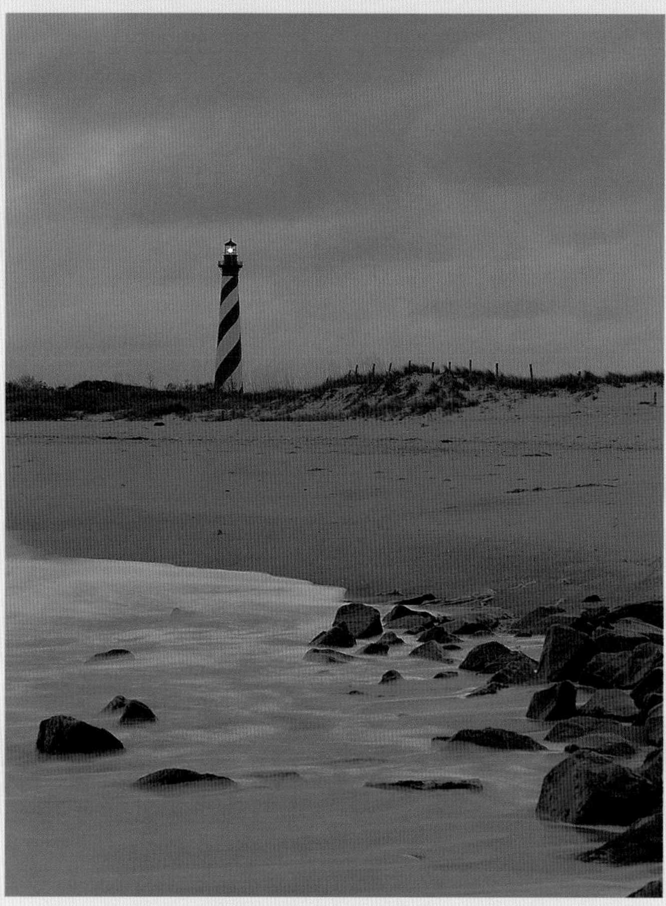

Despite the dangers, no lighthouse marked the Outer Banks until the first Cape Hatteras Lighthouse was built in 1803. Damaged in the Civil War, it was replaced by the present tower in 1870.

Ships faced a plethora of perils as they sailed along the southern coast, and colonists quickly discovered lighthouses were needed in many spots. Waters off the Outer Banks of North Carolina earned the grisly nickname "Graveyard of the Atlantic." More than 2,000 shipwrecks have occurred here, some occasionally uncovered by shifting sands.

its lantern was erected on Little Brewster Island at the harbor entrance. Only a year later the first lightkeeper, his wife, daughter, and a black slave drowned while returning to the island in a boat.

About this same time, Governor Alexander Spotswood of Virginia spoke before the Virginia House of Burgesses on behalf of ship owners and merchants, imploring that a lighthouse be established on Cape Henry at the entrance to the Chesapeake Bay. The project was deemed worthy, provided the lighthouse could be funded and maintained by a duty levied on passing ships and that "the Province of Maryland will contribute" to the building and upkeep of the structure. The Board of Trade in England did not approve the levy of dues, despite Spotswood's argument that a lighthouse was crucial to the burgeoning Chesapeake commerce. A second proposal was brought a decade later, but again it failed.

A Daymark for Savannah

In 1733, General James Oglethorpe and a small group of settlers made landfall at the Savannah River and sailed about fifteen miles inland where they established the colony of Georgia. Oglethorpe soon recognized the need for a navigational aid at the river entrance to assist commerce in this "land of liberty and plenty." He chose an island the Savana Indians called Tybee, meaning "salt," and ordered Noble Jones to oversee construction of a daymark—a tall, unlit tower to serve as a lookout and a landfall marker. Several families moved to the island to homestead, among them master carpenter William Blythemann, who was to oversee the building of the tower. But a year passed with little to show for the effort. Rumor circulated that the Tybee community had grown indolent and were indulging in too much rum. Oglethorpe responded by jailing Blythemann and threatening his crew of workmen. The ploy worked. Once released, Blythemann completed the ninety-foot, octagonal, cedar and brick tower in only a few months.

Life on Tybee Island was difficult for the pioneer families. Nearby marshes bred hordes of mosquitoes. Scouring wind and waves took their toll along the coast. Erosion changed the shape of the river estuary, prompting Oglethorpe to hire a pilot to help ships enter the river and safely navigate its twisting course into Savannah. Erosion ate away at the residents' homes and the watch tower. By 1741, changes in the shoreline left the tower perilously close to the tide line, and a hurricane swept it away that summer.

Undaunted, Oglethorpe called for the building of a new wooden tower, ninety-four-feet tall and shingled, with a flagstaff on its pinnacle to be used for signaling. From time to time, someone on watch may have hung a lantern in the tower at night to serve as a beacon, but no records exist to substantiate this. The architect and builder, Thomas Sumner, was praised for his work, which Oglethorpe called "much the best building of that kind in America." Sumner was rewarded with a large parcel of land south of Savannah. But once again, the builders had placed the tower too close to shore, and the island's restless sands undermined the foundation. While Georgians struggled to keep a daymark at their most critical port, their neighbors to the north built a true lighthouse.

The First Southern Sentinels

Albemarle Point, at the confluence of the Ashley and Cooper rivers, was settled in 1670 and eventually became the city of Charleston, South Carolina. Colonists kept a "fier ball" of oakum (rags) soaked in pitch burning in an iron crib on an island off the point and charged vessels a small duty as they passed the crude beacon. Morris Island, as it would later be called, had restless sands. By 1700, the channel into Charleston had widened and split around the island. A few years later a storm surge sliced the island itself into three smaller isles. Storms further sculpted the shore and, toward the end of the 1700s, reconnected the disparate islands. Throughout these years, the crude beacon light continued to shine. In 1716, tallow candles replaced the flaming bale of oakum, indicating that some sort of enclosure had been built for the light. Candles soon gave way to oil lamps.

The colonial government ordered a lighthouse built on Morris Island in 1750, but could find no money for the project. Again, in 1757, an act of the colonial legislature called for a lighthouse to replace the feeble lamps. Money was allocated but somehow went for construction of a new church steeple, which itself was considered a beacon by reason of the oil lamps hanging in it. As traffic into Charleston increased, much of it from England, ship owners bitterly complained about the lack of a decent light at the harbor entrance. England responded this time, hiring bricklayer Samuel Cordy to design and build a new tower. Its cornerstone bore the inscription: "The First Stone of this Beacon was laid on the 30th of May 1767 in the seventh year of his Majesty's Reign, George the III." A few months later, lard oil lamps lit up the forty-three-foot brick tower of the seventh lighthouse built in the American colonies and the first official lighthouse in the South.

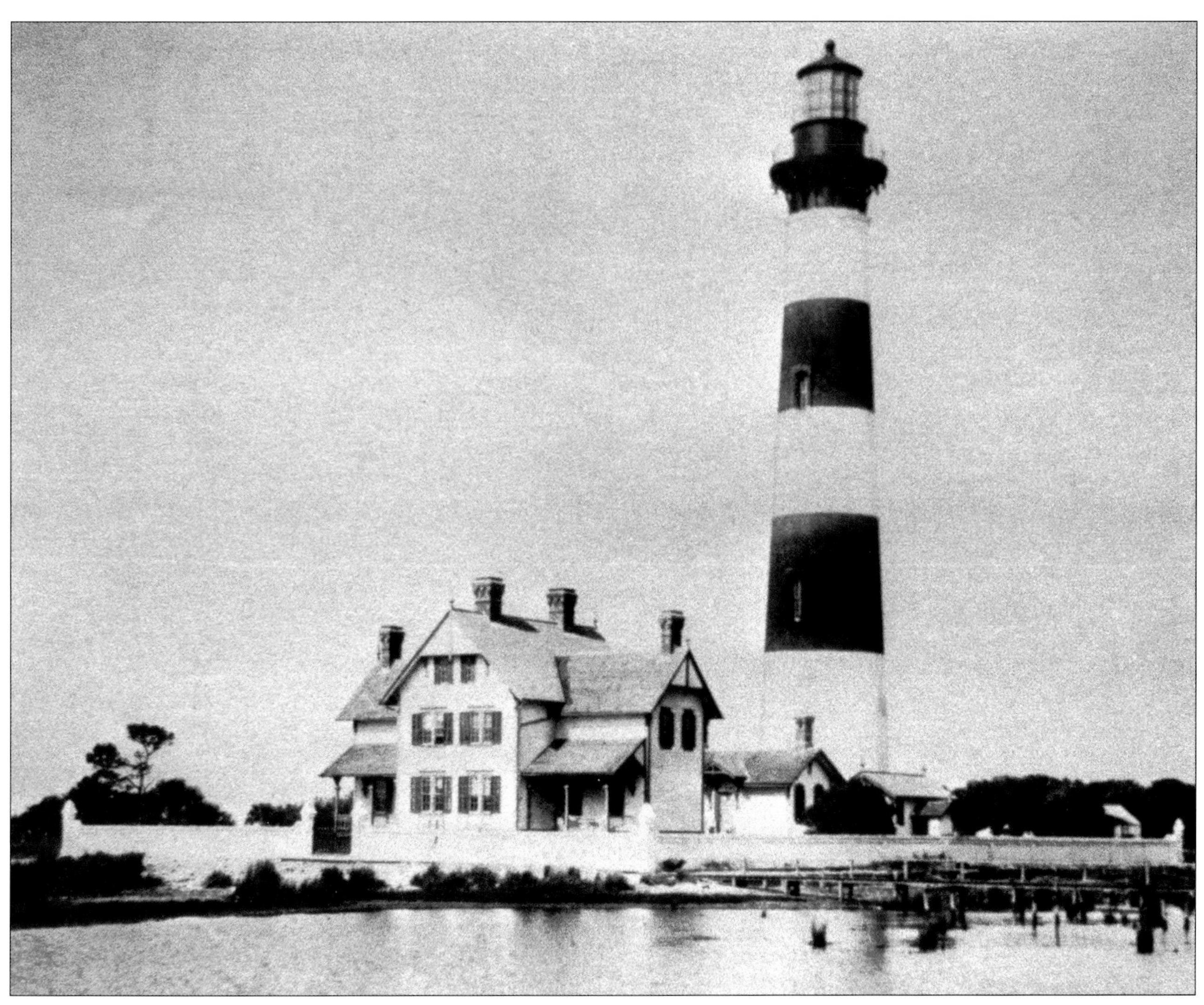

Charleston, South Carolina's first navigational aid was a crude "fier ball" of oakum soaked in pitch. Its first lighthouse was built on Morris Island in 1767 and served until the Civil War, when Confederate troops damaged it. The replacement, built in 1876, was a pastoral assignment for lightkeepers. This view from the 1880s shows the farm-like compound and a seawall that protected it. Erosion has since consumed the entire island and only the tower remains. (Photograph courtesy of the National Archives)

Above: *In the mid-eighteenth century, the only navigational aid for the Chesapeake Bay was a simple oil lamp that glowed from a private home at Old Point Comfort, Virginia, a critical turning point for ships. Nearly half a century would pass before lighthouses would cast beams of light over the bay, first at Cape Henry in 1791 and later at Old Point Comfort in 1801. Both light towers were sturdy octagonal stone designs that still stand today, but only Old Point Comfort remains in operation.*

Facing page: *Looking much different today than when it was established in 1773, Tybee Island Lighthouse wears a daymark of black-and-white bands. Historians call it one of the most complete, extant old-time light stations. It is now a museum in the care of the Tybee Island Historical Society.*

Back in Virginia, arguments were mounting between colonists and England over the construction of a lighthouse at Cape Henry. Although a private beacon was maintained in Hampton Roads at Old Point Comfort, it was probably no more than an oil lamp placed in a window or hung from a post, and the mouth of Chesapeake Bay desperately needed a coastal sentinel. It was the South's busiest ingress. Numerous petitions for the light had failed, but in 1772, the House of Burgesses in Virginia and the British Admiralty reached an agreement and work began. Barracks for the construction crew were built and 4,000 tons of stone were shipped to the site, not far from where the first Jamestown settlers had raised a cross of gratitude in 1607 for their safe voyage from England. The foundation was complete and a few stone courses had been placed when funds ran out. Additional money was requested, but when the American Revolution erupted in 1775, workers abandoned the job. Piles of undressed granite and the foundation of the would-be lighthouse soon disappeared under blowing sand.

Meanwhile, in Georgia, the second daymark tower at Tybee had collapsed when storm waves reached its base. A site was chosen farther back from sea and a new ninety-five-foot brick tower with wooden stairs was completed in 1773. It was sturdy, and this time plans included a lantern and beacon of spermaceti candles. A year later in Florida, the British established a "beacon" at Mosquito Inlet, now called Ponce de Leon Inlet. The exact nature of the original structure is unclear, for the word "beacon" was sometimes used to mean a daymarker. The British Admiralty hired a man named Angelo Vackiere, agreeing to pay him £24 per year to maintain the "beacon at Musquito Inlet and for assisting vessels over the Bar."

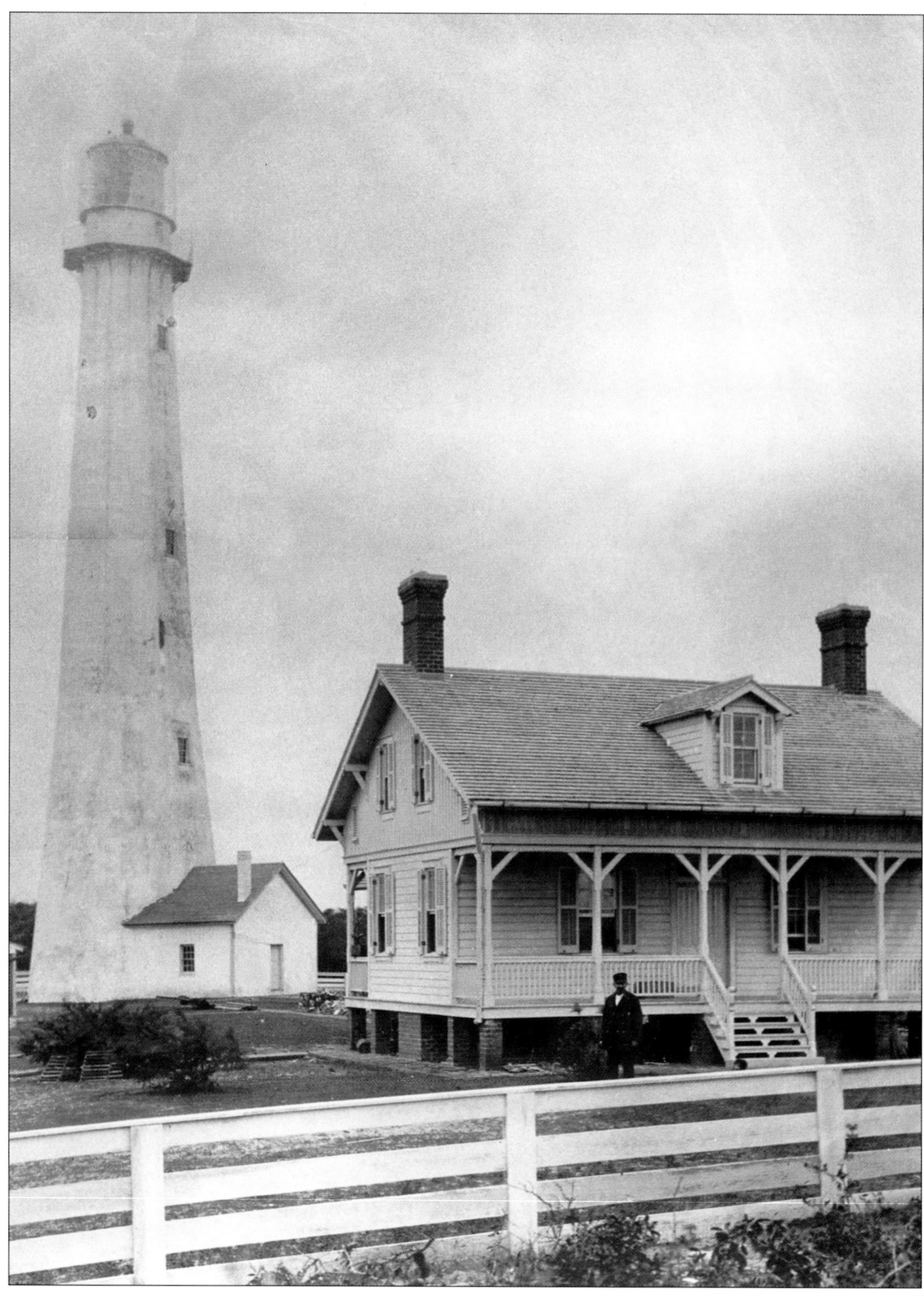

A wooden lookout tower served as the first navigational aid for the port of Savannah, Georgia, in the late 1730s. The first lighthouse in Georgia, a brick tower with a wooden stairway and wooden lantern, replaced the wooden structure in 1773. The beacon's spermaceti candles caused a fire late in 1792 and the tower had to be rebuilt. In June 1885, Major Jared O. Smith, engineer for the sixth lighthouse district, snapped a photo of the station and its keeper. The flared bottom third of the tower is thought to be from the original lighthouse. (Photograph courtesy of the National Archives)

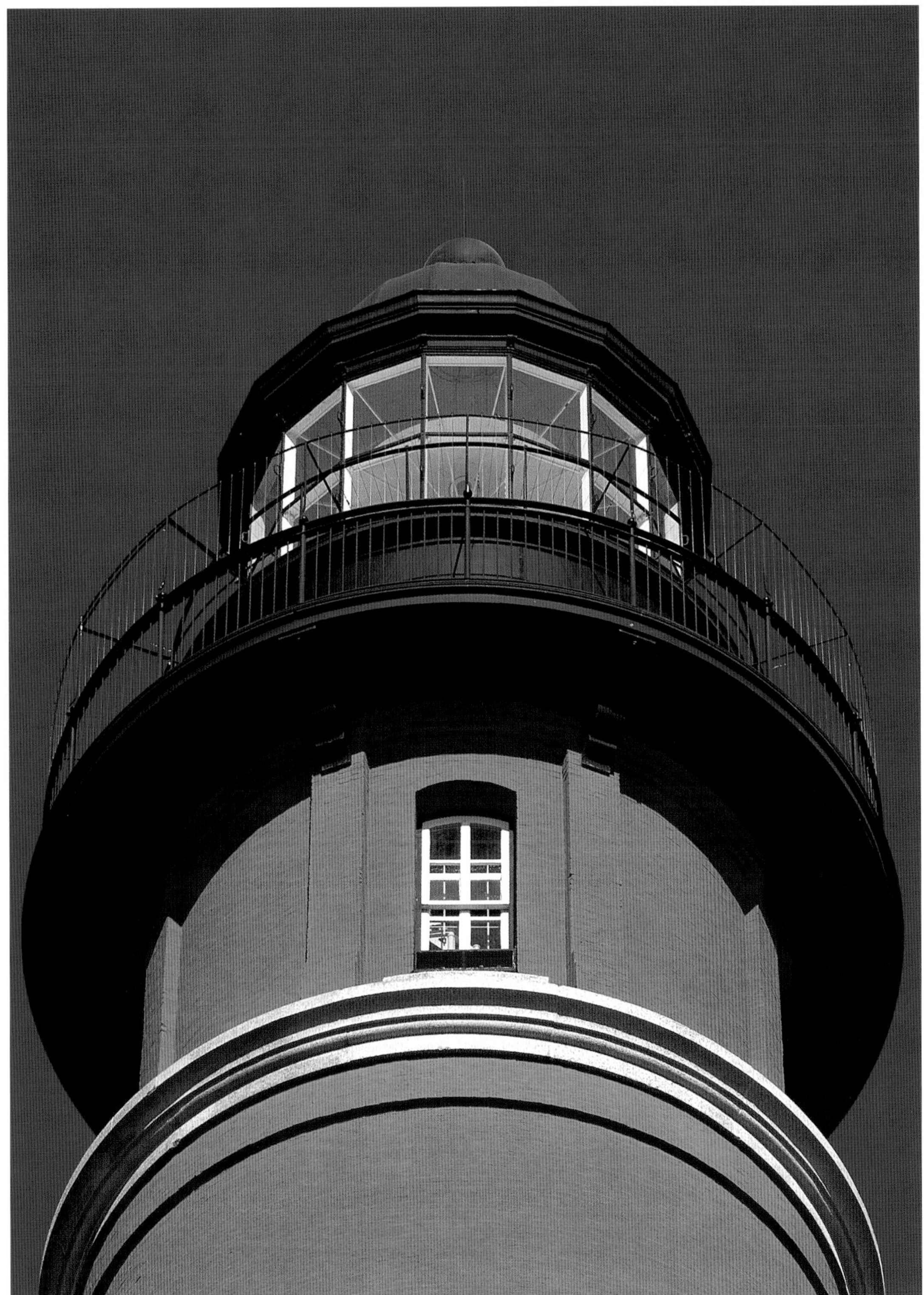

In 1774, the British built a "beacon" at Mosquito Inlet, Florida, and paid a keeper to tend it. The tower probably served only as a daymark, but could have held a light. A century later, in 1887, the present 175-foot lighthouse at Mosquito Inlet was built. The name was changed to Ponce de Leon Inlet Lighthouse in the 1920s.

An evolution of simple beacons and light towers have marked Charleston Harbor since colonial times. Ironically, it is home to the South's oldest and youngest lighthouse sites. Morris Island Lighthouse went into service in 1767 as the first southern sentinel but eventually fell victim to erosion. Almost two centuries later, in 1962, the ultra-modern Sullivans Island Lighthouse took over lighthouse duties for the busy harbor. This is the only sentinel in the nation with an elevator.

Survivors of War

Marking American ports with lights and buoys began in earnest when the Declaration of Independence was signed and the war began. Patriots extinguished all twelve Colonial lights so as not to aid the British Navy in accessing vital ports. In 1775, the lightkeeper of Tybee Light snuffed the lamps and dismantled and hid the illuminating apparatus. It stood dark during the Defense of Savannah from 1778 to 1779. At Charleston Harbor, the royal governor took refuge on the HMS *Tamar* on September 15, 1775, and watched as the Americans seized Fort Johnson and extinguished the lamps in Morris Island Light. During British occupation of Charleston in 1780, the enemy used the lighthouse as a lookout and signaling station.

At Cape Henry, where the rubble of planned construction still lay scattered on the beach, there was no lighthouse to serve British needs. But a curious turn of events that occurred near the cape suggests the lack of a lighthouse worked in the Americans' favor. In 1781, when the weary but confident redcoat army of General Cornwallis marched into Yorktown, they quickly realized the redoubtable General George Washington was closing in from the west, supported by the French infantry under the command of the Marquis de Lafayette. Cornwallis looked east in hopes of seeing British Navy ships for support. What he didn't know was that a decisive battle had taken place at the mouth of the Chesapeake Bay a few nights earlier.

Because no lighthouse marked the ingress, French ships entering the bay were forced to wait until daylight to negotiate the treacherous estuary. As they quietly lingered off Cape Henry, a flotilla of British naval ships—Cornwallis' supposed protectors—appeared from the north. The French met them off Cape Henry and opened fire, sinking three British ships. Realizing they were far outnumbered, the remaining British ships fled out to sea. Without support, Cornwallis was soundly beaten. Had Cape Henry Lighthouse been completed and lit at this time, history might have recorded a different outcome.

The lighthouses at Tybee and Charleston remained extinguished until the end of the conflict. They were among only five light towers in the colonies not seriously damaged during the Revolutionary War. Cannon fire pounded and darkened Cape Henlopen Light at the mouth of the Delaware Bay. British troops bombarded and occupied Sandy Hook Light at the entrance to New York Harbor. Much worse was the fate of Boston Lighthouse. Here, retribution proved too great a temptation as the British passed the lighthouse on their way out of Boston on June 13, 1776. The redcoats tossed a keg of gunpowder into the tower and leveled it.

The colonies successfully gained independence from England, but at war's end the American landscape and shoreline were in disarray. With the same conviction and determination that had won them liberty, they set about rebuilding their lighthouses and establishing a nation of maritime importance.

CHAPTER 2

Marking the Golden Shores

TRIM YOUR FEEBLE LAMP, MY BROTHER!
SOME POOR SEAMAN, TEMPEST TOSSED,
TRYING NOW TO MAKE THE HARBOR,
IN THE DARKNESS MAY BE LOST.
Philip P. Bliss, 1838–1876

Left: *Congress authorized money for the Cape Lookout Lighthouse in 1794 to mark the dangerous Core Banks, but it was 1812 before the tower was completed and entry into the port of Beaufort was made safer. Beach erosion so damaged the tower it had to be rebuilt in 1859. The U.S. Lighthouse Board added the black-and-white-checkerboard daymark in 1873.*

Above: *A red door offers a friendly welcome to Bald Head Lighthouse, the first lighthouse site in North Carolina. The original tower, built at the mouth of the Cape Fear River in 1795, was replaced by the current lighthouse in 1818.*

As the emergent nation struggled to define itself, the need to bolster maritime commerce became paramount. President George Washington, influenced by seamen and merchants alike, urged consolidation of all existent navigational aids and construction of new ones. In its first session on August 7, 1789, Congress passed the Ninth Act, a public works measure that provided for the transfer of all colonial lighthouses into the hands of the federal government. It resulted in the formation of the U.S. Lighthouse Establishment, administered by Alexander Hamilton of the Treasury Department.

Hamilton's first public project was the completion of the lighthouse at Cape Henry, Virginia. The work begun in 1772 was resumed in November 1789, though building materials had been stolen during the war and blowing sand had completely covered the original foundation. New York mason John McComb, Jr. won the bid to construct the ninety-foot lighthouse and ordered new stone, quarried from the Rappahannock River, to be lightered down the bay to the site. In October 1792, he completed the octagonal granite tower, topped by an iron lantern and copper roof. President George Washington appointed Laban Goffigan first keeper of the light at a penurious annual salary of $266.

In the meantime, the Lighthouse Establishment ceded the lighthouses at Tybee Island and Morris Island to the federal government. They had suffered little damage during the war and keepers relit them soon after the British retreat. But a great dark space existed between Cape Henry and Charleston. In 1792, realizing the awesome building task ahead and feeling the nation's heavy fiscal burden, Hamilton created the Office of the Commissioner of Revenue and placed lighthouses under its control. The new state of North Carolina immediately began to pressure the commissioner for lighthouses at Ocracoke Inlet and the Cape Fear River, both critical entry points for shipping.

In order to finance lighthouses, since 1784 the colony of North Carolina had been collecting a duty on ships passing Bald Head. By the time Congress met in 1789, North Carolina had already procured land at Ocracoke and Cape Fear and had ordered bricks. The projects were transferred to the federal government and construction proceeded in earnest. Bald Head Lighthouse went into service in 1795 at the mouth of the Cape Fear River, followed in 1800 by Shell Castle Lighthouse, located on a small islet between Ocracoke Inlet and Pamlico Sound.

Funding plagued both efforts and rendered Shell Castle Light an insubstantial fifty-five-foot-tall wooden tower with only one lamp. More crucial for mariners was Bald Head Light which marked the river entrance at Cape Fear and the treacherous Frying Pan Shoals, so it was constructed of sturdier brick with an iron lantern and an array of spider lamps. Even so, its beacon was too weak to show beyond the shoals and may have caused more harm than good.

South Carolinians implored the first Congress to earmark money to build a lighthouse at the entrance to Winyah Bay, a major artery for the export of rice. A private citizen named Paul Trapier had donated land for the tower at the end of the Revolutionary War, but the new federal government preferred to spend its small purse on northern ports. Not until 1798 was an appropriation of $7,000 made for construction to begin on Georgetown Lighthouse. Completed in 1801, the seventy-two-foot wooden sentry guided vessels past a finger of land separating the Waccamaw River from the ocean. It stood only five years before a storm toppled it.

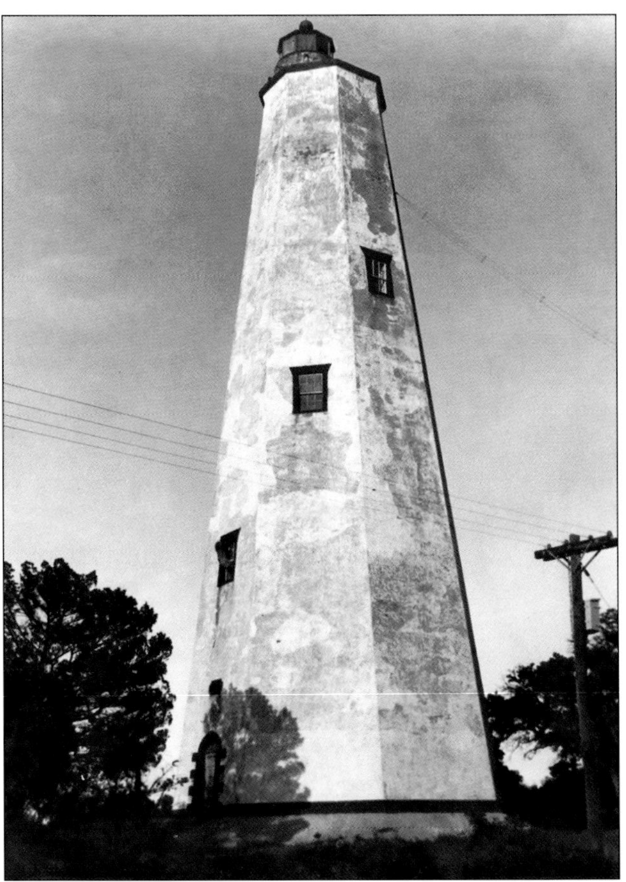

***Above and facing page:** Nearly two centuries of weathering is apparent on the massive walls of the 1818 lighthouse at Bald Head, North Carolina. (Above photograph courtesy of the U.S. Coast Guard Archives)*

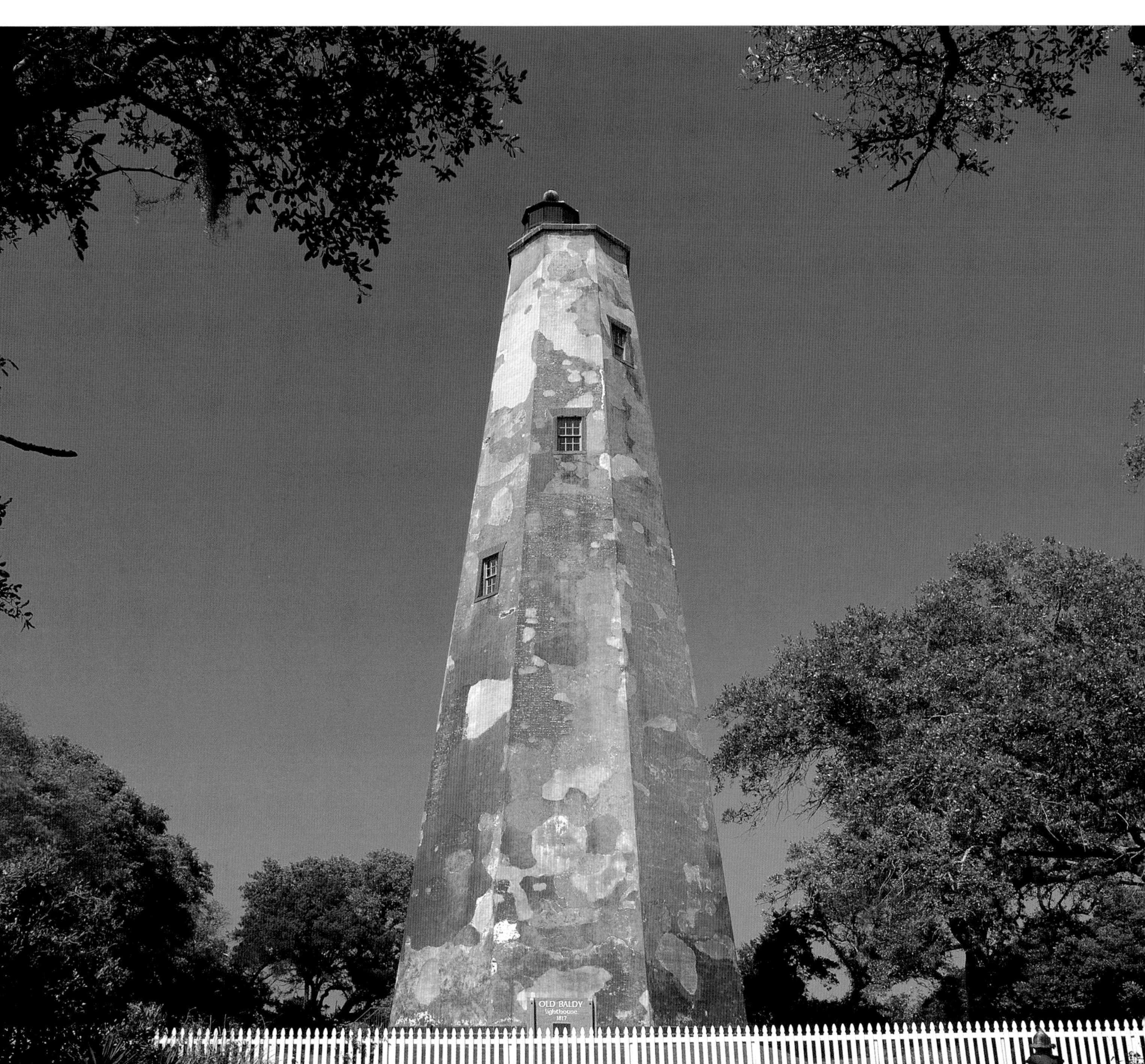
OLD BALDY
lighthouse
1817

Lean Years

The Jefferson administration returned control of lighthouses to the Treasury Department. Albert Gallatin, the department's fourth secretary, faced a national debt of $83 million, but President Jefferson understood the need for more lighthouses in the South. Struggling to find money for the many proposed beacons, Gallatin tightened the budget and prioritized needs. Two Virginia lighthouses, one at Old Point Comfort near the entrance to the James River and another on Smith Point at the mouth of the Potomac River, were under construction when Jefferson took office. Both were completed in 1802.

North Carolina's Outer Banks was now at the top of Gallatin's lighthouse list. Southbound mariners faced numerous perils when passing this area. The Diamond Shoals lay just offshore, prevailing southwest winds buffeted the sea lanes, and the Gulf Stream's northerly push impeded travel. In addition, the southern coastline turned southwest at this point, necessitating a change in course. Such dangers spelled disaster for many ships.

Although Congress authorized Cape Hatteras Lighthouse in 1794, it was 1803 before the tower—the first sentinel on the Outer Banks—was completed. Work was delayed due to difficulty getting materials to the site, along with a bout of fever that swept through the construction crew. The ninety-foot stone tower was described as "a handsome plain edifice" by a visitor who climbed its wooden stairs shortly after it went into service. The visitor also noted that extreme heat generated by the lamps greatly vexed the keeper. Not long afterwards, a fire broke out in the lantern, causing minor damage.

Worse, mariners complained of the beacon's inadequacy almost from the start. It was too short and its light too feeble to show beyond the shoals it was intended to mark: "The light at Hatteras is very often without any light in the most tempestuous and dangerous weather," wrote a Beaufort mariner in 1817. The keeper at the time, Joseph Farrow, who also was responsible for distribution of salvaged goods from shipwrecks, was suspected of deliberately letting the light go out to profit from calamity.

Barraged with complaints and financially strapped, the U.S. Lighthouse Establishment struggled. Northern ports were demanding new lighthouses, and many hazards in the South had yet to be marked. In 1794, Congress authorized money for a lighthouse at Cape Lookout to mark the Core Banks on the approach to the important port of Beaufort. Mariners called this point "Horrible Headland," an apropos nickname considering the frequency of shipwreck. Again, difficulty accessing the site and money problems stalled the project. The ninety-six-foot brick-and-wood lighthouse was not completed until 1812. In the same year, the storm-toppled Georgetown Lighthouse also was rebuilt, this time of sturdier materials. It shone again in 1812.

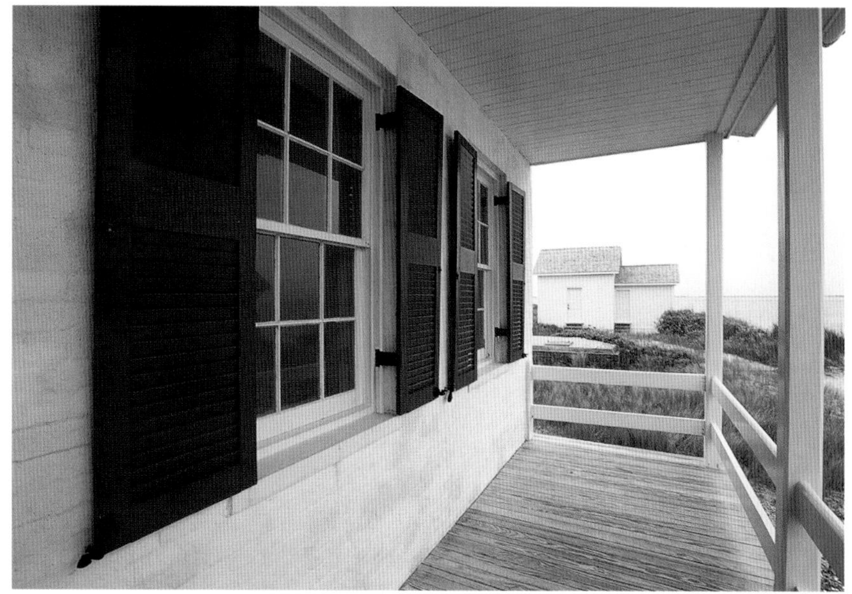

Cape Lookout received its first lighthouse in 1812, flanked by a small residence for the keeper. Scouring wind and rain brought beach erosion that took a toll on the structures. Both the lighthouse and quarters were rebuilt before the Civil War. Antebellum simplicity and sensibility is revealed in the 1860 keeper's house with leeward-facing porch.

Facing page: *Though land was donated for a lighthouse at Winyah Bay, South Carolina immediately following the Revolutionary War, it was 1798 before Congress saw fit to appropriate money to build the Georgetown Lighthouse, and 1801 before it was completed. The wooden sentinel collapsed in a storm a year later. A stone tower replaced it and stood until the Civil War. Too damaged to reclaim, it was rebuilt in 1867.*

Concurrently, a lighthouse was built on St. Simons Island, Georgia, to mark the sound leading into Brunswick. James Gould, a respected local architect who had moved to the area from Massachusetts as a young man, built the tower. Gould won the contract in 1807. Specifications called for brick, but he opted for the more economical local tabby, a cement-like material composed of oyster shells, lime, sand, and water. The finished seventy-five-foot lighthouse was a truncated octagonal shape with an iron lantern, in which oil lamps were suspended with chains. Apparently, the Treasury Department was impressed with Gould's economy and industry, for they offered him the job of lightkeeper at an annual salary of $400. He remained at the lighthouse for twenty-seven years.

In 1812, Congress reinstated the Office of Commissioner of Revenue, and once again placed lighthouses under his management. Perhaps the move was a favor to reward a political friend; more likely it was a desperate effort by the re-elected Madison administration to better control a runaway national debt. Whatever the reason, the change meant instability and stagnation for the Lighthouse Establishment. The War of 1812 further depleted the nation's coffers and brought lighthouse construction to a halt. Another change in administration would occur before more lighthouses were built in the South.

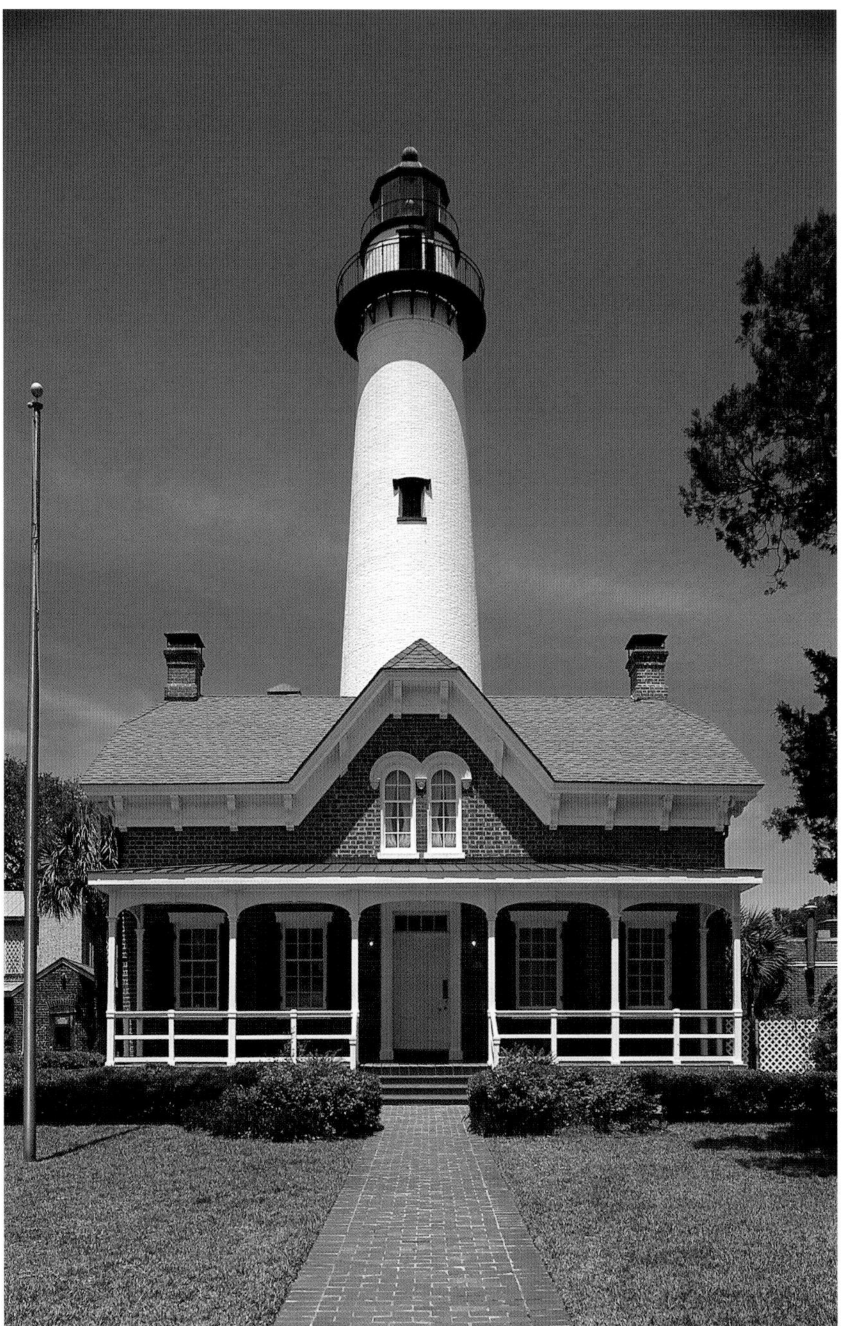

An octagonal stone lighthouse was completed on St. Simons Island, Georgia, in 1811, but destroyed during the Civil War. It was much shorter and simpler than the lofty Victorian beauty that replaced it in 1872.

Period furnishings and a lightkeeper mannequin depict life at St. Simons Island Lighthouse in the late nineteenth century. A large master bedroom (top) and a comfortable kitchen (bottom) were part of the keeper's house. The station was considerably less spacious in 1811, when the original tower and keeper's house stood on the site.

Seeming to stand as a memorial to its builders, many of whom died of malaria contracted in the mosquito-infested swamps surrounding the site in the 1870s, St. Simons Island Lighthouse gives no hint of its bleak beginnings. The glamorous Victorian sentinel is today a popular museum in Brunswick, Georgia.

Costly Thrift

By 1820, lighthouses had landed back in the Treasury Department under the aegis of the Fifth Auditor, a newly created office entrusted with the fiscal business of the growing nation. The man in charge was Stephen Pleasanton, a government accountant who knew little about lighthouses but much about saving money. He set about expanding the chain of coastal sentries with one thought in mind: thrift. Pleasanton tightened the burdensome budget for construction and operation of navigational aids while adding many more lights, buoys, and fog signals.

To achieve the desired economy, Pleasanton consolidated activities within the Lighthouse Establishment and delegated to the Collectors of Customs in various ports around the nation the responsibility for selection of lighthouse sites, building and maintenance of the towers, and hiring of keepers. In all matters, he relied heavily upon the advice of a retired Cape Cod shipmaster named Winslow Lewis who in 1812 had persuaded the government to adopt his patented illuminating apparatus. Historians debate whether Lewis was self-serving or simply in the right place at the right time. Either way, he gained Pleasanton's trust, as well as the majority of contracts for building and outfitting lighthouses. In defense of both men, it bears noting that in 1809 the government passed a resolution that mandated contracts be awarded to the lowest bidder, which prompted Pleasanton to accept rock-bottom bids and hire builders like Lewis in order to penny-pinch and take shortcuts to stay within a budget.

Brick, prized for its durability and uniformity, was the material of choice for many southern lighthouses. It was recommended for the first St. Simons Lighthouse in 1811, but the builder instead chose tabby, a cheaper local material composed of shells, lime, sand, and water. Brick won over in 1872 when the U.S. Lighthouse Board rebuilt the lighthouse, and again in 1890, when an oilhouse was added to the station to store flammable fuel. The use of a wooden door on a structure designed to be anti-combustible seems contradictory.

The first southern lighthouse built by Lewis was Sapelo Island Light, Georgia, an important seamark on the route to the port of Darien on the Altamaha River. Land had been ceded to the federal government for the tower in 1808, but in a scenario played out again and again, construction was delayed by lack of funds and government bias against southern sites due to poor southern representation and influence in Congress. Early in 1820, Lewis completed a sturdy, ninety-foot brick lighthouse and outfitted the lantern with his Lewis Reflector System. He also built a brick keeper's dwelling and sold the government whale oil for the lamps. His bill came to $17,000, a tidy sum for the time. Almost concurrently, he built a similar tower farther south on Little Cumberland Island. This sixty-foot sentinel was lighted July 4, 1820, fetching Lewis another $17,000. In all, Lewis built more than twenty lighthouses in the South.

Pleasanton adopted England's lightship technology to mark offshore hazards in 1820, placing the nation's first lightship, a vessel equipped with one or more lanterns on its masts, at Willoughby Spit, Virginia. A second lightship called *Aurora Borealis* went to work off Pensacola, Florida. Within five years, lightships were anchored at six danger spots on the Eastern Seaboard and Gulf of Mexico, the most treacherous site being the Diamond Shoals, thirteen miles off Cape Hatteras. The first lightship to mark the shoal was blown off-station by storm winds three times in four years. The third incident was so damaging, the Lighthouse Establishment abandoned the vessel and sold it for salvage. Smaller lightboats moored in quiet backwaters and rivers also came into use. Lamplighters tended these boats nightly. Lightboats went out of service in the mid-twentieth century, but lightships continued to work on dangerous offshore sites until the 1960s, when Texas tower lighthouses replaced them. These sturdy, steel, tubular-leg designs utilized the same technology as offshore oil rigs and were anchored firmly into the sea floor.

Sapelo Island Lighthouse, which marked the Altamaha River, was the first southern lighthouse built by Winslow Lewis, a Cape Cod shipmaster-turned-builder. Lewis was known for his thrift, and his contract for $17,000 included a brick tower with lighting apparatus, keeper's dwelling, and cistern. By 1885, when this photo (left) was taken, the lighthouse was in its halcyon days, brightly daymarked in red-and-white bands. (Photograph used courtesy of the U.S. Coast Guard Archives) It fell into disrepair in the mid-twentieth century, but was rescued in 1997 by the Sapelo Island Restoration Foundation. Refurbished and relighted (top), the tower is today the focal point of a wildlife refuge.

The cottage-style lighthouse became popular during the administration of Stephen Pleasanton, Fifth Auditor of the Treasury and the man in charge of the nation's lighthouses from 1820 through 1852. The incorporated house and tower design appealed to Pleasanton's frugal nature, since it reduced construction and maintenance costs. The U.S. Lighthouse Board continued the practice. Haig Point Front Range Lighthouse, built on Daufuskie Island, North Carolina, in 1872, was typical of the cottage-style sentinels of the post–Civil War era. The two keepers, their wives and children, and a dog attest to the family nature of lighthouse work at this time. (Photograph courtesy of the U.S. Coast Guard Archives)

Pleasanton's era also saw the beginnings of a peculiar construction practice known as the cottage-style lighthouse, a commingling of light tower and keeper's dwelling. Designed with economy in mind, these distinct and ubiquitous styles worked well at sites where the expense of building separate structures was prohibitive or a very tall tower was not needed. The diminutive lighthouses at Price's Creek and Federal Point in North Carolina, Haig Point in South Carolina, and Cedar Keys in Florida were all built in this style, as were many screwpile sentinels in the rivers, bays, and sounds of the South.

During Pleasanton's tenure, the Florida Territory became part of the United States, and he faced the onerous task of marking its coastline, the longest in the United States at the time. The task was complicated by sandbar-fringed barrier islands, jutting capes, shallow coral reefs, and the Gulf Stream, which pushed close to shore. An old Spanish watchtower stood at St. Augustine, but it was of insufficient height and strength for a lighthouse, so a new tower was ordered built. Placed in service in 1821, it was the first of twelve Florida lighthouses completed over the next thirty years under Pleasanton's administration. Pleasanton chose important sites, including the St. Johns River, Key Biscayne, Key West, Dry Tortugas, St. Marks, and Pensacola. Lightships were anchored in 1823 at Pensacola; in 1824 in the vicinity of a concealed jagged coral reef at Key Largo, and in 1825 at Carysfort Reef, where the British frigate HMS *Carysfort* was wrecked fifty years before.

Building continued in other parts of the South as well. In 1827, a sixty-five-foot tower went up at Cape Romain on the mouth of South Carolina's Santee River. The following year another important beacon was lit on Cape Charles, Virginia, to mark the northern shore of the entrance to the Chesapeake Bay. Roanoke Marshes Light lit Albemarle Sound in 1831 and a lightship was added to the area in 1835. Assateague Island Lighthouse, closing the dark space between the Delaware and Chesapeake Bays, went into service in 1833, along with Cape St. George Light on a barrier island off Florida's "Big Bend."

The construction of St. Marks Lighthouse near Apalachicola, Florida sadly reflected the poor workmanship and political maneuvering that had begun to plague

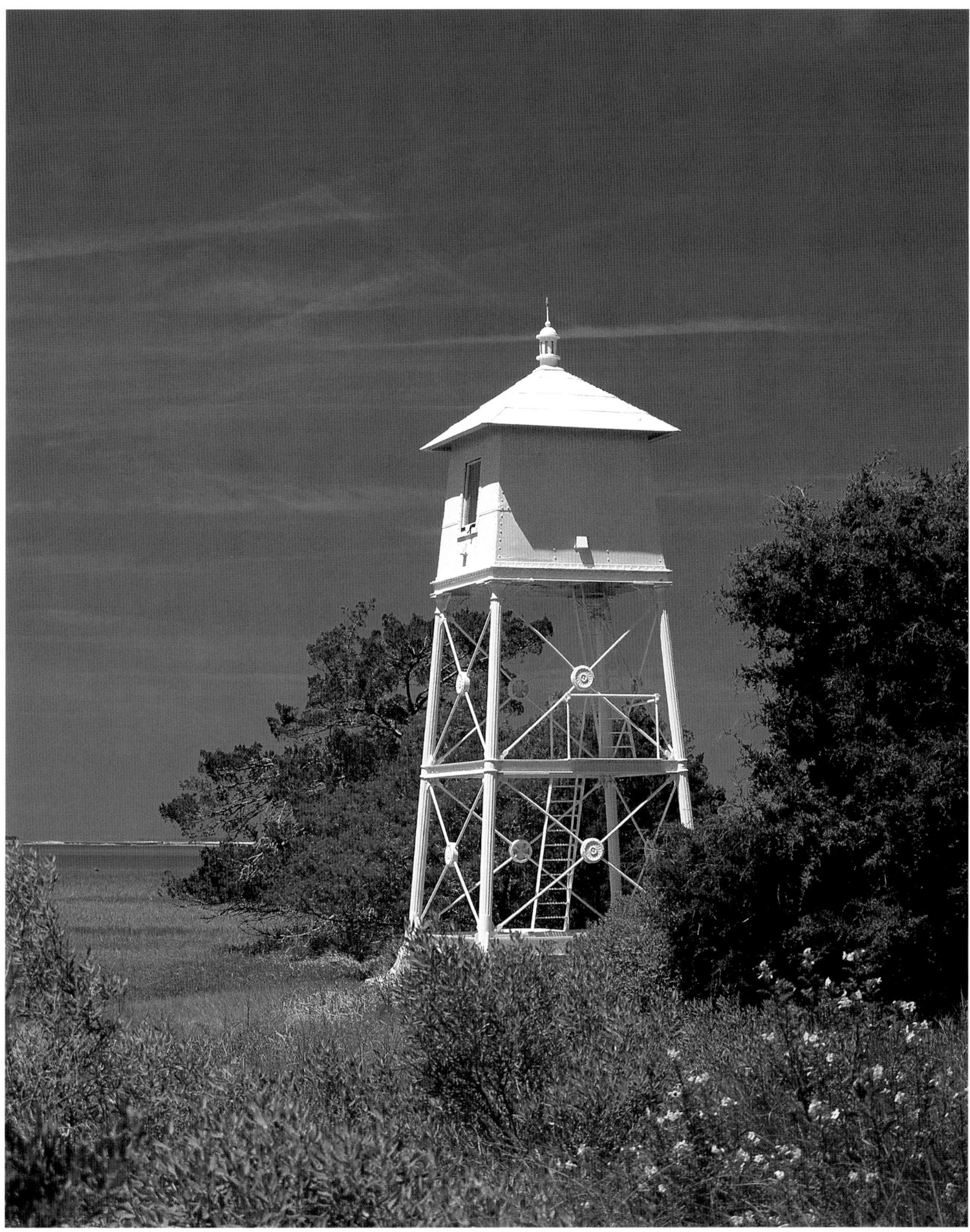

The establishment of range lights to guide shipping through twisting harbor and river channels was a priority for the U.S. Lighthouse Establishment in the 1840s and later the U.S. Lighthouse Board. The Sapelo Range Lights that marked the Altamaha River channel were typical of the many ranges completed in the second half of the nineteenth century. The 1838 Sapelo Island Light served as the back range. Sapelo Front Range Light, a wooden framework tower was the lower of two beacons. When lined up visually, these lights appeared as one beacon and kept a vessel in mid channel.

The Travail of Cape Florida Light

The lighthouse fire blazed
like a star in the midst of the ocean.
Thomas Moore (1779–1852)

South Florida was a dangerous place for lighthouse keepers to work in 1836. Not only was there deprivation and loneliness at the remote lighthouse locations, but also severe storms and heat. In addition, Seminole troubles were escalating. Angry about plans for confinement on a reservation in the Midwest, the Seminoles attacked and burned South Florida homesteads and outwitted military strategists. Ultimately, they set their sights on the most obvious local symbol of the U.S. government—the lighthouse on Key Biscayne.

After Seminoles murdered a family in what is present-day Miami, Cape Florida Light's principle keeper, James Dubose, moved his family to Key West to keep them safe. He was there in July 1836, visiting his wife and children, when the lighthouse on Key Biscayne was attacked.

The assistant keeper, John Thompson, and an elderly black man named Henry Aaron Carter were alone in the keeper's quarters that afternoon. They were resting, taking refuge from the intense afternoon heat, when the Seminoles approached in their canoes. The men fled to the lighthouse with rifles and barred the door. Minutes later they heard the crackle of fire outside and knew the Indians had set fire to the station. The blaze soon reached the wooden door. Realizing the cans of oil and ammunition in the base of the lighthouse would ignite, the keepers raced up the wooden stairs, carrying a keg of gunpowder.

At the top of the lighthouse they exchanged gunfire with the Seminoles, but soon faced a greater threat. Fire broke through to the base of the lighthouse, reached the oil supply, and exploded in a fury of flames that engulfed the wooden stairway. The tower's hollow interior acted like a flue, fanning the fire. Thompson and Carter grabbed an axe and attempted to chop away the blazing stairway, but the incredible heat forced them back. Before long, the iron lantern grew frying pan hot.

In Thompson's own words: "The lantern was now full of flame, the lamps and glasses bursting and flying all directions, my clothes on fire, and to move from the place where I was would be instant death from their rifles. My flesh was roasting."

The men crawled to the edge of the catwalk to escape the horrible inferno, but were greeted by a hail of gunfire from the Seminoles. In agony, Carter stood up to jump from the tower. He was shot and fell to the catwalk floor beside Thompson. Thompson retreated inside the lantern enclosure, but his clothes were now burned away and his flesh was exposed to the hot metal. Screaming and writhing with pain, he spied the keg of gunpowder he had carried to the top of the lighthouse. Thinking to end the horrid ordeal, he rolled the keg into the access hole in the lantern floor and closed his eyes, expecting the entire lighthouse to explode.

The concussion of the blast rocked the tower and threw Thompson against the lantern wall, but the tower was not destroyed, nor was he killed. He crawled back outside where Carter lay with five bullets in his body. The old man murmured something to Thompson and died. Meanwhile, the fire began to subside. The explosion had caused the burning stairs to collapse to the bottom of the lighthouse, snuffing out the flames. Dazed and badly burned, Thompson lapsed into unconsciousness. Thinking both men were dead, the Seminoles looted the house, stole Thompson's boat, and departed.

For hours, Thompson lay inert at the top of the tower, as the fire smoldered in its base. He was burned over much of his body, and several fingers and toes had been shot off in the gunfight. When night came, the lantern cooled, but hordes of mosquitoes descended to feast on Thompson's tortured flesh. With no way to get down, he resigned himself to a slow death.

At dawn he woke to the buzzing of flies and the awful scene of Carter's bloated, bullet-riddled body a few feet away. Scanning the horizon with red, swollen eyes, he saw no sign of help—only a trackless expanse of sea canopied by a clear blue sky and brutally hot sun. Around noon, Thompson roused and saw a ship offshore. He tore a piece of unburned cloth from Carter's trousers and waved it in hopes of being seen. After a few minutes exertion, he collapsed again.

Sometime later he heard voices on the ground below. Pulling himself to the edge of the catwalk, he cautiously peered down, worried the Seminoles might have returned. But the voices did not belong to Indians. The ship had anchored, and men in blue uniforms were searching the burned-out station. They had heard the explosion of the gunpowder keg the day before and found the sloop adrift. Smoke from the burning lighthouse had led them to Cape Florida. Thompson knew he was saved. Feebly, he waved and called out for help.

The seamen of the USS *Motto* looked up at the charred lantern in disbelief. The tormented soul who greeted them had no clothing, no hair, and bloody stumps where many of his fingers and toes should have been. His skin was blistered and raw as a smoked ham. Excitedly, the sailors made plans to rescue Thompson. They tried several ways of getting a line to him, including throwing it with a ball of shot and flying it up on a kite. For twelve hours, they tried unsuccessfully. Thompson was growing weaker and had all but given up on his rescuers. Finally, one sailor devised a ramrod attached to twine and fired it onto the lantern. Cheering loudly, the men encouraged Thompson to pull up a lifeline, which he did after much effort. A man climbed the rope and brought down the near-dead keeper.

Thompson was taken to Key West and hospitalized. The collector of customs for the town sent a letter to Stephen Pleasanton, who superintended lighthouses from an office in Washington, D.C.: "Thompson was brought to this place and is in a fair way to do well. Indeed his recovery is deemed certain, but it is feared he will be a cripple for life. He, being a seaman . . . I have thought it equitable to extend the agreed aid to sick and disabled seamen."

Following his recovery, Thompson moved to Charleston, South Carolina, where it is believed he took up duties at another lighthouse. His story was told around the world, and as an old man it is said he made money telling of his ordeal.

The Cape Florida Lighthouse, gutted and scarred by the conflagration, stood dark for a decade until Seminole troubles died down. When a work crew finally came to assess the damage, they found more than two hundred bullet holes in the lantern. They also discovered the original builder had defrauded the government by constructing hollow walls, thus saving half the cost of bricks. No such shortcut was used in the refurbishment. The tower was repaired, strengthened, and relighted in 1846.

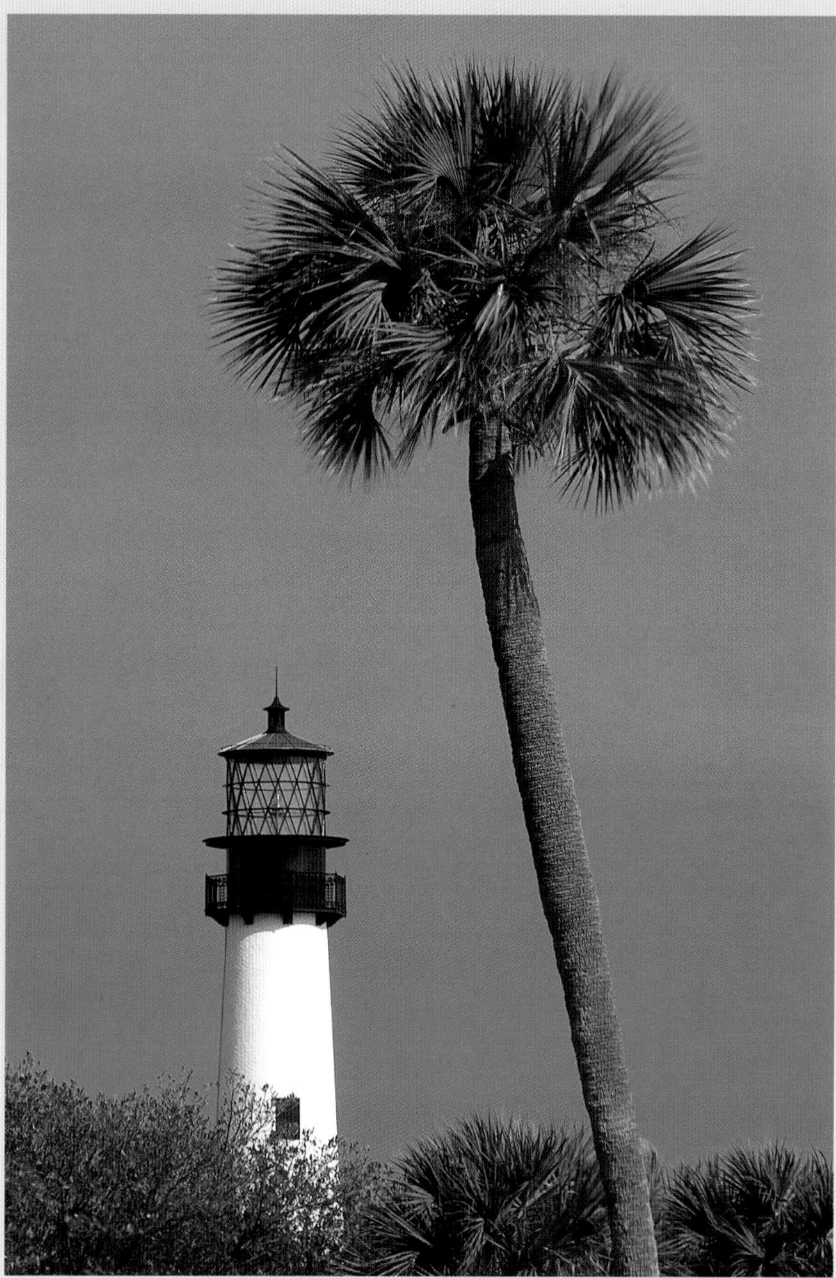

Angry Seminoles lay siege to Cape Florida Lighthouse in 1836, looting and burning the station in retaliation against government demands that they retire to a reservation. One keeper was killed and another seriously injured. The station was not repaired and reopened until 1846. Tempers slowly abated and within a decade lightkeepers were friendly with the Seminoles. The family of Simeon Frow, who lived at Cape Florida Light from 1859 until 1878, often received gifts of fish, turkey, and venison from the Seminoles. On one occasion, an Indian came to the station after dark to barter. Not wishing to disturb anyone, especially Keeper Frow, who was on watch in the tower, the Seminole man went to sleep on the lighthouse floor, where Mrs. Frow found him the next morning.

·1871·

The annexation of Florida in 1819 brought the need for many new lighthouses. The first to be lighted was at St. Augustine, a site which already had a lookout tower that could be quickly outfitted as a lighthouse. The tower survived more than fifty years before erosion and storms necessitated its replacement in 1874. One of the South's loveliest sentinels, it is now a museum. The lofty 167-foot sentinel (facing page) wears a capricious yet functional daymark of black-and-white spirals and is topped with a bright red lantern (bottom right). Elegant appointments dress the workroom at its base (left), where handsome brackets and details on the windows and chimney reflect an architect's eye for beauty. The station's crown jewel is its first-order Fresnel lens made in Paris (bottom left). Initially, the lamps burned lard oil, but an electric beacon operates in the lens today.

the Lighthouse Establishment. Due to the site's remoteness, the lowest bid for construction came in at $11,400, nearly twice the amount for comparable projects in New England and the mid-Atlantic. The contractor, the aforementioned Winslow Lewis, subcontracted the project to Benjamin Beal and Jairus Thayer, who saved money by using local stone from an old Spanish fort rather than the brick stipulated in the contract. They also left the tower walls hollow. The regional collector of customs charged the men with fraud and refused to pay for the project until the tower was rebuilt to contract specifications. This time, Lewis subcontracted to his friend Calvin Knowlton. The second tower went into service in 1830, little better than the first. Only a year later, its walls began to sag and iron bands had to be wrapped around it for stability. The foundation also was giving way. Repeated legal battles between Lewis and the Lighthouse Establishment resulted in a complete reconstruction in 1842.

Scandal and Self-Examination

Amidst the flurry of construction and expansion, mariners complained about the quality of lighthouses. In the 1820s, an average of 100 American ships wrecked each year, often along their own shores. Mariners felt most American lighthouses were not tall enough and were poorly built, maintained, and regulated. A few were considered unreliable, and all were inferior to the magnificent lighthouses of Europe, which featured the Fresnel lens. This remarkable 1823 invention was the masterpiece of French physicist Augustin-Jean Fresnel, who revolutionized illumination with a lenticular system that increased brilliancy while creating a flash unique to each lighthouse to aid in identification. Pleasanton knew about the superior Fresnel system, yet refused to purchase any of the lenses, citing their expense and complexity to maintain and operate. American lighthouses at this time featured fixed white beacons visible no more than twelve miles at sea. Fresnel lenses could be seen from twice as far.

Among Pleasanton's harshest critics were the Blunt brothers, publishers of the widely respected sailing guide *American Coast Pilot*. In a letter to Congress, the Blunts opined that "the lighthouse establishment is badly managed." Another missive to the secretary of the treasury accused Pleasanton of poor judgment and ineptitude, and suggested that the task of managing the nation's navigational aids required the talents of more than one individual. Equally critical of Pleasanton was I. W. P. Lewis, the estranged nephew of builder Winslow Lewis and an engineer in the lighthouse service. The younger Lewis intimated to Congress that Pleasanton awarded contracts based on favoritism, with a pork-barrel partiality toward

A flurry of lighthouse-building in Florida in the 1820s meant safer passage for ships headed around the great peninsula and into the Gulf of Mexico. The mouth of the St. Johns River, which had been marked only by a pole lamp prior to annexation of the territory, received its first lighthouse in 1830. A rendering that appeared in a book some years later revealed the fate of the old St. Johns River Lighthouse (above). After being abandoned in 1835 and replaced by a stronger lighthouse, it became a makeshift barn for cattle. (Photograph courtesy of Picturesque America, Author's Collection) The third and final lighthouse to stand at this site is an 1858 eighty-foot brick sentinel that was decommissioned in 1929 (facing page).

Excessive penny-pinching and political scandal had begun to mark the U.S. Lighthouse Establishment by the late 1820s. Perhaps nowhere were the effects more obvious than at secluded St. Marks, Florida, where an inflated contract, fraud, and poor workmanship produced an inferior tower. It was rebuilt twice before the government accepted it. The 1842 tower still stands watch, a comely edifice that contradicts its checkered history.

A number of classic lenses have been restored for museum display, including the first-order flashing lens of Cape Canaveral Lighthouse (right), which was lovingly refurbished in the early 1990s. Walt Bogert, a lens restorationist at Ponce de Leon Inlet Lighthouse Museum, works on a first-order brass prism panel in the museum shop (bottom left) while another panel (bottom right) awaits repair. The museum is the vanguard of lighthouse lens restoration in the South.

MAGIC LANTERNS

THE BRILLIANT KERNEL OF THE NIGHT,
THE FLAMING LIGHTROOM CIRCLES ME:
I SIT WITHIN A BLAZE OF LIGHT
HELD HIGH ABOVE THE DUSKY SEA.
Robert Louis Stevenson (1850–1894)
The Light-Keeper

The soul of a lighthouse—its reason for existing—is the great cyclopean eye that opens in its lantern each night.

Reaching miles at sea, it probes the darkness in search of a ship needing guidance. The piercing beam is a consummate altruistic symbol, but how is such radiance produced?

Over the centuries, a variety of intensifying devices evolved, but none as elegant and efficient as the Fresnel lens. This opulent jewel of prisms and brass transformed the feeble light of oil lamps into brilliant rays and ushered in a new era of illumination in the 1820s. Its invention was both miraculous and practical. The inventor was a young man whose insight into the nature of light was far advanced for his time.

The French Lighthouse Authority asked physicist Augustin-Jean Fresnel (pronounced fray-nel) in 1822 to create a better lighthouse beacon. France was desperate for such an improvement. Its coastline, particularly on the North Sea, was hazardous and underlighted. Lighthouses stood on every major island, rock, and headland, but with rays too weak to shine beyond the dangers they were intended to mark. Fresnel went to work on a lenticular scheme to harness and concentrate light, intensify it, and then direct it seaward in a powerful beam.

Reflection, refraction, and magnification were at the core of his work. He knew much of the light generated by a lamp was scattered, but if it could be collected and focused, the resulting sharp ray would outshine everything around it. Fresnel placed a single oil lamp at the center of a beehive-shaped lens composed of a central panel of magnifying glass surmounted by concentric rings of prisms angled to bend light toward the focal plane. Held together in a lustrous brass frame, the result was a lens that gathered and intensified light.

Fresnel devised flashing and fixed lenses in six orders, or sizes. First-order lenses for use in landfall and coastal beacons were the largest and most powerful, while sixth-order lenses were the smallest and best suited for rivers and backwaters. Flashing lights utilized a series of magnifying bull's eyes encircling the center of the lens, each one producing a flash as the lens revolved. A smooth drum of convex glass at the center of the lens produced a fixed, or steady, light.

Beacons revolved by means of a clockworks system, with weights suspended in the tower. Keepers wound up the weights every few hours, similar to the winding of a cuckoo clock. As the weights fell, they powered the clockwork, which turned the lens on its pedestal. Early models turned on brass chariot wheels or bearings. Later, heavier lenses rested in tubs of mercury, where high density supported the massive apparatus and low friction allowed it turn almost effortlessly.

The first lighthouse to receive the new Fresnel technology was the enormous ornate tower at Cordouan, France, established in 1610 to mark where the Gironde River flows into the Bay of Biscay. Its experimental Fresnel lens went into service in 1823, and mariners worldwide immediately applauded its superior brilliance. The major maritime nations adopted the system immediately, and companies in France and England began manufacturing them. However, the United States considered Fresnel lenses too expensive and complex for lightkeepers to operate and continued using archaic lighting systems for nearly three decades.

By 1850, American lighthouses had fallen far behind those of Europe in brilliance and reliability. With the reorganization of the lighthouse service in 1851 into the Lighthouse Board, Fresnel lenses were purchased and installed at many major lighthouses. By the start of the Civil War, Fresnel technology had upstaged almost all other systems. French and English companies produced the majority of the new optics, but for a short time the McBeth Evans Company of Indiana manufactured Fresnel lenses in America.

Over the years, these handsome optics have adapted to changing illuminants, from whale oil to kerosene to gas to electricity, even to solar power. Some still operate in old lighthouses around the nation, but as the Coast Guard modernized the towers in the second half of the twentieth century, they donated most Fresnel lenses to museums.

One of the grandest displays is in the lens hall at Ponce de Leon Inlet Lighthouse near Daytona Beach, Florida. Its huge first-order lens, removed from Cape Canaveral Lighthouse in the early 1990s, was lovingly restored piece by piece. As visitors walk around it on an elevated platform, they are at once awestruck by its beauty and intricacy—an aggregate of crystal and brass that, though utilitarian, could easily pass for a ballroom chandelier.

customs collectors. This practice, Lewis said, resulted in a shabby brigade of second-rate lighthouses.

In 1837, Pleasanton requested a large sum of money to build new lighthouses and rebuild crumbling structures. Only twenty-six lighthouses stood in the South at this time. With complaints mounting, Congress launched an investigation to determine how the money should best be spent, assigning twenty-two naval officers the onerous task of assessing the nation's lighthouses. Lieutenant Napoleon L. Coste, who commanded the revenue cutter *Campbell* (a vessel that policed American waters and ensured safety on the sea), surveyed the American coast south of the Chesapeake Bay to determine where improvements could be made to existent lighthouses or where new ones should be built. What he found was disconcerting. Many of the lighthouses Pleasanton had requested were not needed and almost half of all existent lighthouses had structural flaws and staff problems. Foundations were crumbling, dwellings were cramped and drafty, lighting equipment was outdated, and lightkeepers were generally untrained, unsupervised, and poorly paid.

Coste noted that a lighthouse was paramount for Bodie Island on the easternmost point of the Outer Banks. "More vessels are lost there than on any other part of our coast," he reported. Popular legend held that the area got its name from the many bodies washed ashore from shipwrecks. Lieutenant William D. Porter, who investigated Virginia's lighthouses, reported that Smith Island Light was "built of bad materials." The Smith Point lightboat captain was absent and had left the care of the lights to a fourteen-year-old slave boy. Other embarrassments stemmed from Pleasanton's lack of experience in legal matters. A court case against the government at the time asserted that Roanoke Marshes Light stood on private property and that no official rights to the land had ever been obtained. Only eight years after its inception, the Lighthouse Establishment was forced to abandon the beacon when the rightful owners reclaimed their property.

Additionally, the investigators recommended Fresnel lenses for major coastal lights. In 1840, the Lighthouse Establishment purchased from France two such lenses, a first-order and second-order, and installed them for testing in the Navesink Twin Lights in New Jersey. The new lenses shown with more brilliance and used less oil than the Lewis Patent Lamps. Pleasanton refused to purchase additional lenses, however, still believing them too pricey and difficult to operate. Congress conducted subsequent investigations in the 1840s, including a tour of European lighthouses, confirming the need to reorganize the lighthouse service under the supervision of people knowledgeable about and interested in maritime activity. But the wheels of change turned slowly.

In the midst of fiscal turmoil and government uncertainty, building continued. Pleasanton authorized a set of wooden range lights for Oak Island, North Carolina, to mark a dangerous curve in the Cape Fear River. Similar beacons were set up in the Savannah River, the St. Marys River, and the St. Johns River. These double lights consisted of an upper and a lower beacon that when properly aligned provided a safe course for the mariner to follow through a river bend.

Lighthouses were completed in Florida at Cape Canaveral, Cape San Blas, and Egmont Key. The Lighthouse Establishment also moved the lighthouse from Cumberland Island, Georgia, which was built in 1820 and had outlived its usefulness, to Amelia Island, Florida. Then a devastating storm hit the Deep South. On October 19, 1846, winds estimated in excess of 150 miles per hour slammed Key West. A witness reported "wrecks of all descriptions. . . . the lighthouses at Key West and Sand Key washed away, and Key West in ruins." Up until this

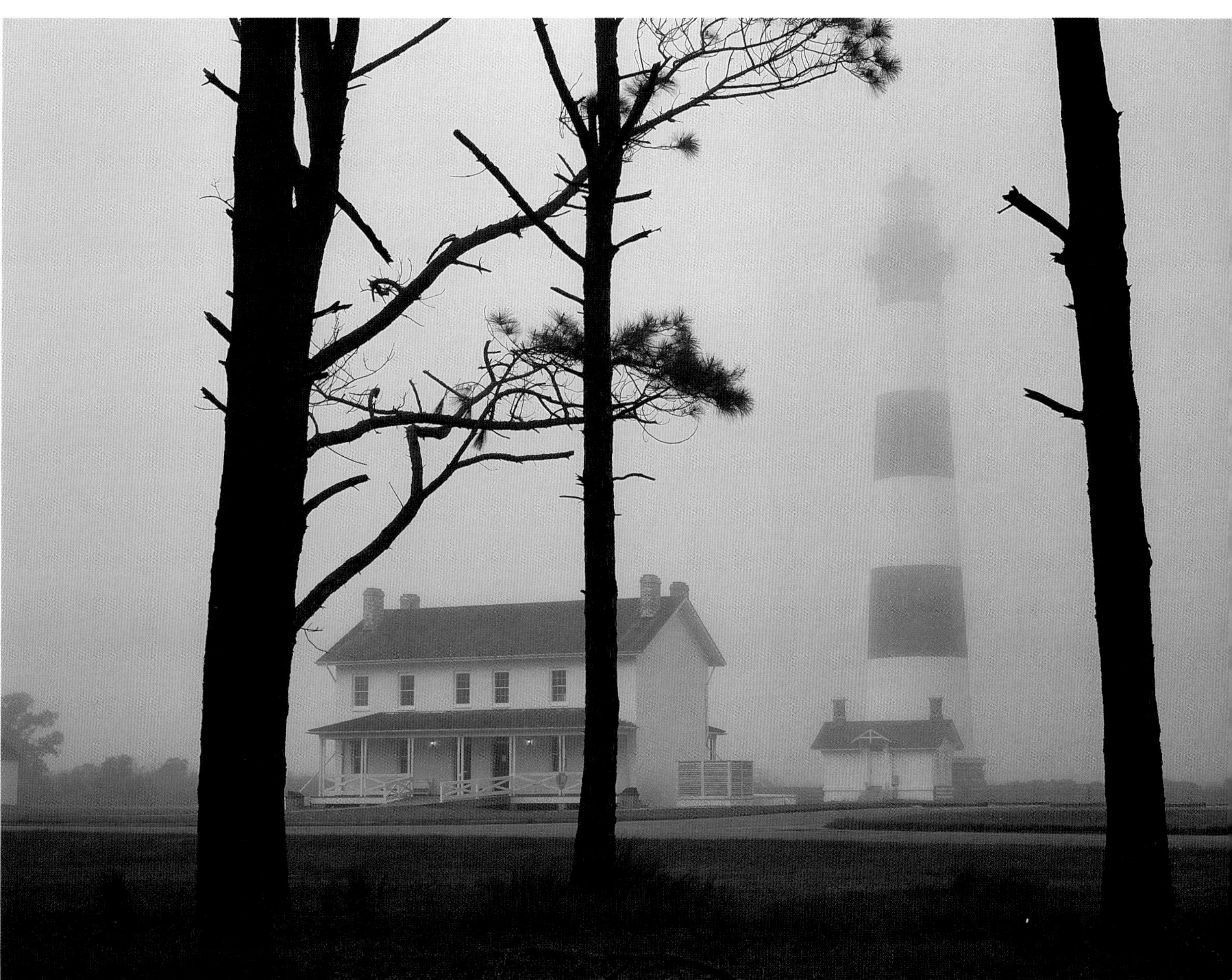

A misty shroud of fog envelopes Bodie Island Lighthouse on the Outer Banks (above). In 1837, after the U.S. Lighthouse Establishment requested a large sum of money to build new lighthouses, Congress investigated the best sites. Among those selected was Bodie Island near Oregon Inlet, a major portal into Pamlico Sound. Frequency of shipwrecks in this area made it a dreadful menace to navigation. Supposedly, Bodie Island was named in memory of the many dead that washed ashore here. The lighthouse was built in 1848 and rebuilt in 1872 following damage incurred during the Civil War. Its graceful lantern holds a classic first-order Fresnel lens (facing page).

All photos: *Cape Canaveral, Florida, was among the sites deemed in need of a lighthouse during an 1840s congressional investigation. A brick lighthouse was built on the jutting cape in 1848, but changes in the shoreline and damage during the Civil War rendered it useless. It was replaced by a cast-iron lighthouse in 1868. Porthole windows in the tower gave it a nautical look (top) and a unique pulley system allowed lightkeepers to lift supplies up the tower (bottom).*

time, and regardless of their location, southern lighthouses had been modeled after New England's masonry towers. Their heavy walls were not suited for sandy foundations and could not withstand severe storms. The hurricane killed twenty people at two lighthouses, including the children of Key West lightkeeper Barbara Mabrity and three people at Sand Key Light. The tragedy underscored the need for better construction methods in areas prone to cyclonic storms.

In 1851, pressure from the maritime industry reached a climax. One mariner called Cape Hatteras Lighthouse "a disgrace to our country." Another claimed he could not see the light until he was within sight of breakers and that the running lights of a ship were brighter. Criticizing the Cape Florida Lighthouse on Key Biscayne, a crucial aid for entering the dangerous Florida Strait, one ship's captain wrote: "The Cape Florida light is a beacon for all persons to avoid . . . badly lighted and badly kept."

Congress responded by passing an act that authorized the secretary of the treasury to upgrade all major U.S. coastal lighthouses with Fresnel lenses. Over the next year, a board of military officers, scientists, and engineers conducted another investigation to assess the condition and management of all U.S. navigational aids and recommend ways to overhaul them. The Board scrupulously examined every detail of the lighthouse system and condemned much of it. In the end, however, they gave Stephen Pleasanton credit for his "zeal and faithfulness" and for "the spirit of economy which he has shown." At the time the annual cost to operate the average lighthouse, including its keeper's salary, was about $1,150—approximately one-quarter of what Britain and France were spending on lighthouses.

Regarding southern lighthouses, the investigative board deemed them "comparatively useless to the mariner for want of sufficient power or range." The 762-page report had little positive to say:

> No part of the United States is so badly lighted as the Florida Reef. In a distance of 220 miles there are but three light-houses . . .
>
> The lights on Hatteras, Lookout, Canaveral, and Cape Florida, if not improved, had better be dispensed with, as the navigator is apt to run ashore looking for them . . .
>
> The light at Charleston is very bad, and like-

> wise the bug lights for ranges about that bar . . .
>
> The Bald Head Light is comparatively useless, owing to its bad location and dimness . . .
>
> On the reef near Cape Largo is the floating light-ship, showing two lights, intended to be seen twelve miles, but they are scarcely discernable from the outer edge of Carysfort Reef . . .
>
> The light-boat on Martins Industry (a most dangerous shoal) scarcely deserves its name; it is neither useful by day or by night.

The Board found equipment and personnel equally lacking. Old Point Comfort Light had "sorry oil," while at Sapelo Island Light the lamp reflectors were "worn out" from abrasive cleaning. The tower at Virginia's Back River Light leaked badly when it rained and needed whitewashing. Its keeper was ill and had given his young son charge of the light, with no lens cloths and "no regular watch kept." At Cape Fear River, the keeper of the lightship was absent when inspectors arrived and had left a young boy in charge of the lights. Similarly, the captain of Wade's Point Lightship, North Carolina, had been "absent nearly a week" and had left the vessel "in very bad order."

At Federal Point, South Carolina, keeper James Newlin did not keep a journal or record of oil consumption, nor did he have any instructions regarding operation of the lamps, which were in poor condition. Oil soaked the lantern floor and soot covered its walls and ceiling. Overall, inspectors found "everything very dirty . . . very bad order throughout."

By contrast, Ocracoke Lighthouse was found "in excellent order, and showing the best light on the coast." The 1823 tower had been built by stone mason Noah Porter of Massachusetts for $11,359, including the keeper's house, and was of sturdy design. Its keeper, twenty-six-year-old John Harker, maintained the oil lamps and reflectors in excellent condition. That this tower still stands today as the oldest operating lighthouse in North Carolina testifies to its fine construction.

On October 2, 1852, as a result of the investigation of 1851, the government abolished the U.S. Lighthouse Establishment and created the U.S. Lighthouse Board. Entrusted with overhauling the nation's navigational aids, this new entity was composed of nine respected military and civilian members, many from the 1851 investigative team. Over the next fifty-eight years, the Board created a system of navigational aids superior to all others and established the U.S. coastline as the best marked in the world.

Through the urging of seamen and merchants, lighthouse technology slowly improved in the early nineteenth century, though only as quickly as funds would allow. Wood, once the material of choice for lanterns and stairways, was upstaged by more durable iron. The metal stairs in Key West Lighthouse, which spiral upward around a central column (facing page), are lightweight and fire resistant. Deck prisms set in the floor of its lantern room bring light into the tower's dark interior (above).

CHAPTER 3

Progress and Regress

NOTHING INDICATES THE LIBERALITY, PROSPERITY OR INTELLIGENCE OF A NATION MORE CLEARLY THAN THE FACILITIES WHICH IT AFFORDS FOR THE SAFE APPROACH OF THE MARINER TO ITS SHORES.
U.S. Lighthouse Board, 1852–1910

Left: *Bathed in soft evening light, rugged old Cape St. George Lighthouse stands a solitary watch over the Gulf of Mexico. Built in 1852 to serve Apalachicola Bay, it has been plagued by encroaching waves and pummeled by hurricanes throughout its career. It sits perilously close to the tideline.*

Above: *Juxtaposing old and new, 1,000-watt bulbs illuminate the antique Fresnel lens of St. Augustine Lighthouse. When the primary bulb burns out, the secondary one automatically moves into position. Bulb changers were developed in the 1960s, yet they work well in the tower's old prism lens that dates from the 1870s.*

The newly formed U.S. Lighthouse Board, comprised of three Navy officers, three Army officers, two scientists, and the secretary of the treasury zealously set to work to improve the nation's lighthouses. In its care were about 300 lighthouses and forty lightships. The Lighthouse Board established twelve new districts, assigning two military officers and an engineer to oversee the operations of each. Southern sentinels were included in the fifth, sixth, seventh, and eighth districts, which extended from the Chesapeake Bay to Lake Pontchartrain, Louisiana. To assist mariners, the Board published a twelve volumn *Light List*, a compendium of information about navigational aids in each of the nation's twelve districts and issued circulars each time something changed, such as the addition of a new light or fog signal or an alteration in the character of an existent one.

Another outcome of the 1851 investigation was more rigorous management of lighthouses. The Lighthouse Board established criteria for hiring lightkeepers, training them, and assigning rank. New rules granted multiple keepers to large light stations, including an experienced principle keeper to train assistants. Lightships now had full-time resident crews. District inspectors conducted regular evaluations of lighthouses and lightships to ensure quality work and well-maintained buildings and equipment. A merit system rewarded those who excelled. By 1880, uniforms were required for all personnel—lighthouse keepers, lightships crews, tender crews, and depot workers. The Lighthouse Board also expanded the fleet of lighthouse tenders to build, repair, and stock lighthouses, and set up a series of depots to handle the needs of each district. The influence of a largely military Lighthouse Board was obvious in the regimentation and discipline that now characterized the service.

Lesser waterways, such as small inlets, coves, and rivers, were amply marked with range lights, post lights, echo boards (intended to assist mariners during fog), and daymarks—colorful patterns painted on the lighthouses to make them easier to identify in daylight hours. Lamplighters, a corps of local watermen who knew their neighborhood well and worked part-time servicing the lights, maintained all of these lights as well as lighted buoys.

Beginning in 1852, the Lighthouse Board worked to address mariners' complaints about individual lighthouses. Cape Hatteras Light was among the first to be upgraded. In 1854, the Board purchased a first-order Fresnel lens from the French firm of Henry-LaPaute and Company of Paris. The magnificent chandelier of crystal and brass was comprised of more than 1,000 shimmering prisms, angled to bend light and focus it through a series of magnifying bull's-eyes. The apparatus was hailed as a thing of beauty and utility, but to house the lens and its massive pedestal, a larger lantern was required. Congress prudently decided to increase the height of the lighthouse before installing the new lantern and lens. The stone base of 110 feet was augmented with an additional forty feet of brick, then topped with a handsome English-style lantern. The change elevated Cape Hatteras Light above the obscuring mists, created when the warm water of the nearby Gulf Stream collided with colder waters nearer shore, and sent its beam twice as far out to sea.

South Florida became a priority for U.S. Lighthouse Board engineers. One-third of the state's commerce moved in and out of Key West, and major fishing and wrecking industries still thrived there, but since the two sentinels at Sand Key and Key West were destroyed in the devastating hurricane of 1846, only makeshift beacons lit the port. Key West Light was rebuilt on Whitehead Point in 1848, but still housed the inferior Lewis Patent Lamps and needed a stronger beacon. In 1858, a third-order French lens was installed in the tower and its thirteen whale-oil lamps were supplanted by a single lard-oil hydraulic lamp with three circular wicks. Keeper Barbara Mabrity, who had lost five of her children in the 1846 hurricane, now maintained a light that sent a much stronger signal to mariners. The Board had chosen a solid masonry design, and Mabrity's fears about another catastrophe were eased, but at sixty-six feet, the tower was still too short. The Board added another twenty feet to the tower in 1886, long after Mabrity's departure, giving the lighthouse a peculiar-looking waistline that evoked a feminine figure. It was an unintended tribute to the woman who had kept the lighthouse for more than thirty years.

Along the tempest-torn Florida Reef, magnificent skeleton towers rose—cast-iron screwpile lighthouses anchored firmly into the coral. The first of these went into service on Carysfort Reef off Key Largo in 1852, followed by Sand Key in 1853 and Sombrero Key in 1858. Three others at Alligator Reef, American Shoal, and Rebecca Shoal were planned but not completed until after the Civil War. These huge metal hulks were unique designs that quickly earned the nickname "Iron Giants." Though screwpile lighthouses had existed for decades, they were used primarily in quiet bays, rivers, and backwaters. The

With the advent of the U.S. Lighthouse Board in 1852, a major overhaul of American lighthouses began. One of the first to be updated was Cape Hatteras Lighthouse, a critical aid for ships passing North Carolina's Outer Banks. Its 1803 tower was increased in height and improved with a new first-order prism lens. The lighthouse survived until the Civil War, when Confederates damaged the structure beyond repair. Its successor, the present barber-pole lighthouse, was built in 1870 and, at nearly 200 feet, is the tallest lighthouse in the nation. It is a major tourist attraction, and thousands of vacationers visit each year, eager to climb to the top for a bird's-eye view of the infamous "Graveyard of the Atlantic."

THE BUILDER OF IRON GIANTS

UP IN THE LONELY TOWER HE SITS,
THE KEEPER OF THE CRIMSON LIGHT.
Fitz James O'Brien
Minots Ledge, *1861*

What do the bloody battlefields of Gettysburg and the treacherous coral reefs of Florida have in common?

They were both conquered by the same man.

George Gordon Meade was a quiet, dedicated engineer who graduated from West Point in 1835 and went on to serve a successful career in the Army Corps of Topographical Engineers. Later, he distinguished himself in the Union Army during the Civil War. Today he is remembered largely for his glorious defeat of Robert E. Lee at Gettysburg in July 1863.

But perhaps his greater achievement lies on the Florida Reef. There Meade designed and built a phalanx of tall screwpile lighthouses to guide shipping through the bottleneck formed as the Gulf Stream moves through the Florida Strait. They are unlike any other lighthouses in the nation, reflecting cutting-edge technology of the day and a revolutionary design.

Meade had distinguished himself with the completion of two lighthouses in the mid-Atlantic in the 1840s. One was a tall brick tower at Barnegat, New Jersey; the other an innovative design for the Delaware Bay's hazardous Brandywine Shoal. The latter was the nation's first screwpile lighthouse, an iron hulk standing in open water over a submerged reef in the main shipping channel for Philadelphia. After its construction, Meade was sent by the Army Corps of Topographical Engineers to survey the waters around south Florida in preparation for his next task—building screwpile lighthouses on the hard coral of the Florida Reef.

Construction of Carysfort Reef Lighthouse south of Miami barely had begun in 1849, when the chief engineer for the project died. The Lighthouse Board sent Meade to complete the task, since he knew the strait well and had received enormous praise for his work at Brandywine Shoal. Carysfort Reef, named for the first recorded ship lost on the site in 1767, had caused more than 100 wrecks in the fifteen years prior to the outset of its construction. The need for a strong sentinel on the site was paramount.

Pieces for the iron lighthouse were prefabricated at a foundry in Philadelphia, preassembled by the construction crew in a kind of dress rehearsal for work on the actual site, then disassembled and shipped to the reef. Meade oversaw the reassembly, but the project soon encountered problems. When surveying the reef, Meade had believed it to be solid, but during construction he discovered that a sandbank lay beneath the hard coral crust. The lighthouse's giant, tubular legs could not be anchored firmly as planned.

Meade quickly went to work and drew up a design for stabilizing disks that would slide over the bottom of each iron leg and anchor it to the coral. He submitted his design to the U.S. Lighthouse Establishment and obtained permission to fabricate and install the disks. Carysfort Reef Lighthouse, rising 112 feet tall, went into service March 10, 1852. Meade also made important recommendations concerning the illuminating apparatus, which he thought required a first-order lens, and a bright red daymark for the Carysfort Reef tower, to show up well against the blue-green sea. He hired two "intelligent and faithful" lightkeepers and impressed upon them the importance of keeping a good light and providing assistance to any vessels wrecked in the area.

Two months after completion of Carysfort Reef Light, Meade was transferred to Sand Key, nine miles off Key West, where another screwpile lighthouse was underway. The 450-ton lighthouse was already fabricated and awaiting delivery to the site while the newly formed U.S. Lighthouse Board sought funds to complete it. In the meantime, Meade was not idle. He designed an improved lamp for the illuminating apparatus to replace the problematic French lamps then in use. Due to a hydraulic system that pumped the oil, Meade's lamp used less oil and the wick had to be trimmed only once during the night. Sand Key Light was lit for the first time July 20, 1853, utilizing a first-order Fresnel lens and Meade's new lamp. The U.S. Lighthouse Board then asked Meade to attend the Crystal Palace Exposition in New York and demonstrate his lamp and a Fresnel lens to the public.

Meade's next project was to design a lighthouse for Rebecca Shoal, which lies between Key West and the Dry Tortugas. Parts were fabricated by a foundry in Philadelphia and shipped to Key West in 1854. Work began on the site the following year, and proceeded well until a hurricane reeled through the Keys and destroyed the unfinished beacon. Attempts in 1856 and 1857 met with a similar fate, and Meade concluded that no site was more exposed or offered "greater obstacles" than Rebecca Shoal. He sug-

Using technology borrowed from Britain, George Gorden Meade (above), an engineer with the U.S. Army's Topographic Corps, began marking the treacherous Florida Strait in the 1850s with iron screwpile lighthouses. The first of these "Iron Giants" to go into service was Carysfort Reef Lighthouse. Meade completed the lighthouse in 1852. Its open framework design allowed hurricane wind and waves to pass through unimpeded. (Photograph of lighthouse courtesy of the U.S. Coast Guard Archives, photograph of George Gorden Meade courtesy of the U.S. Lighthouse Society)

gested buoys be placed there until a more storm-sturdy design was devised.

In the meantime, the Lighthouse Establishment asked Meade to select the next site for a lighthouse on the Florida Reef and submit a design. He chose Sombrero Key and designed a lighthouse 147 feet tall, which was first lighted in March 1858. The light at Sombrero Key used galvanization, a new technology that would strengthen and preserve the tower's ironwork. After its inauguration, Meade took over as superintendent of both the Fourth and Seventh Lighthouse Districts. He continued to tinker with a design for Rebecca Shoal and then surveyed the Northern Lakes before requesting military service during the Civil War. The Lighthouse Establishment adapted his designs for screwpile lighthouses for iron sentinels at American Shoal, Fowey Rocks, and Alligator Reef. Rebecca Shoal finally received a screwpile lighthouse in 1886, fourteen years after Meade's death.

Immortalized for his military genius at Gettysburg, few Americans today know of George Gordon Meade's great humanitarian service as a lighthouse engineer. A drive across the Overseas Highway between the Florida mainland and Key West gives a hint of his contributions. Offshore stand the majestic "Iron Giants," solemn reminders of a different battle waged on the Florida Reef.

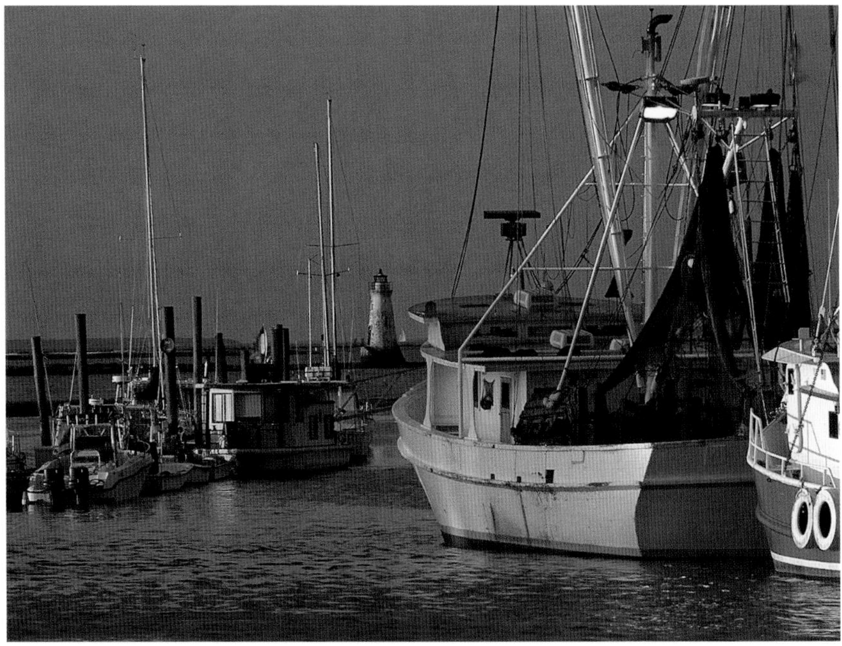

Built in 1849, diminutive Cockspur Island Lighthouse was a range beacon for the Savannah River and Fort Pulaski. It sat on an oyster bed, exposed to the worst the sea could deliver. By the late 1850s, both Cockspur Island Lighthouse and its companion range beacon farther upriver needed extensive repairs. The U.S. Lighthouse Board funded the improvements, but much of the upgrade was lost during the Civil War when the little lighthouse found itself in the direct line of fire between Union gunboats and Confederate batteries at Fort Pulaski.

Florida Reef, however, was a stormy shallow assaulted by wind and waves and baked in semitropical sun. Engineers devised special underwater screw feet on tubular legs to anchor the towers to the seafloor. Sequestered personnel resided in living quarters that were elevated above the waterline. Living on the sea made everyday conveniences a luxury. Water for drinking, bathing, and cooking had to be caught during rainstorms in special roof containers and stored in a cistern. Carrier pigeons bore messages to loved ones and government officials on the mainland. Fishermen brought gifts such as tobacco and sweets to thank the lonely men for their solicitous work.

Of the many improvement projects that took place in the 1850s, the revamping of Cape Lookout Lighthouse was most typical and served as a prototype for many of the masonry towers built in the South by the U.S. Lighthouse Board over the next five decades. At first the Board investigated the possibility of repairing the 1812 Cape Lookout Light and of placing a first-order Fresnel lens in its lantern, but the masonry was in such poor condition and the tower so short that only total reconstruction could provide a satisfactory solution. In 1857, work crews began to build a 150-foot conical lighthouse and completed it two years later. Its red brick exterior served as a daymark before it was painted with white stripes against red brick. In 1873, keepers painted the light with a distinctive black and white diamond pattern to differentiate it from the many lighthouses of the Outer Banks.

The Board rebuilt the aging towers at Hog Island, Virginia; Cape Romain, North Carolina; and Cockspur Island, Georgia, and re-established additional Florida light towers at the St. Johns River, Cape St. George, Dog Island, Loggerhead Key, Egmont Key, and Pensacola. There were smaller projects too. Quaint Jones Point Lighthouse was completed in 1856 to mark shoals in the Potomac River near Alexandria, Virginia, which was then the third largest port in the Chesapeake Bay. The first keeper, George Deeton, lived with his family in the lower level of the cottage-style lighthouse and maintained a sperm oil lamp inside a fifth-order Fresnel lens. His annual salary was $400. A summer kitchen, wood storage house, and a unique, tide-cleansed privy, considered high-tech for its day, were separate from the main structure.

By 1860, the U.S. Lighthouse Board's campaign to make American lighthouses the best in the world was well underway. They had rebuilt crumbling towers, employed new materials and construction methods, and replaced archaic reflector systems with Fresnel lenses. As a result, the string of lighted aids marking U.S. shores grew by the year. A well-trained and well-equipped cadre of keepers and support personnel was hard at work, and the lighthouse service seemed to be approaching its zenith when darkness fell over the nation and its lighthouses.

Prisoners of War

"There is now, we believe, no regularly appointed keeper of the Light House at Jones Point," reported the Alexandria, Virginia, newspaper, the *Local News*, in April 1861.

Like many of its southern compatriots, Jones Point Light suffered an uneasy tenure during the Civil War. Some stood vacant, many were damaged, and several were completely destroyed, vanishing in the smoke of cannon fire and dynamite. In March 1861, aware its southern ports were essential to economic survival, the Confederacy established its own agency to oversee navigational aids—the Confederate States Light House Bureau. Commander Raphael Semmes of Alabama, head of the Confederate Navy, was placed in charge. Lighthouse keepers immediately found themselves in a quandary. Which government should they answer to and what was expected of them if conflict came to their doorstep? Some, like the Jones Point keeper, deserted their posts immediately. Others remained on duty until forcibly removed, and still others played both sides. Their charges, the lighthouses themselves, became innocent pawns in the ever-widening conflict.

After Virginia's secession in April 1861, Cape Henry Lighthouse stood perilously at risk, given its important responsibility as a guidepost for entrance to the Chesapeake Bay. Within days, keeper John B. Drew reported that he was threatened by "men from Princess Anne Country" who raided the station and destroyed the tower's costly illuminating apparatus. They cautioned the keeper to carefully choose his allegiance. Smith Island Lighthouse, standing watch on one of Virginia's barrier islands, was later destroyed and its keeper robbed. At nearby Hog Island Lighthouse, keeper Jean M. Potts feared for his well-being as the war proceeded and requested help. "I was the only man who voted the Union ticket in this precinct," he warned the U.S. Lighthouse Board in 1863. To protect the light and its anxious keeper, a Union ship was anchored off the station. They helped themselves to Potts' garden, chickens, and smokehouse, and soon proved more worrisome than enemy troops.

The State of North Carolina sent an officer of the state militia to various lighthouses in the weeks following secession to oversee their deactivation. He first went to Oregon Inlet and assisted lightkeeper Samuel Tillett with the removal of the third-order lens at Bodie Island Lighthouse. Next came Roanoke Marshes Light, a screwpile sentinel in Pamlico Sound, then Ocracoke Lighthouse, and others. The intent was to quietly remove each light from service and hide its equipment. Lightkeepers would cooperate or be ousted. The

Tiny Jones Point Lighthouse, built in 1856 to mark shoals in the Potomac River and guide vessels into the port of Alexandria, Virginia, was among numerous inland waterway lighthouses commissioned by the U.S. Lighthouse Board. Completed for a mere $5,000, it served until 1926, when a flood destroyed the Chesapeake and Ohio Canal, causing Alexandria to decline in maritime importance. By the end of World War II, the lighthouse was in ruins (left). In recent years, it was restored and relighted by the Mount Vernon Chapter of the Daughters of the American Revolution and the National Park Service (above). (Historical photograph used courtesy of the U.S. Coast Guard Archives)

Confederacy aimed to establish its own republic in the South, after which each sentinel would be gloriously relit.

Not every southern lightkeeper was so sure of a course of action. Benjamin Fulcher at Cape Hatteras Lighthouse felt somewhat insulated from the conflict and was surprised when a courier arrived April 17, 1861, with a letter instructing him to deactivate the lighthouse. He hesitated for a time before following a directive issued by H. F. Hancock, district superintendent of the Confederate Lighthouse Bureau. It was an order he considered unethical—depriving mariners of a guiding light on a stretch of coastline that was notoriously dangerous. But in the end, Fulcher obeyed orders, as did most of his southern peers. He darkened the light, and then helped Hancock's men dismantle, remove, and crate the fragile equipment. Hancock then transported the opulent jewel by steamer up the Pamlico River, where he hid it in an obscure inland warehouse.

At Cape Lookout Lighthouse, keeper Gaer Chawick resisted at first when a rowdy band of Rebels arrived on the beach to dismantle his light. He warned that his cousin, who was an agent for the Confederate Secret Service, would not approve. They ignored his threats and darkened the tower, then carried off and hid the huge first-order lens. The Union would not reinstate the tower until January 1863, and then with a third-order lens. A few months later, disgruntled raiders evaded federal patrols around Core Banks and landed at Cape Lookout. They slipped past the sleeping Union lightkeeper, placed two kegs of gunpowder in the base of the tower, and lit the fuse. The lighthouse survived the blast, losing only its wooden stairs and crystal lens.

Overzealous, self-appointed raiding parties sometimes damaged optics irreparably, but most were given excellent care. Evidence of this is found in correspondence records within individual districts, but also in an appropriation of money that was requested by the superintendent of lighthouses at Beaufort, North Carolina, in April 1861. He asked for blankets, not for human use, but to wrap and cushion expensive lenses for storage. By the time North Carolina joined the Confederate States of America in May, every lighthouse on its coast was out of commission and all illuminating equipment hidden in Elizabeth City and Beaufort.

Admiral William B. Shubrick, a South Carolinian who remained loyal to the Union, chaired the U.S. Lighthouse Board in Washington, D.C. He took a dim view of the Confederate claim of nondestructive deactivation and reported in the summer of 1861: "On 22 August, a gang of pirates from St. Augustine visited the Light House at Jupiter and removed from it all lenses and illuminating apparatus. They then proceeded to Cape Florida Lighthouse, the lenses of which they broke and destroyed."

The Confederate version of the incident, provided to Florida's governor by the accused "pirates," sounded quite different. "At Jupiter we destroyed no property whatsoever, the Light being a revolving one and of very costly make, we took away only enough of the machinery to make it unserviceable. . . . At Cape Florida the Light being within the immediate protection of Key West and most indispensable at this time to the enemy's fleet, as well as knowing it to be useless for us to try and hold it, we determined to damage it so that it will be of no possible use to our enemies."

Similar scenarios played out at many southern lighthouses. At Georgia's Sapelo Light, keeper Alexander Hazard stood by helplessly as Confederates dismantled the Fresnel lens and destroyed the reflectors. His neighboring keeper at Tybee Island Light fled after the lighthouse was set on fire, and at St. Simons Island Lighthouse the new lens was removed and hidden in the town of Brunswick, while the venerable old 1812 tower was destroyed. Florida's St. Johns River Lighthouse remained lit for a time after Union soldiers ran keeper John Daniels off the grounds. It aided Union ships as they traveled in and out of the river, but Daniels surreptitiously returned one night and shot out the lens. Down the coast, Captain Mills Burnham, keeper of Cape Canaveral Lighthouse, quietly removed the lens, lamps, and clockworks from his tower, carefully boxed them, and buried them in his orange grove.

August old Charleston Lighthouse, the first sentinel established in the South and the first to see military action in the war, was completely destroyed by gunfire. Its compatriot at Hunting Island, only four years old when the conflict began, also vanished during the war, probably toppled by Confederate gunfire and then carried into the sea by erosion and storm waves.

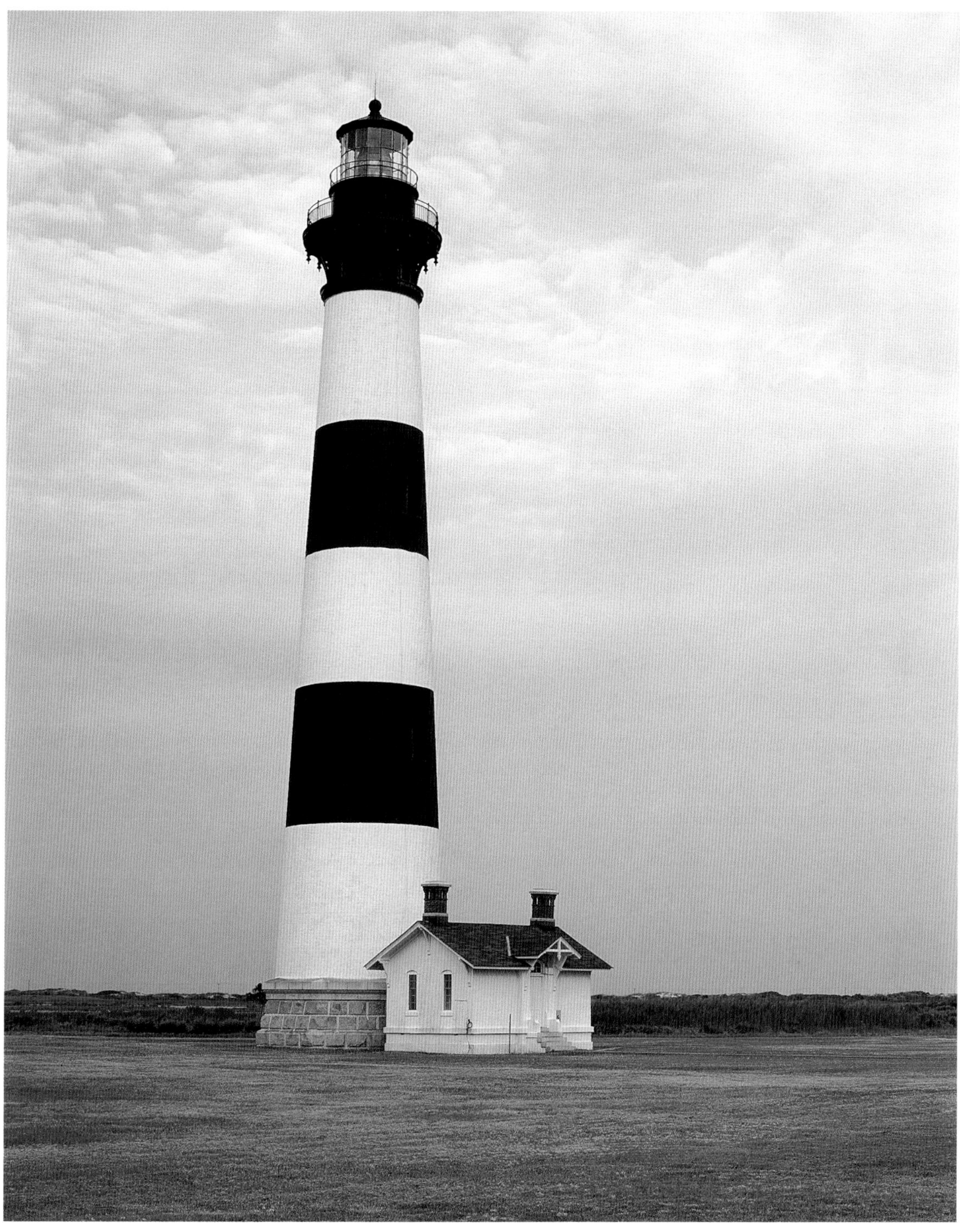

Following secession in 1861, North Carolina sent a military officer to disable all of the state's lighthouses, in order to prevent their aiding Union forces. Bodie Island Lighthouse was the first to be decommissioned. Its third-order lens was dismantled by the Confederacy, crated, and hidden. A few months later the tower sustained heavy damage when Confederate raiders set off explosives inside it. Following the war, it was rebuilt and upgraded to a first-order lighthouse.

Lightships, tenders, and other vessels in the employ of the U.S. Lighthouse Board in southern districts also were affected. Most were decommissioned and stowed at southern depots, but a few were refitted for service in the Confederate Navy. The lighthouse supply schooner *Jasper,* which had run aground on Shackley Banks in 1857 and been taken to Wilmington, North Carolina, for repairs, was seized for Confederate use as a patrol vessel. Confederate troops raided the *Buchanan,* another supply schooner, in the James River on April 18, 1861, taking it to Richmond, where they released the crew and docked the vessel until the end of the war. In the Gulf of Mexico, the Confederacy seized the *Helen* while she was tending southern lighthouses. Confederate troops refitted the tender with cannons and then forced *Helen* to serve the Confederate Navy until Union troops captured her in April 1863 at Cedar Keys, Florida. A Union gunship burned and sank her.

There was great loss during this period, but also gain. In 1867, the U.S. Lighthouse Board rebuilt the Assateague Island Lighthouse in Virginia, despite the rumble of war around it. Farther south, they rebuilt the Cape Charles Light in 1864. The Garden Key Light in the Dry Tortugas Islands of the Gulf of Mexico was surrounded by Fort Jefferson, and thus remained unscathed, continuing to operate throughout the war.

At Key West, a clever officer in charge of the Union barracks anticipated Florida's 1861 secession and took control of Fort Zachary Taylor, preventing the city from falling into Confederate hands. The Lighthouse Board asked eighty-year-old Barbara Mabrity, keeper and matriarch of Key West Lighthouse, to sign an oath of allegiance to the Union or lose her position. Though pro-Southern, she signed and retained her job until 1864, at which time an assistant keeper claimed Mabrity made anti-Union remarks to him. The Board demanded Mabrity's resignation, but she refused. A few days later a Union officer gently removed her from the lighthouse. Key West remained in Union control throughout the conflict.

At war's end, the U.S. Lighthouse Board faced a massive reconstruction assignment; 164 southern lighthouses had been damaged or destroyed, while lightships and tenders were altered or lost entirely. Lenses recovered from the fallen Confederacy were injured or had parts missing, equipment was scattered, and the towers that survived had suffered from conflagration and gunfire. District offices were mostly in ruins. Admiral William B. Shubrick, still chief of the U.S. Lighthouse Board at the end of the war, began the arduous task of reinstating the lighthouse service in the South.

Destruction at southern lighthouses from all natural catastrophes combined—hurricanes, lightning, hail, wind, erosion, and earthquakes—did not equal the enormous losses incurred during the Civil War. One hundred sixty-four southern lighthouses were damaged or destroyed in the conflict. An image of Alabama's Mobile Bay Lighthouse that appeared in an 1865 issue of Frank Leslie's Illustrated Newspaper *served as an emblem of the dreadful travail of war. (Photograph courtesy of Frank Leslie's Illustrated Newspaper, 1865)*

Above: *Though lighthouses were considered Union property, the Confederacy believed it would ultimately gain control of the towers and would reinstate them once the South won the war and became a sovereign nation. Lighting equipment was removed with great care and safely stored, but occasional raiding parties of overzealous southerners took matters into their own hands. The priceless lens and revolving apparatus of Cape Florida Lighthouse was smashed with hammers in August 1861, and its oil stores were poured in the sand.*

Left: *Though many lighthouses were damaged or destroyed by the Confederacy during the Civil War, Key West Lighthouse was protected thanks to the foresight of a Union officer who secured nearby Fort Zachary before the Confederacy claimed it. The lighthouse remained in the care of its southern keeper, Barbara Mabrity, until 1864, when Mabrity was removed for making anti-Union remarks. (Photograph courtesy of National Archives)*

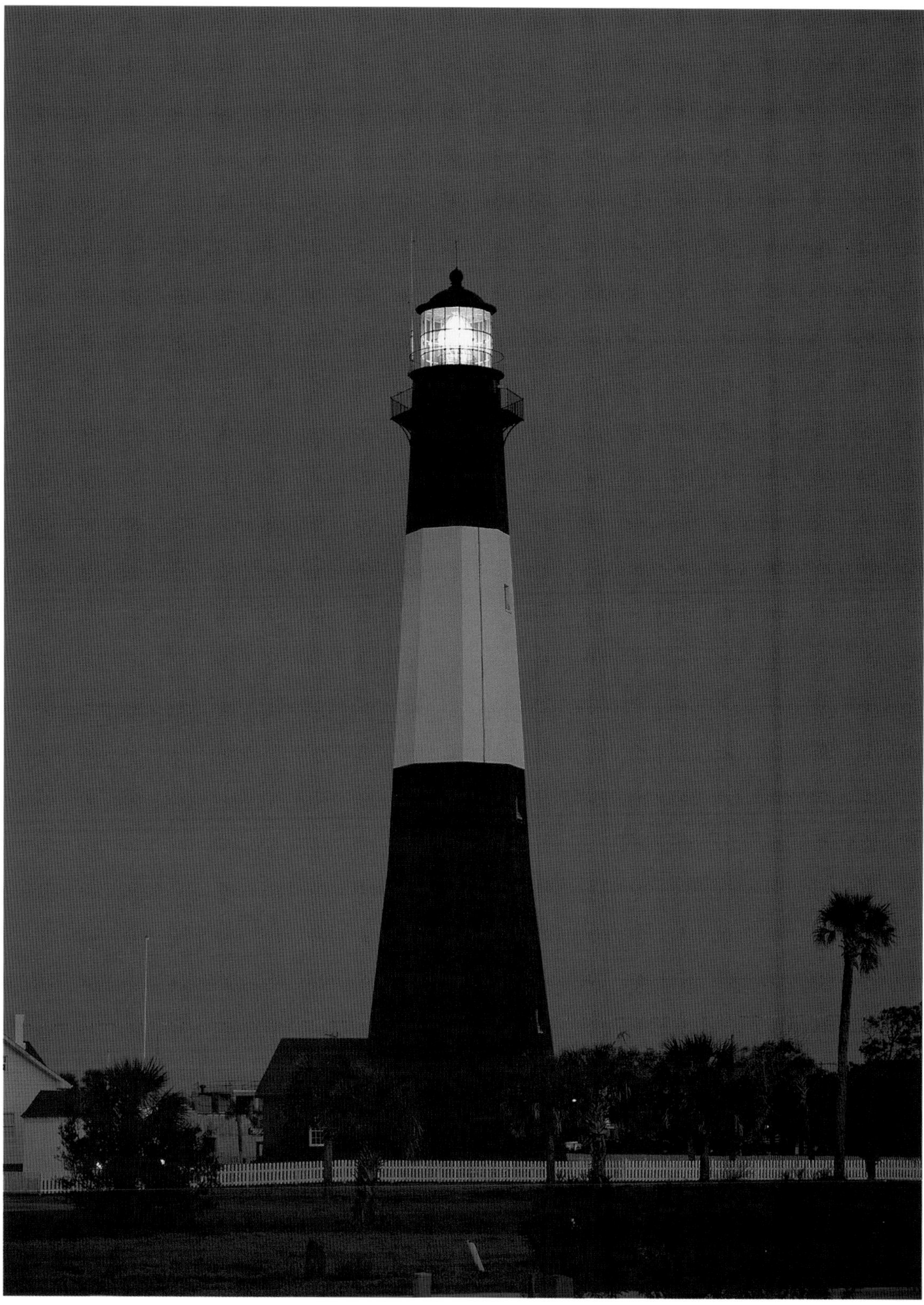

Lightkeepers found themselves in a quandary at the start of the Civil War: they could remain loyal to the Union and risk attack by angry Confederates or extinguish their lights and join the Rebel cause. At Tybee Island Lighthouse in 1861, a Union lightkeeper attempted to stand by his charge but soon fled after the station was set on fire. At the end of the war, the damaged lighthouse was repaired and raised to its present height of 145 feet. The increase is roughly visible in the top black-and-white bands of its daymark.

The Prison Light

Into solitude I went, and wisdom was revealed to me.
Winnebago Holy Song

In 1513, Ponce de Leon named the Dry Tortugas, islands which lie some seventy miles west of Key West, after the many sea turtles his crew harvested there. Many years later, when the government explored Florida for suitable lighthouse sites, surveyors chose the Dry Tortugas. A sentinel here would aid shipping traveling between the Florida Strait and the mouth of the Mississippi River, and mark the dangerous currents and Gulf Stream eddies in the area. More than 200 shipwrecks have been documented around the Dry Tortugas, a third of which were total losses.

Garden Key Lighthouse, surrounded by Fort Jefferson, remained safe during the Civil War since it was heavily fortified as a Union defense. In 1861 it became a prison for captured Confederate soldiers. Its most famous inmate arrived in 1865—Dr. Samuel Mudd, the physician who had given medical treatment to John Wilkes Booth after the assassination of President Lincoln.

The first lighthouse was established on Garden Key in 1826 and fitted with a Lewis Patent Lamps, but by 1847 mariners were calling it "the worst light on the coast." The U.S. Lighthouse Establishment made plans to replace the tower, but before they could act, the U.S. Navy decided to build a fort on Garden Key. When contractors arrived in 1850, they found the lighthouse operating on ground where they were to build fortification walls. After considerable discussion, the Navy and the Lighthouse Establishment decided that Fort Jefferson, named for the nation's third president, would be built around the tower. Eight years later, the Establishment constructed a taller lighthouse on nearby Loggerhead Key, and downgraded the old Garden Key Light to a minor guide for vessels docking at the fort.

When the Civil War broke out, Fort Jefferson was heavily fortified as a Union defense. Both the Garden Key and Loggerhead lighthouses remained functional throughout the war as Union sentinels, and late in 1861, Fort Jefferson became a repository for Confederate prisoners. Dr. Samuel Mudd, the fort's most famous prisoner, arrived in 1865. Mudd had unknowingly given medical aid to President Lincoln's assassin, John Wilkes Booth. A jury found him guilty of conspiracy and aiding a criminal, and sentenced him to serve time at Fort Jefferson.

The good doctor dutifully accepted his sentence and in time became a beloved occupant of the fort. When a yellow fever epidemic swept the prison in autumn 1867, killing the resident physician, Mudd assumed the role of prison doctor. Nearly three-quarters of the prisoners and staff at the fort were sick, possibly also the lighthouse keepers and their families. Dr. Mudd's attentions greatly reduced the death toll. He kept medical records on the fort's many personnel and prisoners, and devotedly wrote in his own diary, often expressing hope he'd be forgiven for his unfortunate misdeed. He constantly maintained he had done only what the Hippocratic Oath decreed. Undoubtedly, the light of Garden Key Lighthouse was a symbol of hope for the physician.

Friends in Washington, prisoners, and wardens wrote letters on Mudd's behalf, praising his compassionate work and urging his release. In February 1869, Mudd received a pardon from President Andrew Johnson. He returned home to Maryland a month later, and lived quietly until his death in 1883.

After a hurricane damaged the lighthouse at the fort, the Lighthouse Establishment rebuilt it in 1874. The new twenty-five-foot tower consisted of iron plates that formed a hexagon on top of the fort walls, which elevated it to sixty-seven feet above sea. The army abandoned the fort that same year, but the government later used it as a quarantine station and buoy depot. The military re-occupied Fort Jefferson during the Spanish-American War, and then, after a fire in the lighthouse privy spread to other structures, they vacated it altogether in 1912. The fire destroyed the keeper's house and part of the fort, but the metal tower survived.

The U.S. Bureau of Lighthouses repaired and automated the tower the following year, and it served until 1921, when it was no longer needed. The National Park Service now maintains the light as part of the Fort Jefferson National Monument.

Rebuilding the Southern Bastion of Sentinels

One of Shubrick's first initiatives was to repair recovered lenses and fund replacements. In a letter to the French lens firm of Lemmonier and Sauttier, his engineers requested repair of nine lenses, one being the third-order revolving lens for Bodie Island Lighthouse: "Lens to be refitted with 65 Sound prisms including 2 annular prisms in place of those which are broken. Astragals, horizontal rings for lens socket, Crown for lens, Pedestal Table, Revolving Machinery." The most damaged among the nine was the optic from Cape San Blas Lighthouse, Florida, which required 137 new prisms.

Rebuilding damaged or lost towers commenced at a feverish pace, and pre-war plans resumed to close dark spaces not only in the South but elsewhere. The need for new lighthouses on inland rivers, such as the Mississippi, Missouri, and Ohio, as well as on the relatively unmarked West Coast, added to the economic burden. The Board's insistence on state-of-the-art materials and technology set it on a focused course to forever quell any suggestion that navigational aids in the United States were inferior to those in Europe or any other part of the world.

To handle the large-scale shipment of materials and construction, the U.S. Lighthouse Board purchased six vessels from the Navy's retired "Flowerpot Fleet," a flotilla of older vessels known for their quaint botanical names. Each was refitted for use as a tender to construct, repair, and provision lighthouses. Slow and somewhat inelegant in appearance, each tender flew the Board's ensign, a triangular white flag with a red border and blue lighthouse. Over the next few decades, the number of tenders increased, as did their work nationwide. When old ones wore out, the Board designed and built new ones especially for the work. Flowery ships such as *Ivy*, *Magnolia*, and *Pansy* served the Gulf of Mexico. *Arbutus* and *Mangrove* tended Florida's lighthouses; *Crocus*, *Water Lily*, *Bramble*, and *Zizania* worked the Carolinas; and *Maple* and *Holly* served the Chesapeake Bay.

The Board completely rebuilt Charleston Lighthouse, which had been damaged beyond repair during the war. Located on Morris Island, Charleston became a much-sought-after assignment due to its pastoral setting. The Board added to the height of the old Tybee Island Light, and completely rebuilt St. Simons Island Light. Taller sentinels went up at St. Augustine and St. Marks in Florida, Cape Hatteras and Bodie Island on the Outer Banks, and Georgetown, South Carolina. Cape Hatteras Light, the grandest tower of all, contained 1,250,000 bricks and rose 198 feet above the sands.

Foundries in the North thundered with the production of iron for new screwpile and caisson lighthouses and tall iron-plate towers. At Cape Canaveral, Florida, where construction crews had started a foundation for a

Iron was the material of choice for many lighthouses in the late nineteenth century. Durable, cheap, and easy to manufacture and assemble, iron pile lighthouses appeared at sites throughout the South. In Florida alone, four iron pile lighthouses were built between 1884 and 1895. Among them was Cape San Blas Lighthouse. The sturdy skeleton lighthouse went into operation in 1885 near Port St. Joe, replacing a brick tower plagued by erosion.

new lighthouse prior to the war, work resumed. They laid a concrete pad for the tower and bolted together huge iron plates to form a graceful conical shape. Then the workers lined the tower with bricks for stability and fitted it with an iron lantern. Beginning in 1868, a first-order Fresnel lens sent a beam eighteen miles seaward. Equally impressive was the iron screwpile lighthouse farther south at Alligator Reef, named for a ship that sank there in 1822. The lighthouse was in the planning phase in 1861 when Florida joined the Confederacy. Work continued after the war using a steam-powered pile driver with a one-ton hammer to force the tower's iron legs deep into the coral reef. When the 136-foot sentinel went into service in November 1873, the U.S. Lighthouse Board called it "one of the finest and most effective lights on the coast." The big iron lighthouse on Fowey Rocks, south of Miami, was built in 1878.

One of the last major nineteenth-century masonry lighthouses built in the Southeast went into service in 1875 at Currituck Beach. The 158-foot tower, with its massive brick walls that were nearly six feet thick at the base and three feet thick at the parapet, closed the dark space between Cape Henry and Bodie Island. At the same time, the Board was busy replacing old wooden stairs with cast-iron stairways, and Currituck Beach Light's great iron spiral was among the loveliest. Two hundred fourteen lacework iron steps were bolted together along the tower's conical walls to form nine elegant spirals. Delicate finials festooned the railing posts, and the entire staircase was painted dark green. A service ladder completed the climb to the lantern, where a first-order lens produced a beam visible nineteen miles at sea.

The U.S. Lighthouse Board made many improvements in the 1870s, including the establishment of more daymarks to make it easier for mariners to identify lighthouses during the day. Prior to 1850, most southern sentinels were whitewashed or had unpainted brick exteriors. Throughout the post–Civil War period, a variety of designs were added to the tall towers of the south to distinguish them from each other. On the Outer Banks, daymarks were crucial for navigation, since light towers were situated close together. Bodie Lighthouse was marked with black-and-white horizontal bands; Cape Hatteras Lighthouse donned its famous spiral black-and-white stripes; and Cape Lookout Lighthouse wore a black-and-white checkerboard pattern. Assateague Island Lighthouse in Virginia and Sapelo Lighthouse in Georgia sported pretty candy-stripe daymarks of red-and-white horizontal stripes.

As the century came to a close, the U.S. Lighthouse Board devoted itself to extending and refining the nation's system of navigational aids. Establishment of lighthouses in Oregon and Washington, and in the new territories of Alaska and Hawaii consumed much of the budget, but the Board continued to improve access to southern ports, especially those in Florida. in 1884, the long-awaited lighthouse for Sanibel Island, an iron straight-pile design for the entrance into the busy cattle-shipping port of Punta Rassa, went into service. Similar iron towers were built in 1885 at Cape San Blas, to guide shipping into Port St. Joe, and in 1887 at Anclote Keys, to aid the approach to Tarpon Springs. The lighthouses at Sanibel Island and Cape San Blas were fabricated at Phoenix Ironworks in Ocean City, New Jersey, and Anclote Keys Lighthouse was fabricated by Colwell Ironworks in New York City. All three towers were shipped to their sites in pieces to be assembled quickly and cheaply. Wooden dwellings on pilings completed the stations.

In 1890, the quaint Charlotte Harbor Lighthouse (now Boca Grande Lighthouse) was built on Gasparilla Island, Florida, to assist the lucrative phosphate shipping industry that had arisen at Port Boca Grande. By now, the government had streamlined the entire process for lighthouse construction, accomplishing the task cheaply, efficiently, and quickly. After appropriating $35,000 to the project, the government solicited bids for construction of the wooden lighthouse and keeper's dwelling, a shed, and two cisterns, plus the manufacture of iron pilings and a metal lantern. Then it ordered an unusual 3.5-order Fresnel lens from France. Within two years of the first appropriation, the little sentinel was completed and placed in service on December 31, 1890. It was the only manmade structure on Gasparilla Island at the time and a lonely assignment for its two keepers, who may have felt much like castaways. Their families lived ashore so the children could attend school. But in summer, the island was alive with activity when the families joined the keepers.

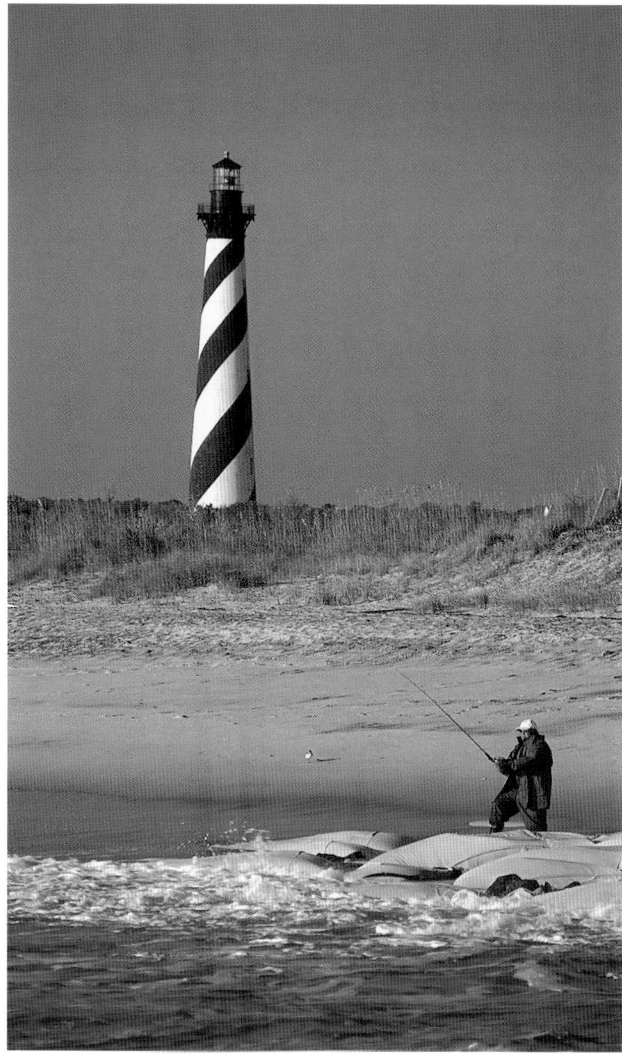

As more lighthouses appeared on the nation's coasts, the need for daymarks to identify them during the day became paramount. Sapelo Island Lighthouse was painted in bold red-and-white stripes in the late 1860s (facing page). On the Outer Banks, where lighthouses stood less than twenty miles apart, a variety of patterns were devised to distinguish the towers. In the 1870s, Bodie Island Lighthouse was given a dress of two white and two black horizontal bands (above left), and its sister sentry at Cape Hatteras was painted in a spiral pattern of black and white (above right). At about this same time, wooden stairs in both towers were replaced with iron stairways and the lanterns were scraped and coated in thick lead paint. The work was done using makeshift scaffolds or a chair slung over the side of the tower and raised or lowered by a pulley system. Today, a large crane does the work of repainting or repairing the tall towers.

Idyllic Sanibel Island, sitting at the entrance to the busy port of Punta Rassa, Florida, was marked in 1884 with a pyramidal-shaped iron pile lighthouse. Kerosene lamps illuminated its third-order lens, and two spacious wooden dwellings, also on piles, flanked the tower. The first keeper, Henry Shanahan, was grateful for the assignment, for it provided plenty of room to raise his thirteen children.

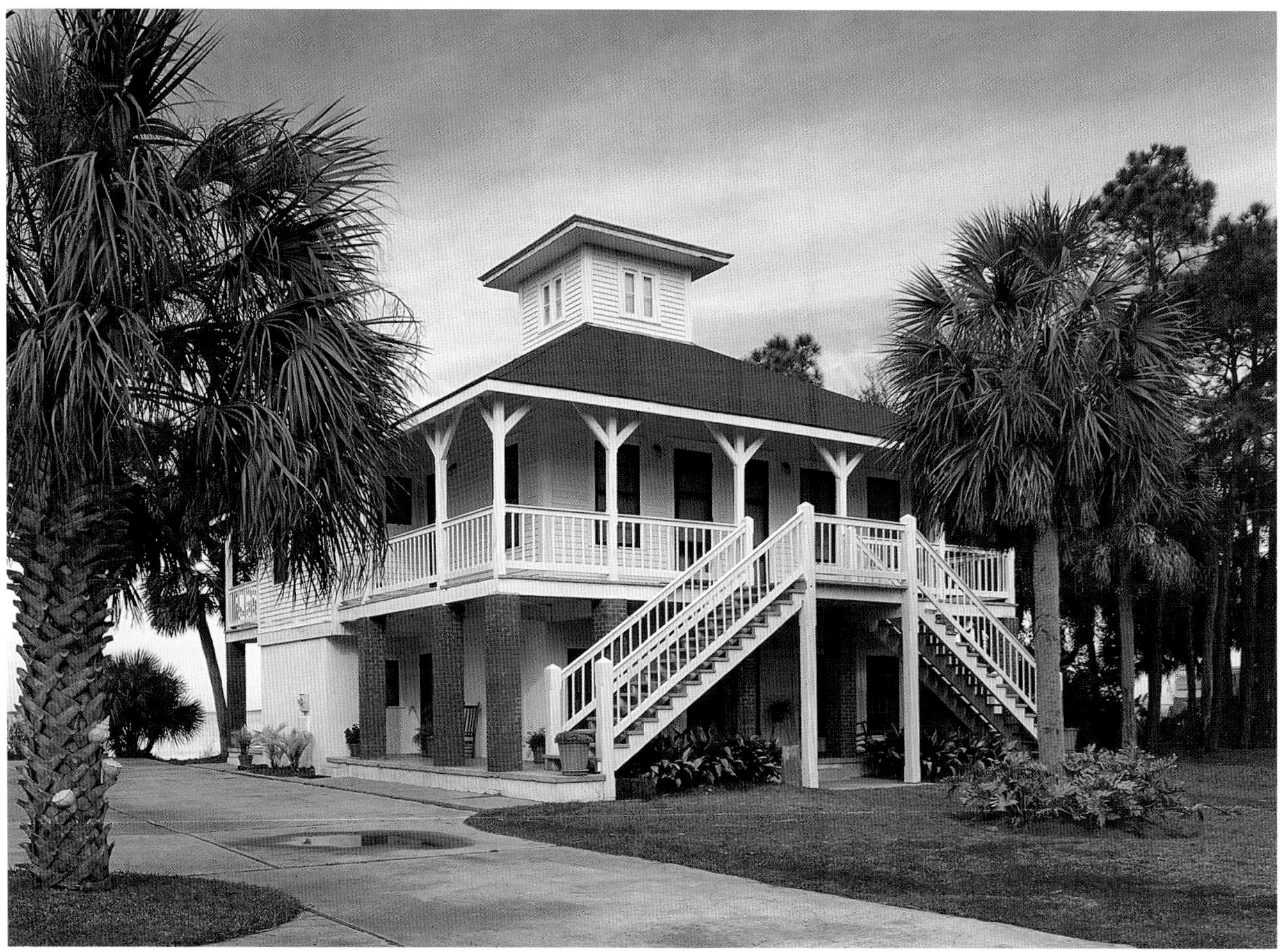

Called Beacon Hill Lighthouse in its early years, all that remains of the 1902 cottage-style St. Joseph Bay Lighthouse is its residence. It served the waters around Apalachicola until 1955, then was "decapitated" (a term lighthouse preservationists use to describe the removal of the lantern) and sold at auction, fetching a mere $300. It has since been moved to Simmons Bayou and restored by its private owner who hopes also to fabricate a new lantern using blueprints from the original structure.

Originally called Port Charlotte Lighthouse, the cottage-style sentinel at Boca Grande, Florida, was the only manmade structure on Gasparilla Island at the time it was constructed in 1890. A simple harbor light, it required neither great height nor a powerful beacon. But its 3.5-order Fresnel lens was an unusual size, of which only a few examples still exist.

Built upon Sand

Like everything built by humans, lighthouses cannot stand forever.

Timothy Harrison and Ray Jones

Lost Lighthouses, *2000*

Many challenges faced lighthouse engineers and builders as they planned and constructed light towers, but none as persistent and costly as erosion. More than half the lighthouses built in the South were lost to shifting sands and changing shorelines. Low barrier beaches posed a serious danger to ships and required lofty navigational lights, but these were difficult sites upon which to build. A sandy foundation is easily undermined by wind and water, and sand moves about seemingly at will. Early on, engineers realized southern sentinels required special technologies.

One solution was to build metal collapsible lighthouses, so that they could easily be taken apart and relocated when in jeopardy. The 136-foot-tall lighthouse at Hunting Island, South Carolina, built in 1875, was made of iron plates bolted together atop a concrete pad. In 1889, after the encroaching shoreline threatened to topple it, workers dismantled the lighthouse and moved it farther inland. Similarly, Cape Canaveral Lighthouse was relocated in 1894. Many lighthouses in the South and elsewhere in the nation were built with this goal in mind.

Pile construction, which used various anchorage methods, was another solution to the problem of erosion. Straight pile towers had legs driven deep into the ground, sometimes as deep as thirty feet, which allowed sand to move about or even wash away without harming the foundation. Virginia's Cape Charles Lighthouse is a straight pile design, as is the old Hilton Head Island Rear Range Lighthouse in South Carolina. Florida has many examples at sites such as Sanibel Island, Boca Grande, Cape San Blas, Crooked River, and Hillsboro Inlet.

Screwpile and diskpile designs provided a stronger anchor for lighthouses that stood in shallow water. Small screwpile sentinels dotted the rivers, bays, and sounds of the South. They usually consisted of wooden cottages perched on iron framework foundations whose screw-tip pile legs extended down through the water. The piles were screwed deep into the muck and sand of the seabed. Diskpiles were used where additional stability was needed. Sand Key Light, nine miles off Key West, is the best example of a diskpile design. Its screwpiles were driven through a hard coral reef into the sand, but each pile also had a shoe-like attachment to hold it firmly in the coral crust.

Another successful solution in the battle with erosion was the caisson lighthouse. A heavy caisson was fabricated ashore, then towed to a water-bound site and sunk into the seabed to a depth of thirty feet or more. The hollow caisson was filled with stone or concrete, capped, and crowned with a lighthouse. Virginia's Thimble Shoal Lighthouse and Newport News Middle Ground Lighthouse in the Chesapeake Bay near Hampton are sturdy examples. More than a century of tidal surge has swept around their bases, and a ship even collided with them, yet caisson sentinels stand strong.

Masonry lighthouses in the South have fought tough battles with erosion. The first two lighthouses at Tybee Island, Georgia, fell victim to erosion. So did Florida's original Sand Key Lighthouse, which began undermining from the moment it was lighted in 1827. Ultimately, it succumbed in an 1846 hurricane after the seawall protecting its foundation washed away. In the Carolinas, shifting sands plagued Cape Lookout Light for much of its career. In 1850, keeper William Fulford reported to the lighthouse inspector that he was constantly removing sand from the front of his house and kept a wheelbarrow parked there for that purpose. Farther south, Cape Romain Lighthouse began to lean only two years after its construction in 1858, because water intruded into the foundation.

Cape St. George Lighthouse near Apalachicola, Florida, has been undermined by surrounding sands too. Established in 1833, its first two towers collapsed.

A masonry lighthouse was built in 1827 at Cape Romain at the mouth of the Santee River to warn ships away from shoals that lie off the river entrance and help southbound ships avoid the northerly flow of the Gulf Stream. Its builder, Winslow Lewis, had trouble with the foundation. The beacon was never adequate, and in 1857 a taller tower replaced the old sentinel. It was built with slave labor and when completed was found to lean slightly due to water intrusion on its foundation. The slight tilt can be seen in this post–Civil War image. (Photograph courtesy of the U.S. Coast Guard Archives)

The current 1852 lighthouse is stable, but nearly toppled in 1995, after Hurricane Opal undermined one side of the foundation and caused it to cant. The Coast Guard feared it would collapse and for safety reasons made plans to raze the tower. But a concerned citizen's group raised money to shore up the historic old beacon. Construction crews excavated its foundation until it leveled, and then placed stabilizing materials around the base. Even so, the struggle is not over. Erosion continues its yearly march on St. George Island, and unless the lighthouse is moved to a more stable site, eventually it will topple.

The resolute old soldier in the battle with erosion is Morris Island Lighthouse at Charleston Harbor. It stands knee-deep on mudflats after more than a century of slow and agonizing erosion. The island once comprised several acres, but over the years it has diminished grain by grain until nothing remains but the old brick tower. The government is partly to blame, since engineers built a jetty along part of the island in 1896 to stall erosion, which ironically changed the movement of sand and accelerated the wearing-away process. Surprisingly, the 1876 lighthouse continues to stand, a testament to its strong foundation. A preservation group called "Save the Light" hopes the Army Corps of Engineers can shore up the site so that the island will rebuild around the old tower. Beyond that, relocation is the only other solution.

By the time Charlotte Harbor Lighthouse was completed, all major U.S. lighthouses were illuminated with kerosene (also called mineral oil). Professor Joseph Henry of the Smithsonian Institution, a physicist who served on the U.S. Lighthouse Board, perfected the new fuel for lighthouse use. He successfully tested kerosene in the 1880s at Navesink Twin Lights in New Jersey, and it was approved for use in all lighthouses soon after. It was much cheaper than lard oil, burned cleaner, and produced a 20 percent brighter light, but it was much more flammable than earlier fuels. The Lighthouse Board designed special lamps for it, and added brick or metal oil houses to light stations to store the incendiary fuel.

A few years later, incandescent oil vapor (IOV) lamps came into use. Similar to today's camping lanterns, they used vaporized kerosene and mantles. Key West Lighthouse was the first southern sentinel to operate an IOV lamp. The changeover resulted in a threefold increase in brilliance and cut kerosene usage in half. Acetylene gas lamps fueled by pressurized tanks came next, often with a sun valve to control the lighting and extinguishing of the beacon. Invented by a Swedish scientist named Gustav Dalen, the Dalen Sun Valve freed lights of the need for daily care, but most lightkeepers remained on duty in case the system failed. The government had yet to completely trust a self-sufficient beacon.

A brief foray into use of natural gas as a lighthouse fuel came in the late 1880s at Jones Point Lighthouse. This experimentation was undertaken due to the little station's proximity to the Smithsonian Institution and Board member Professor Henry, coupled with a nearby gas pipeline in the city of Alexandria, Virginia. The Board ran a pipeline from the city to the lighthouse, and the beacon was rigged to accept the continuous supply. But the system proved troublesome; water intrusion and leaks were constant problems, and by 1900, the lighthouse was converted back to an IOV system.

As the twentieth century began, electricity ushered in a new era of illumination. The torch of the Statue of Liberty, an official lighthouse from 1886 until 1902, was the first electrified beacon. In 1898, the U.S. Lighthouse Board tested electricity for general usage at Navesink Twin Lights, but conversion at many southern lighthouses was not immediate. Their isolated locations required the installation of submarine cables to tap into mainland power sources. Fowey Rocks Light, for example, was not electrified until 1934. With electric lights and fog signals came a plethora of mechanized troubles that resulted in frequent loss of power. All stations maintained kerosene lamps as backups until on-site electric generators were installed to handle periodic outages.

In addition to the advancements in structural technology and illumination, two engineers for the U.S. Lighthouse Board made a complete photo documentation of the nation's lighthouses between 1880 and 1900. These images, now largely housed in the National Archives and U.S. Coast Guard Archives, depict the often bucolic scene of the lighthouse keeper and his light by the sea. Keepers wore their uniforms and families donned their best clothes to pose for the camera, wearing serious expressions that belied their pride and contentment. The Victorian image of the lighthouse as a symbol of goodness and salvation was upheld, and although lighthouses have always been strictly utilitarian structures, the public became enamored of them.

By 1900, the United States had the best navigational aids in the world and the finest people to staff and operate them. By some estimates, as many as 1,400 lighthouses and lightships were on duty in the nation, one-fifth of them in the South, with eighteen tenders to look after their needs. All major ports had depots to handle provisioning, repairs, and the transfer of personnel. President Grover Cleveland had freed the service from political chains in 1896 with the Civil Service Act, ensuring that all employees were hired fairly and on the basis of competence. In fifty years, the U.S. Lighthouse Board had transmogrified an ailing, mismanaged government office, firmly and efficiently moving it into a technological era as the vanguard of world maritime agencies. Even in this glow of accomplishment, there was dissatisfaction. The rigorous management and martial tenor that characterized the U.S. Lighthouse Board was considered unbecoming to an organization whose mission was more about commerce than national defense.

In 1903, lighthouses were shuffled once again from the Treasury Department to the newly created Department of Commerce and Labor, and the swansong of the U.S. Lighthouse Board began. Congress increasingly began to view the transience and strictness of the military officers in charge as detrimental. Congress also criticized the Board for having "moved far from the purpose of its founders." Many believed a civilian chief and permanent staff would provide more consistency and continuity.

In 1910, the government dissolved the fifty-eight-year-old U.S. Lighthouse Board, and placed all navigational aids under civilian control of a new government agency within the Department of Commerce and Labor called the U.S. Bureau of Lighthouses. George Putnam, the first superintendent, was an ambitious man who had distinguished himself with the U.S. Coast and Geodetic Survey in the Philippines and impressed then-governor of the islands William Howard Taft. Putnam had excellent management skills, enormous energy, vision, charm, and, most importantly, the loyalty and admiration of his employees. He seemed the right man for the job and received the highest recommendation from Taft, who had since been elected president of the United States.

But as he sat down at his new desk in Washington, D.C. in 1910, Putnam faced a daunting task as overseer of 46,828 miles of national coastline and river channels equipped with 1,462 lighthouses, 51 lightships, 933 fog signals, 6,704 buoys, and 1,474 daymarks.

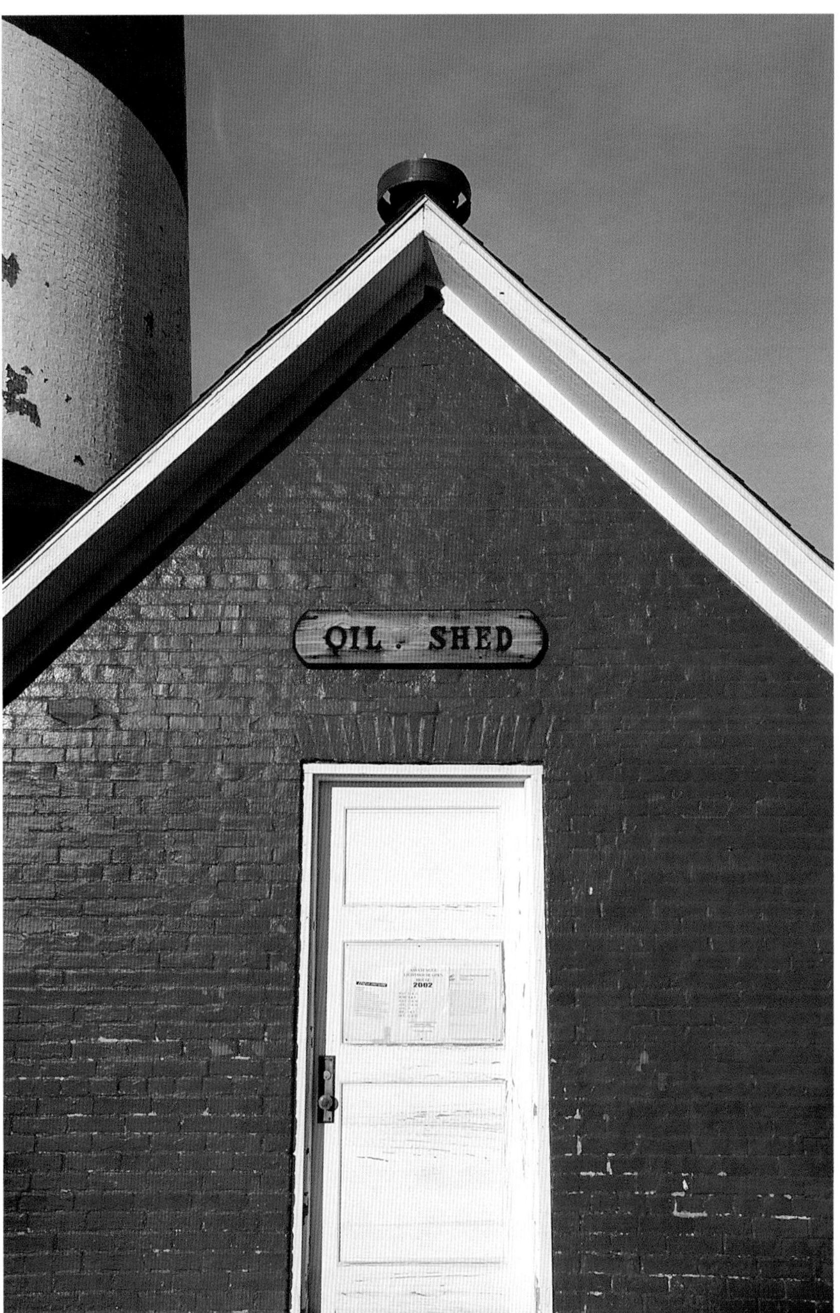

With the adoption of mineral oil, also known as kerosene, lighthouses were equipped with new lamps to burn the cheaper and more efficient fuel and oil houses of fireproof brick or stone in which to store it. The oil shed at Assateague Island Lighthouse was painted bright red to match the tower's candy-stripe daymark.

The Slave Keepers

Ironically, this grand tower built by slaves
was nearly destroyed during the Civil War,
which was fought, in part, to free the slaves.

Ray Jones (referring to Cape Romain Lighthouse)
Southeast Lighthouses, *1989*

The story of lighthouses in the South has many well-known heroes who stand out among the thousands of names listed on government rosters of lightkeepers. But there are some whose work has gone unrecognized. Black Americans, whose service was not recorded, served at many lighthouses and are the unsung keepers of the lights.

Most were nameless slaves and free blacks briefly mentioned in government reports, usually in a negative context. Slave-help at southern lighthouses was probably commonplace prior to the Civil War and, more often than not, an abusive practice that received little approbation from the government. Social mores of the time demeaned blacks as being of inadequate intelligence and reliability for such critical work as keeping a lighthouse. Their service, however, is undeniable and stands as an important chapter in southern lighthouse history.

Somewhat uncertain was the situation of several black boys who were paid in the 1840s to tend the lightboat in the James River, Virginia. The lamplighter assigned to the vessel found it easier to collect his salary and pay the boys a pittance, all the while working another job. Perhaps the coins he gave them encouraged them to keep quiet. Whether they were slaves or free blacks is unknown. An inspector who made a surprise visit to the lightboat found them tending the beacon, and the boys told him of the arrangement they had with the keeper. The inspector dutifully reported the discovery to his superiors. This illegal practice was among many damning pieces of evidence uncovered in an investigation during the administration of Stephen Pleasanton, who was harshly criticized by mariners and maritime interests for his lack of supervision of lighthouse keepers.

At Cape Florida Lighthouse in the 1830s, Henry Aaron Carter was listed as a "helper" and "elderly black man." He may have been a free black, but a written report from assistant keeper John Thompson, relating the horror of an 1836 Seminole attack, suggests Carter was a slave. The Seminoles drove the two men up the lighthouse and then set it on fire. Thompson remarked that from atop the burning lighthouse: "My poor Negro looked at me with tears in his eyes. . . . He called out, 'I'm wounded,' and fell dead." Carter was badly burned before Seminole bullets killed him. He is the only black man known to have died in the service of a lighthouse. Thompson, who was also burned, survived.

At Cape Hatteras Lighthouse in North Carolina in the 1830s, keeper Pharaoh Farrow hired several slaves to tend the lighthouse for him. He paid their owner a small portion of his government salary and pocketed the rest. A few years later, a local mariner reported that a slave was the primary caretaker of Cape Hatteras Lighthouse, with no training or supervision. According to G. W. Blunt, publisher of the *American Coast Pilot*, the station was "badly kept," and the keeper was absent for long periods. These instances occurred during a time when the lighthouse service was being evaluated and reorganized, and undoubtedly use of slave labor was considered just cause to discipline or dismiss a keeper.

In 1852, after the stricter and more regimented U.S. Lighthouse Board took control, an inspector reported that Isaac Foster, keeper of New Point Comfort Lighthouse, had "a negro woman of his own to assist him in keeping the light." This description implied she was a slave, and as such, received no compensation for her work. The Board did not discipline Foster since he reported that the woman was a helper rather than the actual keeper. Inspectors were wary of such arrangements, however. It was easy for a lightkeeper to claim his slaves assisted him when in truth they did all the work.

Following the Civil War, records show no blacks officially employed to work at lighthouses, but lightkeepers subcontracted some as helpers and a few worked as stevedores at lighthouse depots and on tenders, mostly as messmates. Blacks received substandard pay and separate eating and sleeping arrangements.

Beginning in 1944, Clarence Samuels became the only black Coast Guardsman ever to command a lightship. He did his share of mess work and menial tasks, such as driving senior officers, and endured endless derision for his color before earning the rank of warrant officer.

During World War II, the Coast Guard contracted black civilians to help out at patrol stations in the South, many of which were located at lighthouses. A well-

Weathered but strong, the 1804 New Point Comfort Lighthouse remains an active beacon in the Chesapeake Bay, guiding vessels into Mobjack Bay and the York River. It is one of several southern lighthouses known to have been tended by slaves.

known example is Hunting Island Lighthouse, whose lightkeeper and his family were the only white people on the island following the Civil War. The remainder of the island's small population was descended from black slaves. Huntington Island was one of the barrier islands of South Carolina and Georgia that General William Tecumseh Sherman's Special Field Order 15 of 1885 gave to former slaves. When the Coast Guard set up its beach-patrol facility at Hunting Island Lighthouse in 1943, it paid black families to do some of the work. They delivered groceries and did laundry for the twenty-two men, but records do not indicate if they helped with patrols.

With modernization and technological upgrades after World War II, lighthouses began losing their keepers at a fast pace. Although Coast Guard service records show no black lightkeepers in these final years, many worked on repair and automation crews. Today, of course, black Americans regularly serve on Coast Guard ANTs (Aids to Navigation Teams), servicing automated lighthouses and installing state-of-the-art equipment. In a sense, they are still keepers of the lights. The difference is the nature of the work and the parity of employment.

CHAPTER 4

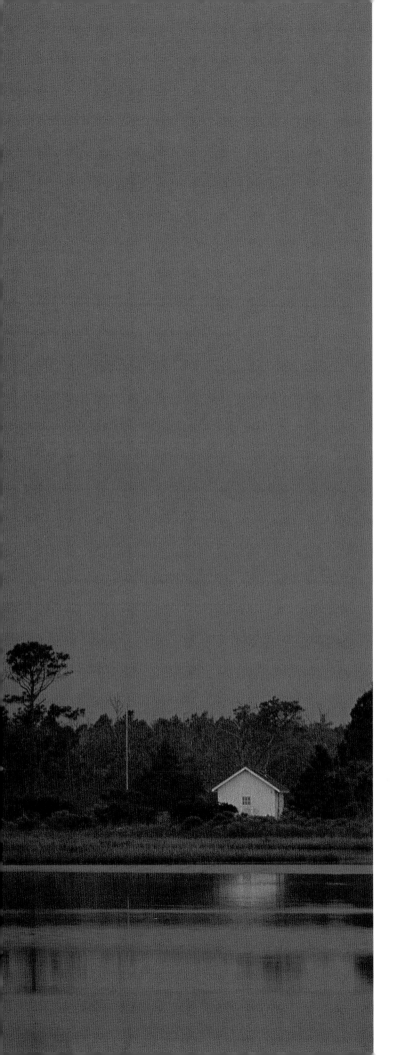

A Bright New Era

THE LIGHTHOUSE WAS THEN A SILVERY, MISTY-LOOKING TOWER WITH A YELLOW EYE THAT OPENED SUDDENLY AND SOFTLY.
Virginia Woolf, To the Lighthouse, *1927*

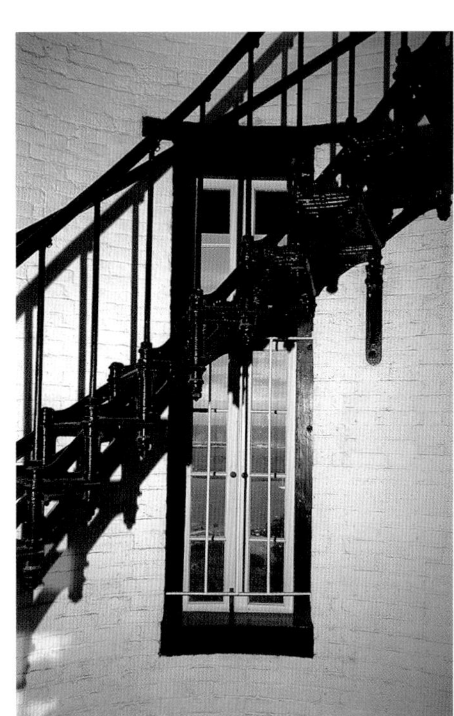

Left: *Dusk paints Bodie Island Lighthouse in lilac light and showcases the soul of the tower—its first-order beacon. The 1872 lighthouse and roomy keeper's dwelling do double duty today as an active navigational aid and museum.*

Above: *Nineteenth-century architects incorporated both function and beauty into the design of a lighthouse's interior. A narrow window in St. Augustine Lighthouse admits light, then magnifies it on white walls. The iron stairway's delicate, airy appearance belies its strength.*

At the start of the twentieth century, the American coastline was the best lighted anywhere in the world. Enormous energy and sums of money had been channeled into research, development, and implementation of the best technologies, and virtually all the nation's dark spaces had been closed. As forty-five-year-old George Putnam took the reins in 1910 of the newly formed U.S. Bureau of Lighthouses, the task ahead of him was clear: keep the nation's navigational aids at the front of world commerce, but trim the budget. It was an assignment that in many ways echoed the mandate of his predecessor, Stephen Pleasanton, a century earlier. Putnam, however, had a well-regulated, highly organized, and firmly established corps working under him. His primary task was to streamline the service and tighten its purse strings. He went a step further by earning for those in his employ much-deserved recognition and a long-overdue pension plan.

Putnam accomplished these objectives in a very public way. The *Lighthouse Service Bulletin*, a monthly in-house publication inaugurated in 1912, detailed much of the work the bureau accomplished. It was a smorgasbord of verbiage, photos, and diagrams, from reports on activities of the lightkeepers and tender crews to updates on new construction projects and cutting-edge technology. Simple and readable, it went far to educate the nation about the venerable work of one of its most charitable government agencies. Putnam also barraged newspapers and magazines, including the respected *National Geographic*, with articles about the bureau that he personally authored, and he regularly spoke on radio, extolling the hard work of lighthouse keepers and their support crews.

Putnam had only begun his work when, in 1914, as part of the Taft Commission's "organization and combination" effort, Secretary of Commerce Charles Nagel suggested that the government establish a maritime safety and law enforcement agency, consisting of the Revenue Cutter Service, Lifesaving Service, and the Bureau of Lighthouses. Nagel's intent was threefold: Revenue Cutters would police the waterways, lighthouses and other navigational aids would guard the coasts and prevent disasters, and the lifesavers would deal with shipwreck and salvage issues. Congress agreed on all but the last entity. Perhaps influenced by President Taft's friendship with George Putnam, the U.S. Bureau of Lighthouses remained independent. It was by far the largest of the three organizations and, in its various forms, the oldest. Nagel

A sister to the U.S. Lighthouse Establishment was the U.S. Lifesaving Service, launched in 1874. Lighthouses were charged with preventing shipwrecks, but when ships did sink or run aground, lifesavers rescued those in peril. More than a hundred lifesaving stations were set up in the South between 1874 and 1915, the year the work was turned over to the newly formed U.S. Coast Guard. The restored boathouse (facing page) of Chicomacomico Lifesaving Station near Rodanthe, North Carolina, and its larger station house, where a crew of fulltime surfmen lived (above), harkens back to an era when shipswrecks were prevalent.

did succeed in merging the Revenue Cutters and Lifesaving Service. In 1915, they joined to become the U.S. Coast Guard.

Progress is often ushered in and sustained by youthful energy, and Putnam knew he needed to transfuse the lighthouse service. More than 12 percent of the lightkeepers on duty in 1916 were past the age of seventy. The reason was simple: the government did not offer a retirement plan. Putnam pressured Congress to pass a bill that would offer retirement after thirty years of service, with a full pension at age sixty-five. It passed, and as President Woodrow Wilson added his signature to the bill in 1918, he commented to Putnam, "I know how important their work is and feel that nothing but justice has been done them."

During World War I the government transferred the U.S. Bureau of Lighthouses to the War Department, and a number of keepers left their positions to serve in the Armed Forces. Those who stayed behind planted victory gardens, purchased war bonds, and maintained round-the-clock watches on the sea for any sign of enemy activity. The War Department installed telephones at nearly every lighthouse so that keepers could report problems or suspicious vessels. Outside lightships operated on alert, for they anchored at sea and often were the first to spot enemy activity. The danger of lightship duty was underscored in 1918 when a German submarine torpedoed and sank the *Diamond Shoals #117* off Cape Hatteras after its crew tried to alert U.S. warships of the submarine's presence. The twelve-man crew escaped in lifeboats.

The War Department continued to expand and refine navigational aids during the war. In 1918, the government automated Charlotte Harbor Lighthouse, which had diligently signaled to cattle ships and phosphate barges for twenty-eight years, outfitting it with acetylene gas tanks. Its keepers remained on duty until the end of the war to keep watch for enemy ships; then it became the first lighthouse in the South to operate self-sufficiently. Putnam had been experimenting with automatic gas lights in Alaska and Hawaii, and he now applied the technology elsewhere.

During the difficult postwar recovery period, keepers who had served overseas came home to their lighthouses and resumed work. Other veterans, by virtue of their military service, got jobs as new lightkeepers. Edward Meyer, a U.S. Merchant Marine sailor, applied for and received an assistant keeper's job at St. Augustine. Captain Unaka Jennette, who had bravely commanded the Diamond Shoals Relief Lightship during the war, was rewarded with the principle keeper's position at Cape Hatteras Lighthouse.

Meanwhile, Putnam was busy with new ideas. In addition to his pension program, Congress agreed to allow Putnam to test untried technologies. During the war, Putnam had urged experiments with a radio compass, and approved it for use on three lighthouse tenders, including the *Arbutus*, which served southern waters. In 1917, the navy was in the process of developing a radiobeacon, a silent signal that worked in all weather, and the beacons became almost commonplace at lighthouses within a decade after the war. The Bureau of Lighthouses installed a radiobeacon at Dry Tortugas Light on Loggerhead Key in 1926, making the light among the first in the South to receive one. During this same time, the government installed telephones in the final few lighthouses that still did not have them. A seven-mile-long submarine cable connected Fowey Rocks Light to the mainland by telephone in 1923.

Putnam reorganized tender service based on areas of operation. The largest tenders served the coastal lights and larger aids; smaller ones served rivers. Medium-sized tenders serviced bays and sounds. The smallest tenders were often no more than shuttles for moving personnel. Larger tenders mainly worked to connect electric cables to lighthouses, first at mainland stations and then at more remote offshore towers. Ten years after Fowey Rock Light's telephone went into service, another submarine cable provided electricity to the beacon. Underwater cables were problematic, however, especially when storms caused outages or the cables snapped in rough seas. The Bureau of Lighthouses retained old oil lamp systems as backup, and later generators were installed at lighthouses in case of power failures.

Radio broadcasts began in 1921, and Putnam was quick to realize that lighthouse keepers would benefit from radios. Budget constraints hampered his effort to place receivers at every lighthouse, but the public rallied. In 1931, a woman in Key West, concerned for the spiritual edification of keepers, donated radio sets to all the offshore reef lighthouses so that the crews could listen to church services. A bonus, of course, was that the radios also provided access to news and weather reports, as well as another means for communicating with shore in an emergency.

Putnam envisioned aviation as part of the lighthouse service and worked in 1926 to add the Airways Division to aid "ships of the air." The division built new steel skeleton towers to provide beacons for flyers, and painted large numbers on top of lighthouses near major airfields to help pilots navigate their final approach. Steel skeleton towers, the backbone of lighthouse construction between the world wars, were also used as radiobeacons for both ships and aircraft. The Airways Division lasted eight years before the government transferred its duties to the Federal Aviation Administration.

The series of range lights that earlier administrations had built in the South to mark harbor approaches and river channels was well established by this time, but Putnam continued to refine inshore navigational aids. In 1927, he ordered the addition of a rear range lighthouse at Boca Grande to work in tandem with the Port Boca Grande Lighthouse at the entrance to Charlotte Harbor. The tower was one that had been discontinued at Lewes, Delaware, a few years earlier. Construction crews disassembled the light and shipped it by train to Florida, where workers rebuilt it on Gasparilla Island. Adding to the sentinel's economy was its gas-fueled fourth-order optic that required no keeper to tend it. Recycling the Lewes tower was one of many cost-effective moves that characterized Putnam's tenure. At this same time, Putnam ordered that automatic equipment be installed at the Barrancas Range Lights at Pensacola. These self-sufficient beacons were harbingers of a larger scheme to streamline and mechanize all lighthouses.

Robotic Lights and Unneeded Keepers

High on Putnam's list of improvements were automatic devices that could operate the lights and fog signals. He proceeded cautiously, however, knowing that advancements in robotics would mean a reduction in the number of lightkeepers. His justifications were numerous, not the least being the cost savings. But there also were the "stag stations" to consider, dangerous and isolated lighthouses where only men were permitted to live, without their families. The reef lighthouses of Florida were among them, each with a principle keeper and two assistants. Putnam knew lightkeepers would gladly abandon these places.

New lighthouses also could be made automatic. In 1921, the government marked Pacific Reef and Molasses Reef with forty-five-foot steel towers, one brown and the other black, with automatic gas beacons. A few years later, similar steel towers and automatic lights replaced lights at Smith Shoal, Cosgrove Shoal, and Tennessee Reef. These important sentinels lacked the beauty of traditional lighthouses, but they marked danger spots along the Florida Keys without risking human life.

Putnam proudly reported in the *Lighthouse Service Bulletin*, "During the year ended June 30, 1925, lights were changed to automatic at 74 stations at a total cost of $50,748, and this resulted in a reduction of annual operating cost of $17,785." He went on to add that he had arranged for keepers who lost their positions to automatic machinery to be transferred to other jobs in the bureau.

What seemed, at first, to be a good thing, eventually proved troublesome. Lighthouses without human keepers were vulnerable to vandalism, and if the automatic machinery failed, there was no one on site to take over. The public seemed unruffled, but mariners asked: Who will keep watch for ships in distress? Who will maintain the buildings on a regular basis? Who will respond if the light fails? Without keepers on site, many lighthouses quickly fell into disrepair and became eyesores. Putnam's vision of a robotic lighthouse service still drove much of the research he commissioned, but he proceeded cautiously. Signs warning vandals of the consequences of damaging government property went up at all automated lighthouses.

One of the first reef lighthouses to be automated was Rebecca Shoal Light, a screwpile sentinel off Key West. It was a dangerous place, and no one complained when machinists aboard the tender *Sundew* went out to the site in July 1925 to convert the lamp to acetylene gas, complete with a sun valve to turn it on and off. The lightkeepers were transferred to other lighthouses in the Florida Keys. Boaters continued to stop by the light, holding parties, which culminated in defacement of the property. District machinists regularly repaired the damage to the beacon and its robotic machinery.

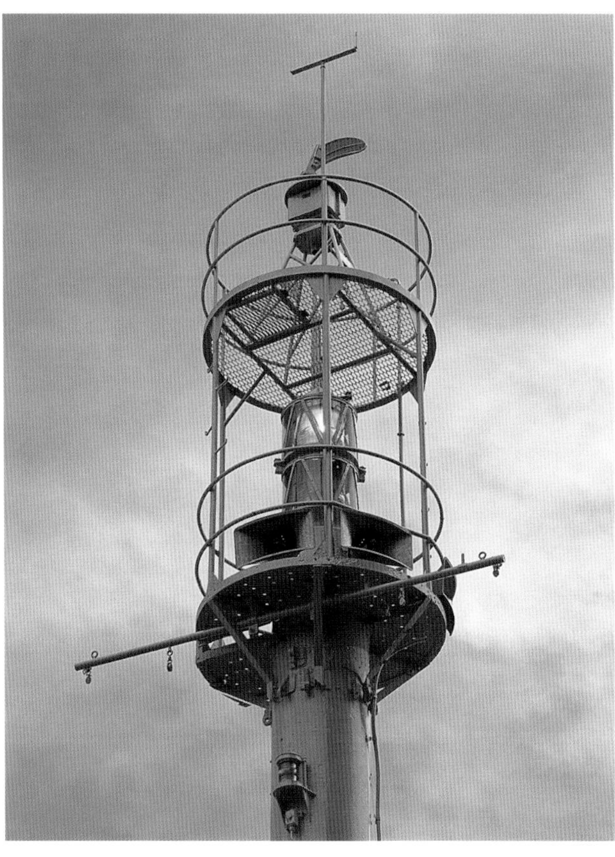

Lightships have been described as floating lighthouses stationed on the sea. First used as navigational aids in the 1820s, they remained a vital part of the U.S. Lighthouse Establishment and the U.S. Coast Guard until the 1980s. Portsmouth Lightship (right), now a museum, served on several ocean stations off Virginia, Delaware, and Massachusetts before retiring from duty in 1964. Its single light basket was elevated on a mast to shine a beacon at sea. (above)

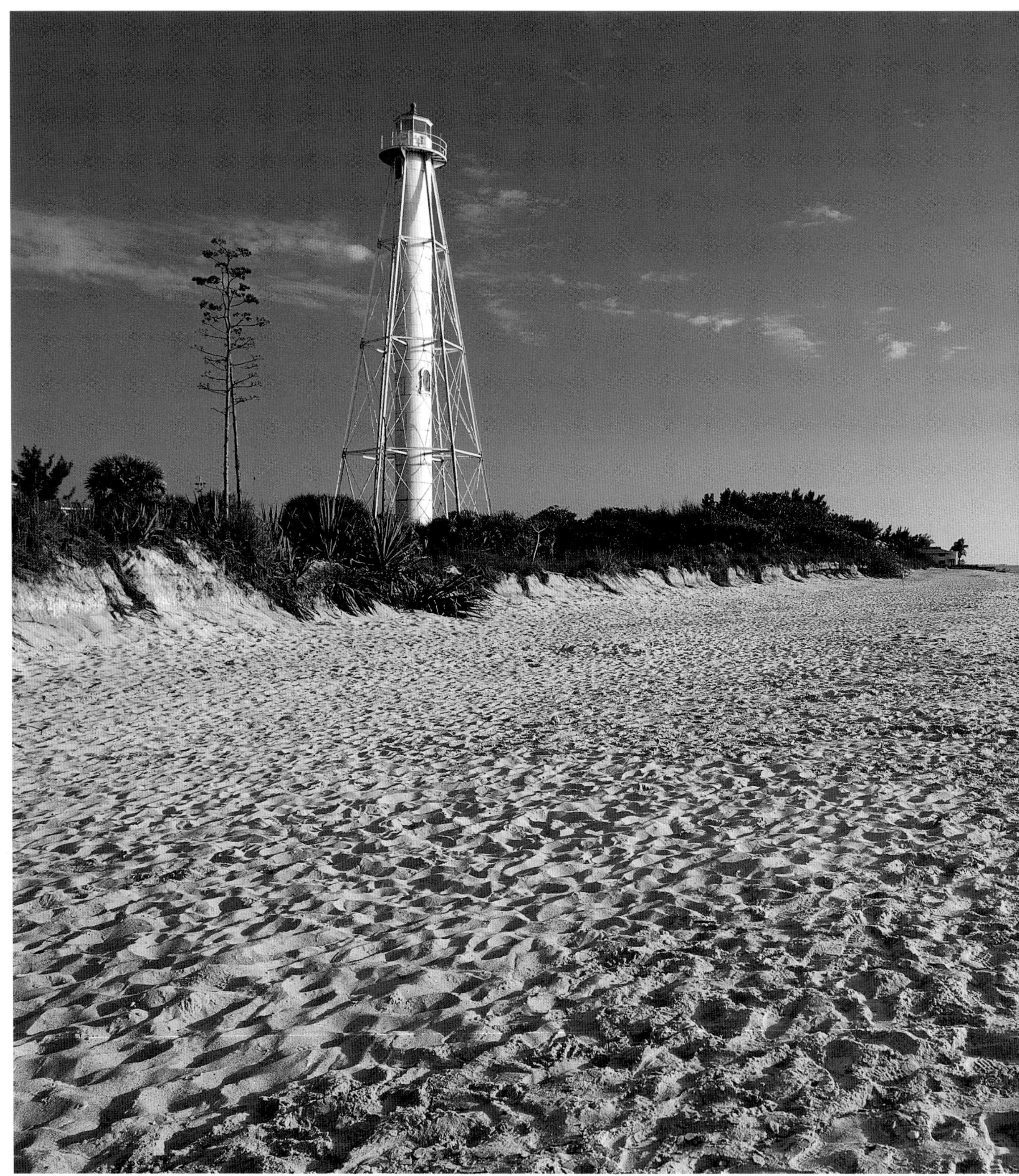

George Putnam's tenure as Commissioner of Lighthouses was marked by frugality and modernization. When the 1881 Green Hill Light was discontinued at Lewes, Delaware, in 1918, Putnam recycled it. The tower was moved to Gasparilla Island, Florida where it resumed service in 1927 as the Boca Grande Rear Range Light. Its beacon was among the first in the nation to run automatically, so no resident lightkeeper was needed.

At some lighthouses, installation of more modern equipment resulted in a need for fewer keepers. A new thermostat with a warning bell, called a "mechanical keeper," went into service at Bodie Island Lighthouse in the early 1920s. It brought an end to the nightly rotation of watches, since the warning bell alerted a sleeping keeper if the light was not burning adequately, eliminating the need for an assistant keeper. A decade later, the station was electrified, and there was even less need for an assistant. In fact, electricity was one of the earliest automating devices, reducing the workload and the need for multiple keepers. At most stations, one man could handle the responsibilities of an electric light.

Ironically, as the number of keepers decreased with automation, the number of navigational aids increased. In 1924, Putnam proudly boasted 16,888 aids, including lighthouses, lightships, buoys, and fog signals. At the same time, he noted a 20 percent reduction in employees since his administration took office fourteen years earlier. Automatic devices were far less expensive to maintain than lightkeepers, who needed quarters, provisions, medical care, inspections, and a regular salary. No one in government questioned the cost-savings Putnam pursued, for no sooner had the war drained the nation's coffers than the Great Depression hit. Economy became the watchword of the lighthouse service.

Changing of the Watch

Putnam retired in 1935, handing over the U.S. Bureau of Lighthouses to Harold King, one of his district superintendents. King oversaw the decommissioning of Cape Hatteras Lighthouse, due to erosion at its base, and ordered the automation and unmanning of Sand Key Light and Charleston Light. He barely had time to set his own agenda of stepped-up automation and modernization before President Franklin Roosevelt decided to reorganize the service once again. In July 1939, in order to save money and consolidate commerce operations, Roosevelt placed lighthouses under the control of the U.S. Coast Guard. The secretary of commerce had suggested this in 1914, and now that Putnam was gone, the government could make the change without offending him or his political backers. But not everyone was pleased. The Navy objected strongly, believing it had the right to administer lighthouses, rather than the U.S. Coast Guard—an organization that was a mere twenty-four years old.

Employees of the now defunct U.S. Bureau of Lighthouses were stunned too. Harold King had been finalizing plans for a nationwide celebration commemorating 150 years of lighthouse service in the United States. Instead, he informed his employees they would segue into the Coast Guard, either as civilians or at ranks commensurate with experience. "Many chose to keep their civilian status," said Edith King, daughter of superintendent Harold King. "I think a few were rankled at the thought of having to answer to young Coast Guard officers whom they felt knew little about lighthouse work."

On July 1, 1939, the official transfer occurred amid quiet protest from the navy and old bureau employees. To allay dissatisfaction and perhaps divert attention from the unpopular move, President Roosevelt declared August 9 as "Lighthouse Day." The government hastily planned small celebrations to be held throughout the nation at various districts, depots, and individual lighthouses. The site chosen for the national ceremony was Cape Henry Lighthouse, which stood on a sand hill overlooking the spectacular entrance to the Chesapeake Bay where the nation's first colonists had arrived more than 300 years earlier. Harold King, the outgoing chief, and Admiral Russell Waesche, Commandant of the U.S. Coast Guard, spoke at the ceremony. The Coast Guard band played, and ministers held religious services to give thanks for the long service of lighthouses. The ceremony was broadcast via national radio.

Despite differences of opinion, the transition went smoothly. The Coast Guard took control of 405 manned lighthouses and forty-two lightships, one-fifth of which were located in the South. The government established thirteen Coast Guard districts to cover the large coastal territories, and appointed managerial boards within each district to handle the affairs of the 5,275 assimilated employees. Lighthouse keepers were offered ranks of chief or first-class petty officer, depending on experience. Masters of tenders were offered warrant officer ranks. Only engineers and district superintendents became full-fledged officers. Few, however, opted for transfer to the Coast Guard, feeling their status would be greatly reduced.

A dichotomy of ranks ensued, a bit troubled at first but assuaged as time passed and old-timers retired. Young Coast Guard boatswains and machinists apprenticed under veteran keepers and tender crewmen, but keepers complained that short tours of duty did not impart the sense of "home" and commitment needed to bond a keeper to his light. Families continued to serve at many stations, but the Coast Guard uprooted and moved them frequently if they were not of civilian status. Automations continued, sometimes with public censure and the realization that someday the occupation of lighthouse keeper might become obsolete.

Within a year, the Coast Guard realized a cost-savings of 10 percent of the entire lighthouse budget, confirming to the Roosevelt administration that the change was a success. But an undercurrent of discontent still ran through the service, especially when the Coast Guard automated the big lighthouse at Currituck Beach, a beloved southern landmark with a century of connections to Outer Banks families. Salve came, ironically, with war. The attack on Pearl Harbor and subsequent entry into the Pacific and European war theaters diverted attention and unified the Coast Guard, which now fell under the aegis of the U.S. Navy. Personnel at lighthouses and lightships went on alert.

With 90 percent of the Allied sinkings off Florida's east coast occurring at night, and most of those within the arc of lighthouse beams, military intelligence officers in Miami soon realized that lighthouses were aiding enemy ships. In order to protect ships at sea from being silhouetted by lighthouses, the Coast Guard decided to shut down major coastal lights or reduce their power. Keepers remained on duty to assist with surveillance operations and to reinstate the lights if needed. The Coast Guard instituted a special system that used radio signals to send messages to lightkeepers or to remotely extinguish and relight unmanned beacons. Keepers also were forbidden to drive along beaches with car headlights on and were issued black shades to darken their house windows at night.

At many light stations, old civilian keepers worked alongside Coast Guard patrols. The omnipresence of enemy submarines, coupled with the fact that the majority of saboteurs were captured in remote areas between Virginia and Florida, demanded stepped-up security. The Coast Guard established a training station for beach patrols near St. Augustine Lighthouse, and dispatched well-equipped patrolmen to outposts all along the coast. Lighthouses were prime destinations, since the high towers could be used for observation. The government housed young Coast Guard patrolmen in lighthouse quarters, and built stables and kennels nearby for the horses and dogs used during patrols. Some stations had Jeeps. The lookouts were to report any suspicious activity, as well as

July 1, 1939, marked the end of the U.S. Lighthouse Establishment. Lighthouses and all other navigational aids were transferred into the hands of the U.S. Coast Guard, an organization not yet twenty-five years old but entrusted with the safekeeping of American waters. A national ceremony was held at Cape Henry to mark the official transfer. President Roosevelt, though he did not attend, felt the site represented the positive change he envisioned for the nation's 405 lighthouses and forty-two lightships. Old Cape Henry Light, the first sentinel commissioned by the nation's first Congress in 1789, had retired and passed its torch to New Cape Henry Light. The symbolism was obvious to all in attendance.

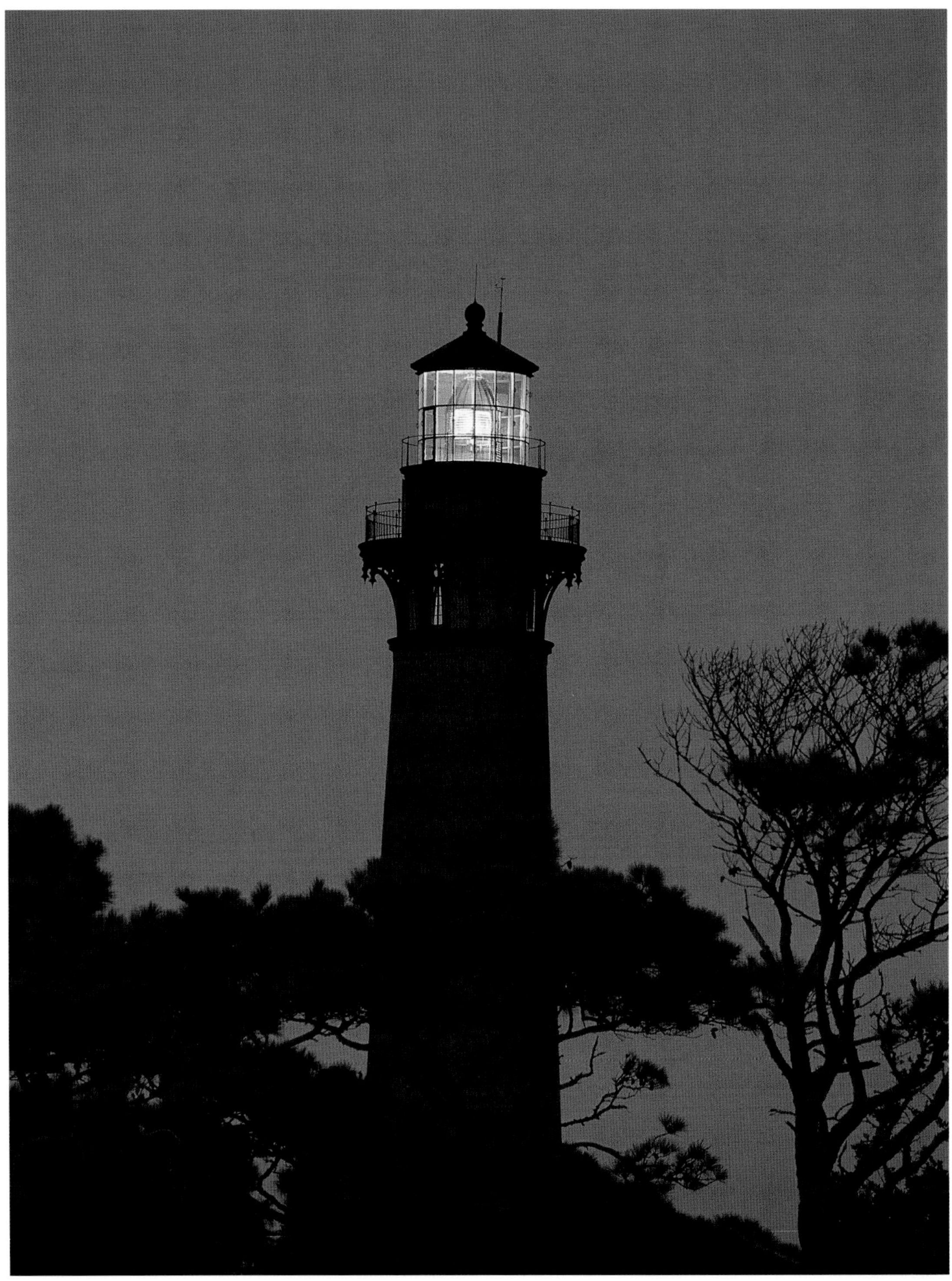

Automations began in earnest with the transfer of lighthouses to the Coast Guard in 1939. Offshore and remote beacons were among the first to be equipped to run self-sufficiently. There was little objection, since these were sites where personnel suffered the most hardship. But public acceptance went cold when the beautiful brick lighthouse at Currituck Beach, North Carolina, was unmanned and automated. Outer Banks families felt a strong connection to the lighthouse and worried it would be vandalized. Their concerns were still new when World War II began and the Coast Guard reactivated the compound to use as a patrol station, complete with stables and kennels for the beach patrols.

instruct lightkeepers in marksmanship (the government issued guns and ammunition to all lighthouse keepers during the war) and response to chemical agents.

The automated Currituck Beach Lighthouse, close to the important naval station at Norfolk, Virginia, was augmented with a patrol station in 1943. The Army built stables and provided horses, which they trucked in from the Front Royal Army Remount Center. The government housed Coast Guardsmen in hastily erected wooden shacks around the lighthouse. At Hunting Island Lighthouse, twenty-two patrolmen guarded the barrier beach. Their commander lived in the empty lightkeeper's house, since the keeper had been transferred elsewhere during the war. Watchmen in the tower communicated twenty-four hours a day by radio with beach patrols. Anclote Keys Lighthouse was similarly staffed, but with a smaller crew of four patrolmen who kept constant lookout from the top of the tower. They lived in the assistant keeper's quarters. The head keeper J. L. Pippin had little work to do, since the Coast Guard had automated the beacon before the war.

Crooked River Lighthouse gained critical importance during Word War II, after the government laid a gasoline pipeline from Carrabelle to Jacksonville. This pipeline allowed for the shipment of fuel to the East Coast without sending ships along the dangerous route around the Florida Keys, where German submarines lurked. The keepers of Crooked River Light, long cloistered in the wilderness of coastal Florida, welcomed their first neighbors when the government built Camp Gordon Johnson, an amphibious training base, nearby. The beach here was very much like landing sites in Europe, and lightkeepers saw firsthand the daily drills of the men who would eventually invade Normandy on D-Day.

Working together in the cause of national security unified the civilian and Coast Guard crews, but some remained discontent about their assignment. Many active-duty "Coasties" resented lighthouse duty, which they considered dull and unimportant. Equally, civilian lightkeepers carped about having to do beach patrols and port security or, in some cases, be transferred away from their stations while the lights were downgraded or extinguished.

The Advent of Automatic Machinery

When the war ended, the Coast Guard once again became part of the Department of Commerce, and closed down most of its patrol stations. One of the Coast Guard's first postwar programs was to use floodlights to illuminate light towers that had become obscure in the glare of surrounding city lights. A nighttime floodlight brightened Old Point Comfort, making it easier for ships to spot the lighthouse from the bay and giving it a much more dramatic facade. Photographers flocked to the site to snap pictures of the handsome old sentinel shining against the backdrop of Newport News.

Also at this time, the Coast Guard assessed the upgrades that had taken place at various lighthouses and determined they could save considerable money and manpower if all lighthouses were equipped to run on their own. In 1944, after water intrusion damaged Egmont Key Lighthouse, the Coast Guard removed its lantern cap, shortened the tower, and installed an automatic, enclosed electric lamp. The experiment was a success, as the beacon required little maintenance and had an excellent record of duty. Though keepers remained at the station after 1944, there was little work to do in the lighthouse. Instead, keepers constantly monitored the harbor entrance, as Tampa was Florida's busiest port.

Lighthouse building slowed greatly prior to the war, and afterwards the Coast Guard constructed only a few lighthouses. In 1954, a concrete art deco sentinel at Mayport, Florida, replaced the aging *St. Johns River Lightship*. Its narrow lantern room and plastic Vega beacon, manufactured in New Zealand, were among the many the low-maintenance features of the light. Four years later, Oak Island Lighthouse went into service at Wilmington, North Carolina. This state-of-the-art tower had its tricolor daymark poured directly into the concrete for a maintenance-free paint scheme, and was also constructed to sway three inches from vertical during high winds, adding stability. It exhibited a dual intensity beacon that could be brightened during severe storm conditions when visibility is poor. Keepers wore green glasses in the lantern room to protect their eyes when tending the powerful beacon. In 1962, the Coast Guard built the Sullivans Island Lighthouse, a triangular porcelain-coated

Few lighthouses were built in the second half of the twentieth century. Oak Island Light at Wilmington, North Carolina, was constructed by the Coast Guard in 1958. State-of-the-art technology is seen in its tricolor daymark, poured directly into the concrete, and its dual-intensity beacon, which is the strongest in the nation. Coast Guard personnel take great pride in the station's appearance.

Lighthouses were critical to coastal security during World War II. Crooked River Lighthouse, established in 1895 for commerce on St. George Sound at Florida's Big Bend, gained importance during the war when a gasoline pipeline was laid from Jacksonville to Carrabelle. This line allowed the transport of fuel from the East Coast to the Gulf of Mexico without sending tankers through the submarine-infested Florida Strait.

tower with an elevator and a powerful beacon. All three of these modern lights were manned until the late 1960s.

The Coast Guard also built two Texas tower lighthouses in the 1960s, one on Frying Pan Shoals off Cape Hatteras and another at the entrance to the Chesapeake Bay. They stand on tubular steel legs driven into the seafloor, and each has a superstructure for the beacon tower and quarters, and a helicopter pad. The 130-foot Frying Pan Shoals Light was built in 1964 off Cape Fear, North Carolina. It had a resident crew of keepers until 1979 when the light was automated. Chesapeake Light, fabricated by the same company that constructed the Chesapeake Bay Bridge Tunnel, was built in 117 feet of water, fourteen miles off the entrance to the bay. Commissioned in 1965, it was automated in 1980.

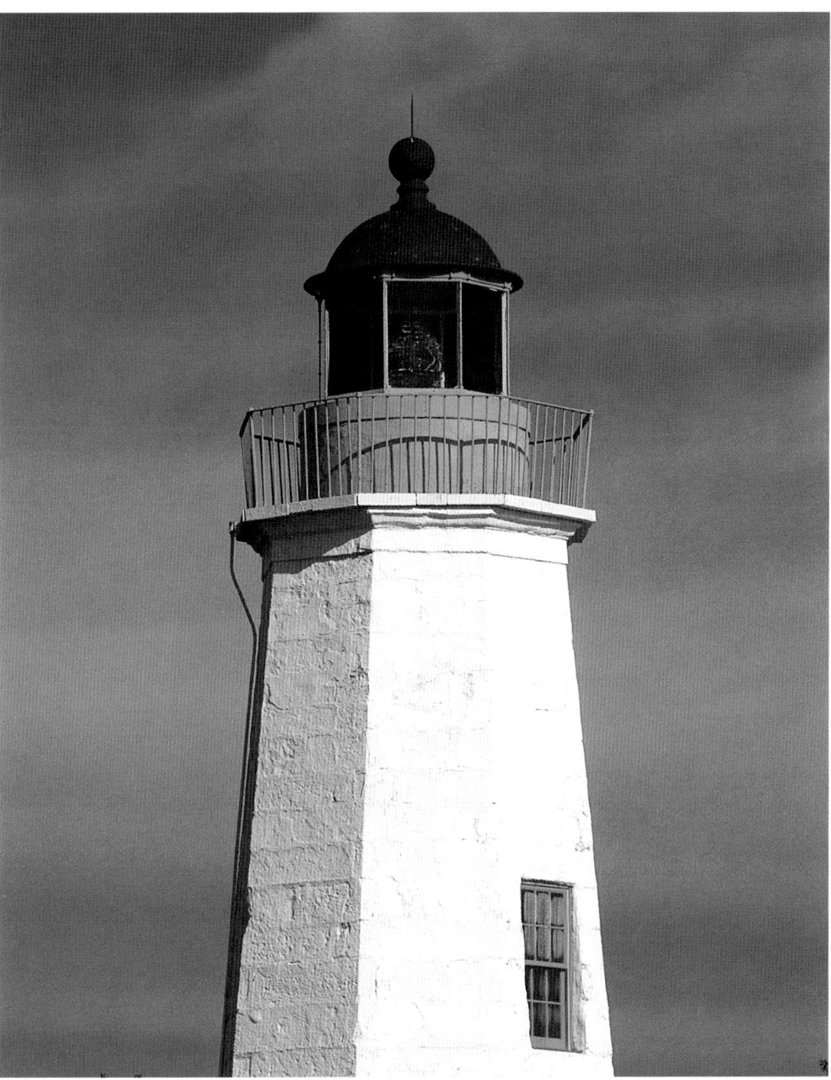

As the coast became more populous, lights from industry, businesses, and homes drowned out lighthouse beacons. This was especially troublesome in the Chesapeake Bay, where several major cities inundated the shore with light. When mariners complained they could not easily find Old Point Comfort Light amid the many lights along Hampton Roads, the Coast Guard illuminated the tower with floodlights. A bright white daymark and red lantern identified it by day.

By 1960, when the last of the modern lighthouses was in the planning stages, many civilian lightkeepers had retired, and Coast Guard keepers were the only ones still tending lighthouses. The men jokingly called themselves "switchies," a parody of the old "wickies" who cared for oil lamps by keeping the wicks trimmed. Electrification meant a simple switch on each night and off each morning. The Coast Guard converted more and more lights to run automatically. As elsewhere in industry and commercial ventures, robotics seemed the wave of the future. Offshore light stations and those where it was difficult to house personnel were automated first, due to their isolation and high maintenance costs. Cape Lookout became self-contained in 1950, Ponce Inlet in 1952, Anclote Keys in 1953, Bodie Island in 1954, St. Augustine and Ocracoke in 1955, and Cape Canaveral in 1960. Egmont Key Light at Tampa, Florida, the last southern sentinel to lose its crew of resident keepers, was automated in 1989.

Instead of human hands, light sensors switched the beacons on and off each day, and a carousel of lightbulbs, mounted on a rotating changer, moved a new bulb into position when an old one burned out. Classical lenses were replaced by smaller, more durable plastic lenses that required little upkeep and could be exposed to the weather. In some cases, lantern enclosures were removed

The Sacrifice of Joshua Appleby

Greater love hath no man than this,
that a man lay down his life for his friends.
John 15:13

For a lighthouse keeper, Joshua Appleby was a curious contradiction. It's said that in his early life, he caused a shipwreck at sea and profited from it. Later, he worked to avert such disasters and ultimately he paid the highest price for his effort.

For his bravery and supreme sacrifice in staying by his light during the October hurricane of 1846, lightkeeper Joshua Appleby was honored in the naming of a buoy tender in 1998. The Joshua Appleby *(WLM-556) tends navigational aids in waters near Appleby's home at Sand Key Lighthouse, nine miles off Key West, Florida. (Photograph courtesy of the U.S. Coast Guard Archives)*

Like many lightkeepers of his day, Appleby came to his job after a seafaring career. Born in 1773 in Rhode Island, he went to sea as a cabin boy and years later settled on Key Vaca in Florida. There he began a lucrative business as a wrecker—one who salvages shipwrecks. Wreckers earned a bittersweet income, profiting from the misfortunes of others. Appleby, like most wreckers, was often under suspicion of causing wrecks in order to earn a bigger income.

In 1823, he was accused by local shipmasters in Key West of conspiring to "run ashore gently" several pirate ships captured by a privateer so that he might gain the rights to salvage them. He may have done this by showing a false light to mimic a ship safely at anchor in an attempt to lure other vessels to the reef. Had he been successful, he could have boarded the wrecked ships and claimed 20 percent of the value of the salvage of each vessel and its goods. Appleby was arrested and sent to trial in Charleston, South Carolina. Evidence against him must have been meager, for he was acquitted of all wrongdoing and the secretary of the navy ordered that he be released. He returned to the Florida Keys with his wife and children, and continued to work as a wrecker.

On July 27, 1837, Appleby gave up wrecking and salvage and took a job as the lightkeeper at Sand Key Lighthouse, a stone tower on a small key nine miles southwest of Key West. Local residents who knew Appleby's background and past confrontations with wrecked crews were surprised at this turn of events. The local collector of customs, however, obviously had faith in Appleby, and awarded him the appointment at a salary of $600 per year. Now a widower and getting along in years, Appleby considered lighthouse keeping an innocuous duty compared to the rigors of wrecking. But life on Sand Key soon proved otherwise.

Hurricanes in 1841 and 1842 caused considerable damage to the key, destroyed Appleby's house, and threatened the foundation of the heavy masonry light tower that had been built there in 1827. The government replaced the dwelling and built a seawall around the station in hopes of protecting it. Another hurricane in 1844 swept away half of the key, part of the seawall, and the new house. Appleby diligently rebuilt his home, seemingly oblivious to the constant danger he faced.

The decisive storm came October 11, 1846. Appleby's daughter was visiting the key that day with her young son, easing the loneliness of her widowed father. The hurricane that slammed Sand Key that morning was a horrific corkscrew of wind and rain. It leveled everything—house, tower, seawall—and obliterated the key to a depth of six feet below the water. Joshua Appleby, his daughter Eliza, and his grandson Thomas died. Their names were added to a long list of citizens in and around Key West who perished in the storm.

Joshua Appleby paid dearly for his work, but his sacrifice was not forgotten. On November 20, 1998, 152 years after his death, the keeper-class buoy-tender *Joshua Appleby* (WLM-556) was launched at Marinette Marine Corporation in Marinette, Wisconsin. The 175-foot vessel, now home ported in St. Petersburg, Florida, has 1,335 square feet of buoy deck area and carries a crew of eighteen. Its work often takes it into the waters Joshua Appleby sailed in his wrecking days.

altogether, ending the long tradition of cleaning windows. The Coast Guard rigged stations with radio transmitters that emitted a signal if robotic systems failed. Radar towers provided the Coast Guard with a continuous picture of ship movements.

In the meantime, the public became increasingly dismayed as the Coast Guard boarded up and decapitated old lighthouses and razed ancillary buildings. Before long, weeds overtook the once well-groomed grounds. Although Aids to Navigation Teams visited lights periodically to maintain them, paint peeled, bird feces piled up on the catwalks and railings, and rust gripped metal surfaces in the interim. Mariners expressed doubt that a mechanized light could serve shipping as effectively as a human lightkeeper, but the cost-savings was enormous. Most automations paid for themselves within four years, and operating costs at some lighthouses were reduced by 75 percent.

Unmanning proceeded with alacrity. In 1968, the Coast Guard officially announced the Lighthouse Automation and Modernization Program (LAMP), a plan to convert all navigational aids to automatic operation by the twenty-first century and eliminate unnecessary lights. Master computer centers would monitor all activity and all districts would be networked. In the end, LAMP meant the end of a long and treasured chapter in American maritime history—the tradition of the lighthouse keeper living on-site to tend a beacon and fog signal.

Putnam's dream of a self-sufficient lighthouse service was on its way to fulfillment. Automation teams worked steadily to install new equipment, seal up towers to protect them from vandalism, and decommission unneeded aids. By 1980, only seven lighthouses in the South still had resident keepers, and by 1989, all were gone. The venerable occupation officially ended in 1995 when the Coast Guard chose Boston Harbor Lighthouse as the only American lighthouse that would continue to be tended by human hands. The State of Massachusetts passed legislation that gave the light memorial status and mandated that its three lightkeepers be retained as a symbol of the much-revered institution that had served our nation's maritime needs for 279 years. The number of keepers was reduced to one in 2003 when the National Park Service took over the site. Dr. Sally Snowman, a Boston Light historian and member of a local Coast Guard Auxiliary, oversees the station and handles its interpretive programs.

Over the course of a little less than three centuries, lighthouse keepers had come and gone. The legacy of LAMP was bittersweet. Hundreds of efficient and economical robotic lights—the best in the world—had replaced a colorful and unforgettable corps of men and women whose sturdy hands and devoted hearts had forged a chain of safety from coast to coast. But even as the lights hummed and clicked with new high-tech life, an echo of footsteps on lighthouse stairs could be heard. A new breed of lightkeeper began to emerge, a steward of sorts, who would preserve both the past and the future of lighthouses.

In the 1960s and 1970s, large navigation buoys and Texas tower lighthouses gradually replaced lightships. Following thirty-three years of service marking shoals fourteen miles off Virginia Beach, Chesapeake Lightship *relinquished its duties to Chesapeake Light in 1965. The Texas tower resembles an oil rig and is the newest lighthouse in the South. It stands in 177 feet of water. (Photograph courtesy of the U.S. Coast Guard Archives)*

CHAPTER 5

Wickies and Switchies

For the lighthouse should have a keeper. And the keeper should be a warm, fatherly man.
Claire Leighton
Where Land Meets Sea, 1954

Left: *The bucolic setting of Currituck Beach Lighthouse on the Outer Banks made it a preferred station for lightkeepers and their families. Built in 1875 at Whalehead, it guided ships as they approached or left the Chesapeake Bay.*

Above: *The interior door to the stair column of Cape Canaveral Lighthouse stands open, as if at any moment a lightkeeper will descend from his watch. He departed years ago, however, superceded by a cadre of sophisticated automatic gadgets. Cape Canaveral Lighthouse has not had a resident keeper since 1965.*

The Coast Guard's Lighthouse Automation and Modernization Program eventually brought an end to a very old occupation. Few Americans have served our nation with the simple devotion and selflessness of lighthouse keepers. Often impelled to answer a call of duty beyond the expected, they became the great solicitous heroes of their timehardworking, thankless individuals whose names are mostly forgotten but whose collective work has earned an honored place in the hearts of all who love the sea. Though lighthouse keepers have disappeared in the traditional sense, the idea of the lighthouse keeper endures. White-whiskered, leather-faced, and hobbling about on retired sea legs, he sits beneath his light with a cat in his lap, looking for a ship in distress. It's a cherished romantic image, but largely inaccurate.

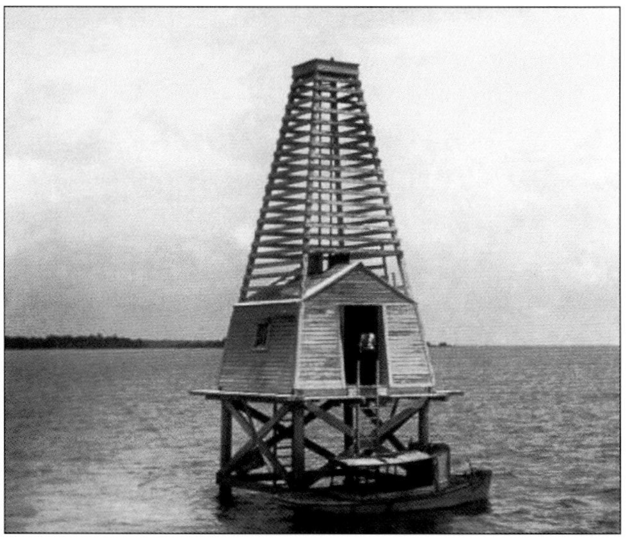

The unsung keepers of the lights were those who tended small range beacons and river post lamps. Their work was as important as that of coastal and landfall lightkeepers, but their lights were less impressive. This humble wooden range light on Florida backwaters was typical of hundreds of small beacons in the South that made inland navigation safe. A small shed held the beacon, which was projected out the door, while the wooden framework above it served as a daymark. (Photograph courtesy of the U.S. Coast Guard Archives)

Working at a Lighthouse

The popular notion of lighthouse life is one of relaxation punctuated by excitement. Pastimes such as reading, whittling, tying fancy knots, or making ships in bottles are thought to have occupied most of the lightkeeper's time, along with the quiet chores of lighting and extinguishing the beacon and keeping watch over the sea for ships in distress. Occasionally, a storm or other catastrophic event might have interrupted the monotony.

This romantic portrayal is accurate to a certain extent. However, there was considerably more work at most lighthouses than the public realized, especially at large mainland stations. Location of a lighthouse and its category—coastal landfall, harbor entrance, or river channel, for example—dictated the nature and volume of work to be done. The time period of a light's service also was relevant, since technological and administrative changes constantly transformed the job, from the tending of simple oil lamps and fogbells in the colonial and early federal years to the maintenance and operation of sophisticated mechanized beacons and sound signals introduced during the Industrial Revolution and streamlined by automatic equipment in the modern era.

Lamplighters who tended the small oil lamps of channel and river post beacons in the early nineteenth century had the fewest responsibilities. They usually maintained the lights as a part-time job and were required to do little beyond cleaning and fueling the lamps and reporting any problems to the district office of the U.S.

The lightkeepers' lifeline to shore and civilization were the lighthouse tenders. These small, homely vessels moved the keepers from station to station, hauled provisions and fuel for the lights, and brought succor to families on remote islands and water-bound towers. Tenders were named after trees, flowers, and shrubs native to the regions they serviced. Hibiscus *supplied southern lighthouses beginning in 1908. (Photograph courtesy of the U.S. Coast Guard Archives)*

Lighthouse Establishment. Large coastal mainland stations in the late nineteenth century and early twentieth century were the most demanding. Their intricate lighting and fog signal mechanisms required hours of service to operate and maintain, and the U.S. Lighthouse Board instituted a rigorous watch schedule for lightkeepers and conducted regular inspections to assure quality work. These stations operated much like small farms with the additional work of tending a lighthouse. Keepers kept livestock and gardens and maintained numerous buildings, including their homes, privies, a fog signal house, tool shed, oil house, and barn, as well as performing their mandated duties in the lighthouse tower.

Some tasks were universal, such as keeping a logbook and weather records. Keepers had to meticulously maintain an inventory of fuel, tools, and various kinds of equipment used for the lighthouse and fog signal. The Lighthouse Board monitored every item it issued, down to paper and pencils, and rags used to clean the lens. Keepers daily recorded fuel usage on a tally sheet, and listed passing ships in a special book. In addition to all of these duties, keepers had to meet visitors, escort them around the station, and record their names in a guest register. When the district inspector arrived, usually once a quarter, the station and its uniformed attendants, even their family members and homes, were thoroughly scrutinized and rated. Those who scored highest within a district were awarded special pins and allowed to fly a pennant to announce their excellence. Less than acceptable work brought negative consequences, usually in the form of disciplinary letters, docked pay, or dismissals.

A typical day in 1900 at a large mainland light station, such as Cape Hatteras Lighthouse on the Outer Banks, Tybee Island Lighthouse near Savannah, or Pensacola Lighthouse in Florida, began with extinguishing the beacon a half-hour after dawn. The keeper on duty in the lantern went off watch to breakfast and then to bed while co-workers tended to work around the station. One or two keepers cleaned the lighting apparatus and readied it for the next night. This involved polishing the prisms and brass, removing dirt from the revolving machinery and oiling it, winding up the weights to power the clockworks that turned the lens, filling lamps and trimming wicks, sweeping the tower stairs, and cleaning the lantern windows. Keepers reviewed and updated the logbook and stocked the tower with cans of kerosene for use during the coming night.

Meanwhile, other keepers and their family members began various station maintenance tasks, housekeeping, and farm chores. Everyone pitched in, whether on the payroll or not. The principle keeper laid out the work plan for the day and the assistants and families complied. Scraping and painting or whitewashing was an ongoing task. The salt air was destructive to exposed surfaces, and paint was the cure. Keepers repaired leaks as soon as they developed and promptly replaced rotted wood. Mildew and dirt were never allowed to build up anywhere on the station.

Daily care of livestock was crucial, especially the station horses, which provided the only transportation. After milking the cows and gathering eggs, family members cleaned the barn and tidied the chicken coop. Then the horse and wagon may have been prepared for a trip to the nearest village to shop for supplies, shuttle children to school, or collect the mail. On very remote stations, parents home-schooled their children or arranged for a traveling teacher to periodically visit. Wives cooked for the families, tended their gardens and pantries, and kept their houses white-glove clean, since the inspector could arrive unannounced at any time. A few women were official keepers and took their turn at watches and other lighthouse duties.

A half-hour before dusk, the keeper assigned to the first watch took up duties in the lantern and lighted the beacon. The watch rotation was normally four hours, but sometimes six, depending on the number of keepers assigned to the station. During this time, the keeper on duty remained in the watchroom just below the lantern, checking the light frequently and attending to paperwork. Keepers refilled lamps as needed. Every four hours, they wound up the weights to keep the clockworks running and the lens revolving. If a problem arose, the keeper on duty would wake other keepers. On stormy winter nights, it took more than one keeper to clear the windows of freezing rain and snow. Several keepers were on watch during a hurricane, which brought manifold concerns, especially if the tower was damaged or the light went out.

The Lighthouse Board expected the beacon to operate efficiently every day. If it failed, officials held the keepers accountable, unless the problem was beyond their control. The keepers knew the workings of the light and its every quirk, and were expected to remain on duty, even in the worst conditions. If they couldn't reinstate a failed light or fog signal, they notified the district immediately and sometimes placed an auxiliary beacon or bell in service until a repair crew arrived.

Sunday always was designated as a day of rest, and though no other work was required, keepers still had to tend to the light. Sunday also was typically a day when visitors stopped by to tour the station. Thus the families sometimes were as busy on their supposed day of rest as on regular work days, but they seldom groused. They were proud to show off their beneficent tower. The Lighthouse Board did not allot regular vacation time, but leave was granted for personal and business reasons with a letter of application to the district office. Only one of the keepers could be on leave at once. An illness in the family or attendance at a funeral or wedding was the most frequent excuse for leave.

When the Coast Guard assumed control of lighthouses in 1939, much of the manual labor had disappeared. By that time, lights and foghorns were electric and required little everyday maintenance. Civilian staffing slowly declined as active duty Coast Guard personnel replaced time-honored lightkeepers. Machinists, electricians, and boatswains took over as keepers, each specializing in unique aspects of light station work. Tours of duty for Coast Guard families usually lasted only two to four years, unlike their predecessors who often spent

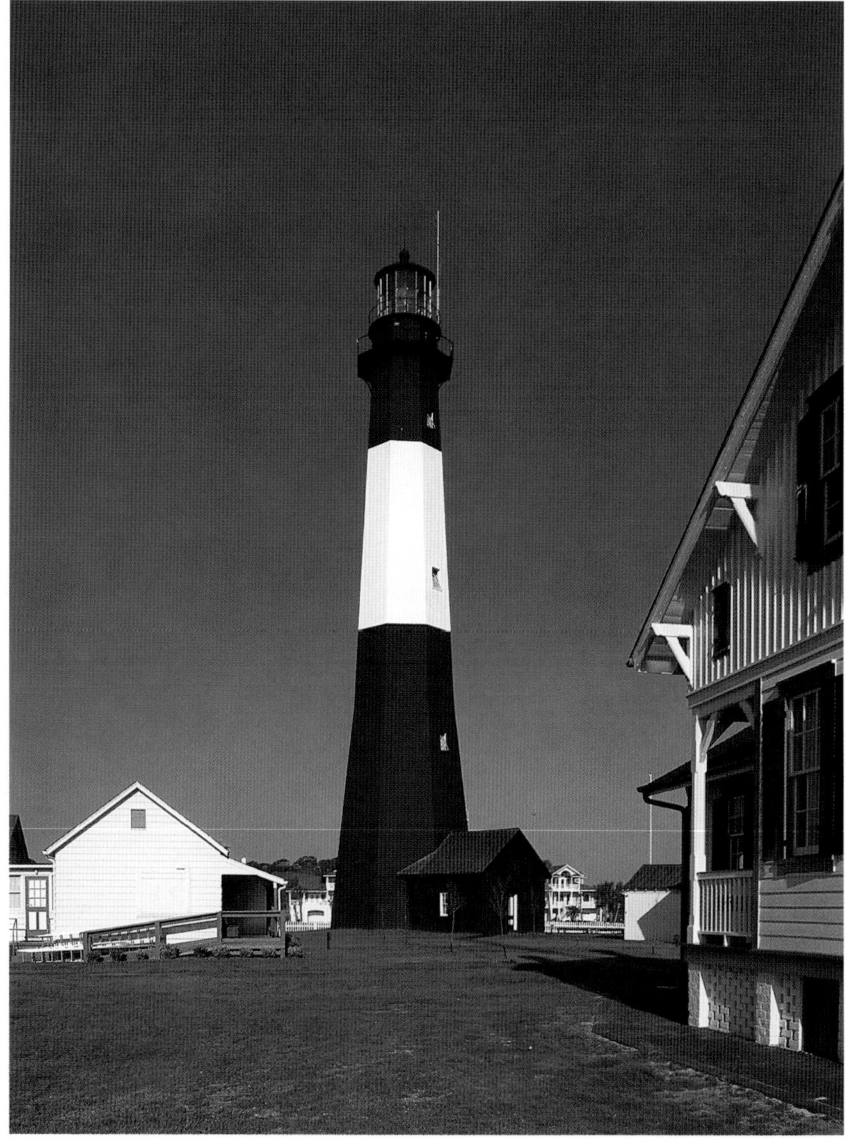

Large mainland light stations, such as Tybee Island Lighthouse (right) at Savannah or Pensacola Lighthouse (above) in West Florida, required several keepers to handle the work. Stations of this size operated much like a small farm, with livestock and a large garden to maintain, in addition to tending the lighthouse and fog signal. Everyone, even wives and children, worked to keep the station in good shape.

decades at a particular lighthouse and considered it "home." Eventually lightkeepers were entirely upstaged by compact, durable plastic optics and automatic devices to run them, and the profession disappeared.

The public was not willing to forget the venerable occupation, however. "Lighthouse keepers and their families had been part of the American consciousness," said Cheryl Shelton Roberts, founder and president of the Outer Banks Lighthouse Society. "The names of those who had served above and beyond the call of duty had become household words." Lighthouses, in truth, had grown as enchanting as medieval castles, and lightkeepers as beguiling as knights in shining armor. The contributions and character of three centuries of dedicated work begged to be documented. Historians ardently set about answering the question: who was the American lighthouse keeper and how was his or her work defined by time and place?

The Right Person for the Job

The first American lighthouses and the earliest lighthouses in the South were simple structures that required more dedication to operate than intelligence. Lightkeepers often came from local communities and obtained their jobs through various means. In colonial times, British governors selected keepers based on counsel from important merchants or naval captains. Similarly, after the founding of the nation, the president appointed lighthouse keepers based on recommendations.

George Washington approved the nation's first lightkeepers and noted that their work was a grave responsibility. In 1802, Thomas Jefferson was pleased to employ the first keeper of Smith Point Lighthouse in his home state of Virginia: "The appointment of William Helms to be the keeper of the Lighthouse at Smith's Point is approved. Salary $250." By 1820, the service had so expanded that the Fifth Auditor of the Treasury, who superintended the nation's lighthouses, made appointments, but presidents were still willing to comment on the appointment or removal of a keeper. John Quincy Adams wrote: "Let John Whalton be appointed keeper of the floating lights on Carysfort Reef with a salary of $700 a year." The retired Thomas Jefferson, upon hearing that the man he assigned to Cape Henry Light had been derelict in his duties, responded: "I think the keepers of lighthouses should be dismissed for small degrees of remissness, because of the calamities which even these produce."

Owning the land where a lighthouse was built sometimes netted a keeper's job, as did being its architect and builder. James Gould of Massachusetts, who designed and built the first St. Simons Island Lighthouse in Georgia in 1808, was deemed a man of good character and was appointed the tower's first keeper by President Thomas Jefferson. He remained on duty twenty-nine years. Elzy Burroughs, who in 1804 built New Point Comfort Light, Virginia, received the appointment as its first keeper. Jacob Meyers superintended the construction of Dog Island Lighthouse at Carrabelle, Florida, then became its first keeper in 1839.

Other lightkeepers came to their posts by association. Temple Pent, who served at Cape Florida Light from 1852 to 1868, had been a state senator. Families passed the duties down from generation to generation, and not always based on skill. Thomas Jefferson eschewed this practice, saying: "I have constantly refused to give in to this method of making offices hereditary." However, Jefferson was among the few who felt this way. According to various letters of recommendation the Lighthouse Establishment received over the years, candidates did benefit from being "a firm friend of the Administration." Adam Gaskins, the first keeper of Cape Hatteras Lighthouse in 1803, was known to be "a good party man."

Political affiliation was considered more important than fitness for duty, and many capable lightkeepers lost their jobs when a new administration came into office. When Abraham Lincoln was elected in 1860, his administration fired 70 percent of keepers and replaced them with Republicans. Political parties continued to control lighthouse positions until the Civil Service Act of 1896, which stipulated that federal employment be based on merit and experience. Even after this time, some keepers earned their assignments by virtue of an acquaintance in government. Political satirist Ambrose Bierce glibly pointed out in his 1911 *Devil's Dictionary* that a lighthouse was "a tall building on the seashore in which the government maintains a lamp and a friend of the politician."

War veterans received special consideration, possibly as a means of propitiation for injuries suffered while serving their country. Government officials appointed Amos Latham, a Revolutionary War veteran, to tend Little Cumberland Lighthouse in Georgia. When the tower was dismantled and relocated to Fernandina Beach, Florida in 1838, Latham moved with it. In 1834, when Captain Henry Hunter of the revenue cutter *Taney* visited Bald Head Lighthouse, he noted that it was tended by "an old Revolutionary War soldier . . . unable to give the light his constant personal attention."

Retired sea captains were favored lighthouse candidates too, and were hired regularly. George Wilson, a Civil War navy veteran, was assigned to Rebecca Shoal Lighthouse, a screwpile structure off Key West. In April 1903, an inspector noted, "Wilson has defective vision, and on testing . . . I found his eyesight with glasses was 7/20." The Lighthouse Board blamed Wilson's poor vision for damage that occurred to the lens after the lamps, which he had not properly adjusted, melted and cracked several prisms. Wilson was not removed, possibly because sympathies toward veterans and sea captains forbade firing them on account of infirmity. He died in 1903.

A few applicants recommended themselves. In 1859, L. H. Dunlop of Jacksonville, Florida, wrote to the U.S. Lighthouse Board asking for the appointment to the new Jupiter Inlet Lighthouse: "I would most respectfully offer my services as keeper. My intimate knowledge of the whole of that section of the country, owning lands there, and earnest desire to get that portion of our state settled, induces me to make application." Dunlop did not get the job. He had applied during a period when the lighthouse service was in the midst of reorganization due to a scandal and accusations that navigational aids in the United States were inferior to those in Europe. The Board carefully selected lightkeepers after 1852. Lightkeepers received training, uniforms, rank, and a merit system, as well as better pay and benefits.

Before the advent of the U.S. Lighthouse Board, however, the work was simple and not highly regulated. Various types of oil lamps lit the beacons, and the need to trim the flax wicks of the lamps during the night to remove sooty residue earned keepers the nickname "wickie." Keepers had to light the beacon shortly before dusk, extinguish it soon after dawn, and keep it immaculately clean. Lighthouse keepers kept records of oil consumption, wick use, and other supplies. Reporting the weather, the number of visitors, and calamitous events such as shipwrecks and rescues was also part of the job, but logbooks contained little else unless a lightkeeper had a garrulous character. Few did.

In fact, some lightkeepers were barely literate and only made marks on a tally sheet to account for oil usage. After the U.S. Lighthouse Board mandated that keepers maintain a logbook, some keepers still balked, insisting that recording day-to-day operations in a logbook was a

Dapper in his summer white uniform, lightkeeper Carl Svendsen leans on the fence surrounding St. Simons Island Lighthouse at Brunswick, Georgia (Bottom: Photograph courtesy of Coastal Georgia Historical Society). He served at the station from 1907 to 1935. The 104-foot sentinel and roomy keeper's house, pictured about 1885, was a coveted assignment (Top: Photograph courtesy of the U.S. Coast Guard Archives).

waste of good work time. Captain Joe Burris, who served forty-five years at lighthouses in Virginia and North Carolina, probably was the best-known of the curmudgeon keepers who refused to write in a logbook. By contrast, Dwayne Snydam, assistant keeper at Amelia Island Lighthouse in the 1870s, wrote in the logbook daily, often adding personal details. For example, he proudly mentioned giving up tobacco. Upon his retirement he wrote: "Twenty years ago I commenced in the Light House Service; have been absent but one night during that time."

A Varied and Ever-Changing Duty

Before 1850, lighthouse keepers had few directives or regulations by which to abide. The collector of customs for a local port visited the lighthouses within his district on occasion, sometimes only at the behest of mariners who complained about a particular lightkeeper's work. In 1826, Captain Samuel Franklin of the revenue cutter *Marion* visited Garden Key Lighthouse, some seventy miles offshore at Dry Tortugas, Florida. He found the station in the care of John Flaherty and in wretched condition: "very dirty, the window glasses very black with soot, the lamps were stopped up with plugs of burnt wicks . . . some of the lamps had no wick, nor oil." Franklin's crew listened to Flaherty's impassioned excuses that he was overworked, ill, and needed an assistant. They helped him clean up the station. William Pinkney, the customs collector from Key West, made a subsequent visit, possibly in response to a letter Mrs. Flaherty wrote to First Lady Mrs. John Quincy Adams, detailing the deplorable living conditions on the island and blaming the government for her husband's illness. Pinkney suspected the Flahertys were conniving to get a mainland assignment and a pay increase. Under duress from the First Lady, he transferred John Flaherty to Sand Key Light, a station nearer to shore and to Key West, where the Board could keep a closer watch on the man. Five years later John Flaherty died and his wife took over his duties.

The keepers were not to blame for all problems, however. In the years prior to the advent of the U.S. Lighthouse Board, the service was inadequately managed and equipment was poor. Complaints about Cape Hatteras Lighthouse in 1817 surrounded keeper Joseph Farrow, who was charged with letting his light go out during the night and with not cleaning the reflectors properly, reducing the light's visible range. Upon investigation, Farrow was absolved of blame. The government had provided oil of such inferior quality that it would not burn properly, and the government had not supplied the proper cleaning fluid for the reflectors. Farrow had been doing his best to shine the reflectors with whatever was on hand. Further investigations turned up several physical factors that obscured the beacon, including mists that hung over the warm Gulf Stream waters just offshore and a too-short tower. Pharaoh Farrow replaced his father in 1821. Nine years later the collector of customs dismissed the younger Farrow after discovering he was subcontracting his duties to another man for less pay and keeping the difference.

After the U.S. Lighthouse Board reorganized the service in 1852 and instituted new technologies in illumination and fog signaling, they were more rigorous about examining and monitoring applicants for lighthouse positions. Candidates took a simple written exam, which underscored the need to read and write. Mechanical skill was a plus, as were letters of recommendation or experience at sea. Once hired, there were years of apprentice-type training in lower ranks before a lightkeeper could be promoted to a top position. Most importantly, lighthouses were adequately provisioned and staffed, and a corps of inspectors and support crews were available to handle the lightkeepers' needs.

Retired sailors and fishermen often edged out farmers and tradesmen, since the former had experience at sea and could handle a boat. Records show a few ministers and teachers who became lighthouse keepers. There were unexpected segues too: William King of Old Point Comfort Light was a former shoe salesman appointed in the 1850s, and Robert Fletcher, who kept three Florida lighthouses between 1836 and 1862, was a druggist. Some keepers believed tending a lighthouse was their calling in life. The first keeper of the Tybee Island Lighthouse, an Irish immigrant named Higgins, was said to have been so smitten with his job as a lightkeeper that he made a ceremony of kindling the oil lamps each night, as if lighting them were a solemn religious rite.

There was also the notion of lighthouse keeping as a quiet occupation and the lighthouse as a place where great minds could be nurtured. Henry David Thoreau said as much in his book *Cape Cod*: "I had a classmate who fitted for college by the lamps of a lighthouse, which was more light, we think, than the University afforded." A century later, Albert Einstein concurred: "I notice how the quiet life stimulates the creative mind . . . I think of such occupations as the service in the lighthouses." Lightkeeper William Hunt Harris, who served at several

Florida lighthouses in the 1880s, was a case in point. Harris studied law in his free time, passing the bar in 1890. He resigned his lighthouse duties and eventually was appointed to the Florida Supreme Court.

At some stations, particularly those offshore, there was ample opportunity to read and study. Recognizing the need to address idle hours, the U.S. Lighthouse Board initiated a lending library program in the 1870s. Special oak bookcases that held about fifty volumes circulated among the lighthouses every few months. The Board described the content as "a proper admixture of historic, scientific, and poetic matter." The spiritual life of the keepers was also important. The Lighthouse Board gave keepers a day off on Sunday to attend church, though they still had to maintain the light. Those on remote lighthouses conducted their own services. Ministers who voluntarily came aboard the tenders to visit distant lighthouses performed events such as weddings and baptisms. One such wedding occurred in 1834 and was reported in the *Florida Herald*: "Mrs. R. F. Flaherty [keeper] . . . was married to Captain Frederick Neill. . . . The Ceremony was performed by Richard Fitzpatrick at the Sand Key Lighthouse."

Long tenures of service were not unusual, nor were dynasties of keepers, all from the same family. George Clifford spent thirty-one years at Pensacola Lighthouse, and Lester Williams served at several Gulf Coast lighthouses for a total of forty-two years. Clement Brooks was keeper at various Florida lighthouses from 1884 to 1937. Patrick O'Hagen began as a temporary keeper at Hunting Island, South Carolina, in 1876 and retired fifty years later from Amelia Island Lighthouse. The Gresham family tended St. Marks Lighthouse from 1892 to 1957, and descendents of Benjamin Fulcher were appointed to Cape Hatteras Lighthouse for some seventy years.

Not all lightkeepers fit the dutiful, solicitous archetype we imagine. Benjamin H. Kerr, who served at Loggerhead Key Light, appears to have been a difficult man. He had a series of problems with assistants and with his family in 1859 and 1860 that culminated in an "incident," as recorded by an officer assigned to nearby Fort

Lightkeepers came from diverse backgrounds and often obtained their jobs by association. Many were humble fishermen and sailors who "swallowed the anchor" and found lighthouse work to be the next best thing to shipboard life. A few keepers had influential friends or positions in government. Temple Pent, a Florida state senator, was appointed to Cape Florida Lighthouse from 1852 through 1868.

Jefferson. Kerr's wife, a daughter, and both of his assistants had made an attempt on his life, sending him fleeing from the island. He took refuge in Key West for several weeks until the dispute was resolved. He resigned the next year.

Dismissals were not infrequent and usually involved alcohol or desertion. In August 1874, J. K. Buckley, head keeper at Sombrero Key Lighthouse, reported that his assistant Josiah Butts "got several drinks of gin so that he could hardly keep his watch in the light. He growled at me and insulted my wife." The following month Butts was found asleep on watch, and he was reported for drunkenness and insubordination again in November. Before the Board could fully investigate, he quit.

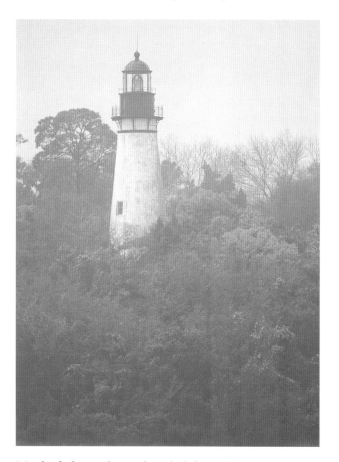

Much of what we know about lighthouse life comes from the logbooks of lightkeepers. Details of daily work at the stations, fuel consumption, weather, visitors, and passing ships were recorded, but so were personal notes. Some keepers were more verbose than others. At Amelia Island Lighthouse in the 1870s, lightkeeper Dwayne Snydam proudly wrote of giving up tobacco and noted that during his twenty years at the lighthouse he had been absent only one night.

An article in *Frank Leslie's Popular Monthly* in 1896 summed up the U.S. Lighthouse Board's view of keepers who left their stations unattended: "it is as cowardly for a keeper to desert his light as for a soldier to turn his back upon the enemy."

A few went mad before deserting. At Rebecca Shoal Light in 1902, assistant keeper James Walker grew more despondent day by day, finally disappearing from the waterbound lighthouse. His superior speculated that he drowned himself. The isolation of lighthouse duty sometimes led to murder. In March 1880, the assistant keeper of St. Simons Island Lighthouse got into an argument with head keeper Frederick Osbourne and shot him. More than fifty years later, on March 16, 1938, assistant keeper E. W. Marler of Cape San Blas Lighthouse was found stabbed to death in his garden. No motive was ever discovered, nor was the murderer apprehended. The remote lighthouse was deemed an easy target for an intruder.

A Plethora of Perils

Southern lightkeepers had advantages over their northern counterparts in many ways. Snow, ice, and fog seldom hindered their work, if at all, and the semitropical sun and warm waters offered recreation. But heat, storms, and a bestiary of unpleasant creatures posed myriad problems not found elsewhere in the nation.

"Sometimes the mosquitoes were so thick we'd be breathing them," remembered John Gaskill, whose father served at Bodie Lighthouse early in the 1920s and 1930s. Another lighthouse took its name from the pesky insects. Construction of the Mosquito Inlet Lighthouse south of present-day Daytona was hindered by an outbreak of malaria in the 1830s. Lightkeepers at other stations died of mosquito-borne yellow fever. Smudge pots burned to repel mosquitoes, and keepers were admonished to drain ditches and standing water where the insects could reproduce. Despite these precautions, Michael Mabrity succumbed to yellow fever in 1827 at Key West Lighthouse.

Other worrisome denizens included birds, which sometimes slammed the towers and damaged the lighting apparatus. The crew at Loggerhead Key Lighthouse in 1909 reported a severe thunderstorm in which hundreds of birds, mostly sooty terns, were thrown against the tower during the night by wind: "They covered the ground like a multicolored blanket . . . the lighthouse

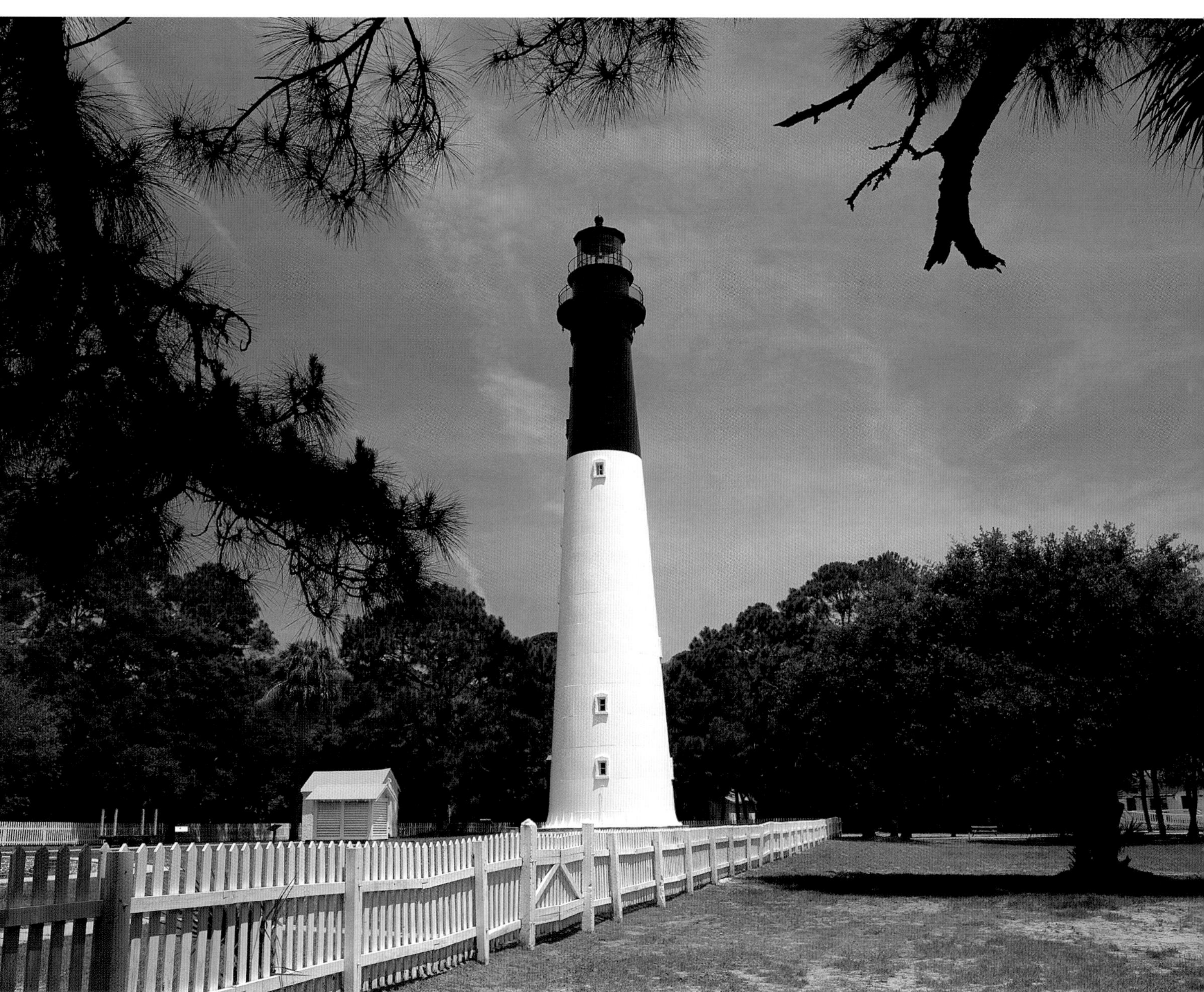

A beach is never still, a fact that plagued lighthouse engineers as they sought solutions to ever-changing shorelines. One answer was to build prefabricated towers that could be easily taken apart and moved when erosion threatened or nature redrew the beach. Hunting Island Lighthouse, built in 1873 on a restless barrier beach in South Carolina, was dismantled and moved to a safer location in 1885.

had been newly-painted, and in the morning it was literally plastered with brilliant feathers." At other times, birds seemed drawn, even maddened, by the powerful beacon. Virginia's Hog Island Lighthouse suffered a bird attack one cold, calm night in February 1900, when hundreds of migratory birds stormed the tower and put out the beacon. The two lightkeepers tried to repel the feathered marauders for several hours, using anything at their disposal, and then took refuge in the base of the lighthouse until the assault ended at dawn.

An alligator was blamed for the loss of chickens at St. Marks Lighthouse in the 1880s. Eleanor Bishop, in her history of Coast Guard activity during World War II, described Hunting Island as "an alligator infested, jungle-like barrier island, with a lighthouse on it." Snakes were a constant menace too, so serious that in the early years of the twentieth century, lightkeepers in the South requested anti-venom kits. Others simply endured the threat. Carl Svendsen, keeper of St. Simons Island Lighthouse, came down the tower stairs one night after tending the beacon to find a huge snake coiled against the door. Terrified and unsure if it was venomous, he jumped in surprise and dropped his lantern, which promptly snuffed out. Alone in the dark with the unidentified reptile, he yelled for help and roused his family from bed. They arrived with a lantern and found the snake coiled around the bottom step. It was a large, harmless black snake that stubbornly refused to leave. Svendsen was forced to overcome his revulsion and remove it by hand.

Captain Mills Burnham at Cape Canaveral Lighthouse took a more lighthearted approach to his slithery companions. A popular legend about Burnham tells how he ran out of lubricating oil for the lighthouse lens and used snake oil, found in a small cavity in a viper's head, to tide him over until the lighthouse tender came calling. The intrepid keeper had no trouble finding a few snakes to supply the oil. They crawled onto the the stone walkway at the base of the tower on cool nights to capture residual heat. Burnham is said to have swept them off the pad each morning with a broom.

Truth can be stranger than fiction. In May 1912, the lamplighter of the Wadmelaw River Lights in South Carolina ascended the ladder on a river-post beacon to tend the light and was greeted by a loud buzzing sound. The *Lighthouse Service Bulletin* later reported: "Peering around for the cause he was amazed to discover a huge rattlesnake that had coiled itself just under the light box . . . arming himself with an oar he succeeded in making it plunge overboard . . . to his amazement, as well as discomfiture, the now thoroughly angered reptile, instead of making off, swam back to the beacon, and proceeded to ascend, weaving its body in and out between the steps. Fortunately, he managed to give it another well-directed blow with the oar, which caused it to drop back in the water and float off apparently dying."

The iron door of Hunting Island Lighthouse at Frogmore, South Carolina, closed on sixty years of history in 1933, when the lighthouse was deactivated. While the light was in service, one of its keepers, Patrick O'Hagan, came to the lighthouse to fill in for a few weeks while the principle keeper took leave. O'Hagan became so enamored of the work he stayed on to replace an assistant and served a total of fifty years as a lightkeeper in the South.

The sheer elevation of southern lighthouses assured their beams showed a sufficient range out to sea, but caring for such tall towers was dangerous. Lantern windows were fitted with handholds around 1820 to give the keepers something to grip while cleaning the glass panes on windy days. Painting the towers was a task that exacted courage, however. Most keepers rigged scaffolding or slung a chair down from the lantern on ropes. The faint of heart despised the chore, and with good reason. Few were injured, considering the amount of work accomplished over the years. Joseph Andreau was among the fatalities. He fell from St. Augustine Lighthouse in 1859 while working on the tower. He was sixty years old.

At times, bizarre events occurred. On the night of September 3, 1886, a rare earthquake, centered in Charleston, South Carolina, rumbled along the coast. Lightkeepers from Maryland to Florida reported the quake. George M. Quarterman at Cape Canaveral Lighthouse wrote that the tower shook for several minutes, accompanied by a sound much like thunder. During the worst of the quake the lighthouse swayed about ten inches from southeast to northwest. Putty crumbled off the windows and pendulum clocks in the house and tower stopped. Nearly 500 miles up the coast at Currituck Beach Lighthouse, Etta Dunton was inside the lantern of the lofty tower with her baby. When the shaking began, she rushed for the stairway but was unable to stand due to the swaying of the huge lighthouse. She sat down and slid down the 214 stairs, one by one, with her baby in her arms.

Storm-Tossed Lightkeepers

New England had its nor'easters, the Great Lakes its numbing ice storms, and the Pacific its powerful windstorms, but in the South there were tempests to exceed all others. Even thunderstorms raged with a ferocity seldom seen in other parts of the nation. Lightning destroyed the Shell Castle Lighthouse on Ocracoke Island in 1821, only seventeen years after its commissioning. In May 1831, a thunderstorm swept over the Chesapeake Bay and pounded Old Point Comfort Light. The keeper took cover in his house as hail stones "as large as chicken eggs" pummeled the station. The hail battered the roof of the house and shattered most of the windows, including those of the lighthouse lantern.

At Bodie Island Lighthouse in the 1880s, the lightning rod became detached from its grounding wire. The keeper was unaware of the danger until one afternoon when he was descending the tower in a thunderstorm. Lightning struck the cupola and traveled down the iron stairs to where he had hold of the railing. The jolt entered the man's hand, coursed through his body, and knocked him down. He lay on the stairs for a several hours, partially paralyzed, before his wife found him.

Near dawn in February 1967, a waterspout (tornado at sea) struck Diamond Shoals Light, a Texas tower beacon thirteen miles off Cape Hatteras. Winds estimated at 100 miles per hour tore out windows and snatched away the radiobeacon antenna. The crew, most of whom were asleep, suffered no injuries. The lighthouse had been in commission only three months when the cyclone hit.

Southern lighthouse logbooks occasionally recorded unseasonable weather. On February 8, 1885, the keeper of Tybee Island Lighthouse noted a temperature of 0°F. His co-keeper farther north at Charleston Light reported 1°F. Fourteen years later, almost to the day, two inches of snow fell on the St. Johns River Lighthouse and the temperature at Pensacola Lighthouse was a frigid 14°F below zero. Three winters later, the logbook at Currituck Beach Lighthouse noted: "Snow, very cold, fresh breeze. Snow frozen on storm panes." Due to the rarity of such harsh weather in the South, keepers were not issued tools for ice or snow removal.

Hurricanes were probably the worst natural disasters. When others fled for safety, lighthouse keepers remained by their lights and sometimes paid the ultimate price. At the very least, they lost personal property and incurred, at their own expense, the comfort and succor of storm refugees. High winds tore down buildings and battered the towers, but it was the storm surge accompanying a hurricane that did the most damage.

When a terrible hurricane hit the Florida Keys in 1846, widow Barbara Mabrity was on duty at Key West Lighthouse. Mabrity, who had served as keeper since her husband's death, was in the tower with her six children, who had come to assist her, plus several neighbors who had taken shelter there after their homes were swept away. A horrific storm surge arrived at high tide and undermined the lighthouse. As it began to collapse, Mabrity somehow escaped with one child. But all others in the tower, including five of her children, perished in the falling rubble. Gone too was the lighthouse her husband had kept from its inception in 1826 until his death six years later.

In 1848, Sherrod Edwards and his family endured a powerful storm at Egmont Key Lighthouse, which marked the entrance to Tampa Bay. As the storm surge breached the island, the lower level of the house was inundated. Edwards, his family, and his pregnant dog took refuge in an upstairs bedroom. In his journal Edwards wrote that at the height of the storm the terrified dog lay down on the bed and gave birth to premature puppies.

Jupiter Inlet Lighthouse survived a violent 1928 hurricane, though the storm badly damaged the tower and sorely tested the stamina of the keepers. The station's new electrical system failed shortly after the storm began. Franklin Seabrook, the head keeper's sixteen-year-old son, turned the huge lens by hand for nearly forty-eight hours, until his father was able to repair the generator. During this time, wind and rain broke through one of the lantern room windows and shattered a bulls-eye panel of magnifying glass in the expensive French lens. After the storm, the Seabrooks carefully collected the shards and shipped them to the lighthouse service depot in Charleston where the shards were painstakingly fitted together and braced by a metal framework. The repaired panel was shipped back to the lighthouse and reinstalled. It still serves today.

In August 1933, a hurricane raged over the Chesapeake Bay, carrying a high storm surge. At York Spit Lighthouse, keeper W. J. Diggs documented the storm's progress in his journal: "Floors began to burst up . . . sailboat broke away . . . sea breaking over deck . . . oil tanks broke away . . . cookstove completely gone." The station was in near ruins afterwards, but Diggs had done what lightkeepers pledged to do—he had stayed by his light.

Haunted Lighthouses

THE LIGHT STILL SHONE PALELY
DOWN THE STAIRS;
WE SAW NOTHING COMING;
WE ONLY HEARD THE STEPS.
James Thurber (1894–1961)
The Night the Ghost Got In

A lighthouse is the perfect setting for the supernatural. Its penchant for eerie events probably derives from the nocturnal work and the extreme isolation and loneliness of lighthouse duty, combined with the many tragedies that take place at or near the sea. Hardly a lighthouse exists that does not have stories of shipwreck, drowning, fire, and storm embedded in its history—all prime material for a good ghost tale.

Southern lighthouses have their share of colorful wraiths. Some believe these spirits polish the lantern windows and brass, and clamber about on stairways and catwalks. Their spectral shadows glide over the grounds and flit about in buildings, sometimes opening and closing doors or causing rocking chairs to suddenly come alive. They moan and sigh, scream, and exhale clammy breath on visitors. Some have even plagued lighthouse pets.

St. Simons Island Lighthouse has phantom footfall on its iron spiral stairway, attributed to the restless climbing and descending of a lightkeeper murdered at the station in 1880. The harmless shade never bothered lightkeeping families, but it seemed to delight in tormenting one keeper's dog. Jinx, owned by keeper Carl Svendsen, reportedly growled and bristled in fear each time the muffled footsteps sounded in the tower. At times, he seemed to see something others could not, and snarled loudly or backed away.

St. Augustine Lighthouse has multiple ghosts, including a little girl in a rose-colored dress who appears in various parts of the house, then slowly fades and vanishes. There's also the occasional mysterious smell of cigar smoke, attributed to a past keeper whose spirit roams the grounds. The basement of the keeper's house is the haunt of another ghost. One evening as a staff member was straightening the benches in the basement's video room, he was mortified to discover some invisible help. He lifted one end of a bench, and then watched in horror as the opposite end lifted on its own—or did it? The museum staff is convinced the ghost was to blame.

A headless ghost supposedly haunts the beaches of Gasparilla Rear Range Light in Florida. She was a Spanish princess kidnapped by the fabled seventeenth-century pirate, Jose Gaspar, for whom the island and lighthouse are named. Gaspar's existence remains in doubt. It's likely he was invented by a local storyteller many years ago. Truth or fabrication, his evil deeds continue to fascinate. Gaspar is said to have held his kidnapped princess captive with the intent of marrying her. But during the shotgun wedding she spit in his face. Enraged, Gaspar brandished his sword and cut off her head. Quickly filled with remorse, he scooped up the head and wrapped it in cloth, to be kept as a souvenir of an unhappy love affair. Her body was taken ashore and buried in the sand near the present-day site of the lighthouse. Naturally, it rises from the grave on eerie nights to search for its lost head.

The South's most comical lighthouse ghost is Captain Johnson, the inveterate clanking, groaning, screeching poltergeist of Carysfort Reef Lighthouse, a screwpile tower standing a lonely watch in the waters off Key Largo. Charles Johnson was the first keeper of the lighthouse, transferred to the station in 1852 from the ship *Florida*, which he captained. Acquaintances knew Johnson as a "terrible sinner," prone to drink, swear, and throw hot-tempered fits. But he was also a very religious man who worried about his destiny in the hereafter. He died only a few months after taking up his duties at the lighthouse. Not long afterwards, horrible groans and howls began sounding throughout the tower each evening. Witnesses quickly attributed these inexplicable noises to the ghost of Captain Johnson. The eerie sounds continued year after year, habitual in the summer months and acceptably supernatural, until a young man named Charles Brookfield came to visit the tower in the 1920s.

As one who questioned ghost tales and put great stock in science, Brookfield began a quick study of the big iron tower and the temperature dynamics affecting it. Within hours, he had a plausible explanation. On hot summer days, the lighthouse's ironwork heated up in the intense sunlight, causing its joints to expand. As the temperature rapidly dropped with nightfall, the joints contracted, sending frightful groans and screeches through the ironwork. The sounds were remarkably human. Naturally the keepers attributed them to old Captain Johnson, whose restless spirit, they claimed, was having difficulty getting into heaven. Like all lighthouse ghosts, Captain Johnson exists in the fertile imagination, fueled by dark and lonely nights on a storm-battered tower washed by the sea.

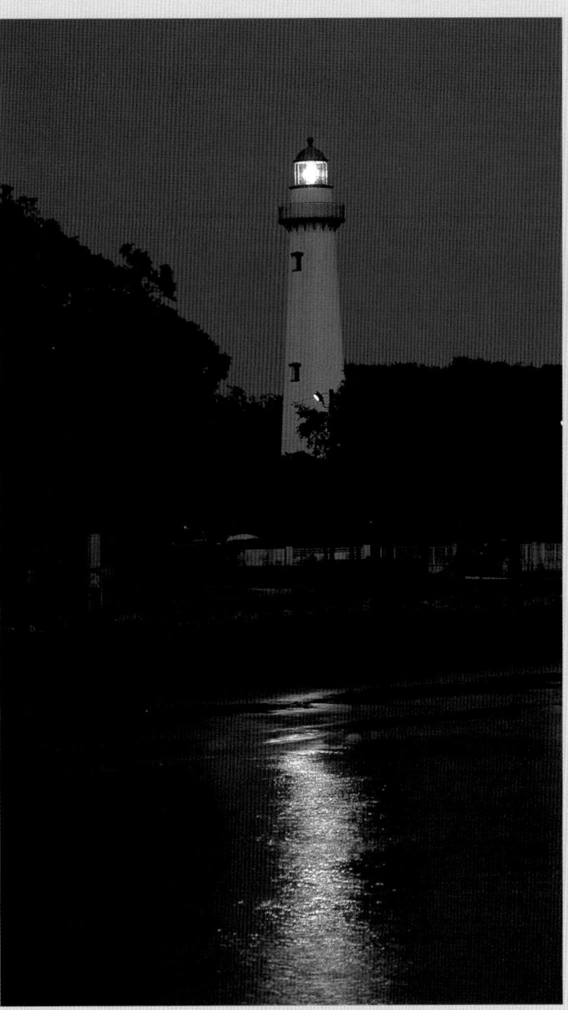

Phantom footfall sounds can be heard on the great iron stairway of St. Simons Lighthouse from time to time. Docents say the ghost of a lightkeeper killed at the station in the 1880s is the cause of the eerie clamor.

Both photos: *A rare earthquake rumbled through the South on the night of September 3, 1886. Its effects were recorded at a number of lighthouses. The tall sentinel at Currituck Beach swayed so badly a woman in the tower was forced to descend the stairs in a sitting position, holding her infant in her arms.*

After 1852, the U.S. Lighthouse Board improved living conditions for lightkeepers, who often were poorly compensated and assigned to posts far from the pleasantries of society. Keeper's homes were designed with comfort in mind. A broad porch on the head keeper's house at the 1875 Currituck Beach Lighthouse provided space to escape the heat and relax during leisure hours (right). The station's spacious kitchen (facing page) was the center of activity, a place where family gathered and the all-important meals were served. A bedroom at Currituck Beach Light was heated and had an adjoining washroom (above).

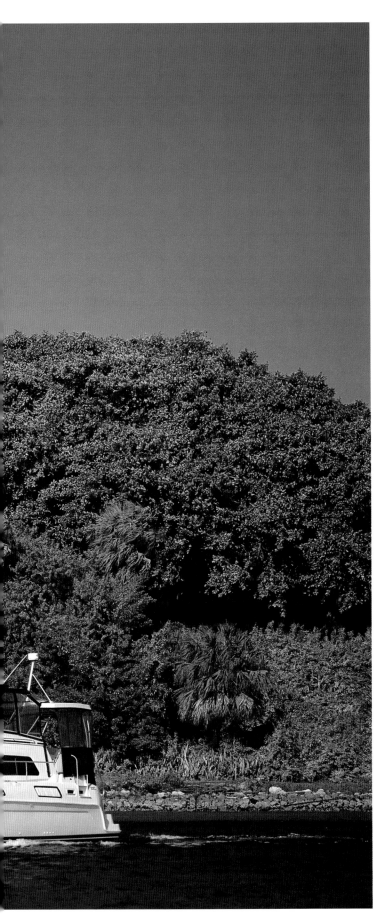

Diversions, Ingenuity, and Valor

"A certain peculiarity describes some of the lighthouse keepers," according to lighthouse historian and former president of the Florida Lighthouse Association, Tom Taylor. He might have been thinking of Dwight Allen of Jupiter Lighthouse, who derived a bit of comic relief from his work by standing on his head at the top of the tower, or Edward Meyer, who had his Model T lightered to Morris Island Lighthouse by boat so his family could joy-ride around the island on Sundays. Perhaps he also enjoyed perplexed visitors asking, "How did you get a car out here?" and "Where do you drive to?" In 1935, a hurricane washed the car into the sea, along with Meyer's livestock.

Boredom and the need for self-amusement sometimes afflicted lightkeeping families. At Ponce Inlet Lighthouse, the Meyer children put an SOS message in a bottle and tossed it into the sea as a prank. The Coast Guard recovered it and brought it to the lighthouse, suspecting the children were to blame. Keeper Meyer disciplined his progeny accordingly. Farther up the coast, Cracker Daniels, the young and enterprising son of Cardell Daniels, keeper of St. Augustine Lighthouse, made a handkerchief parachute for the family cat and launched the unsuspecting feline from the top of the 165-foot tower. "Smoky" survived the frightening descent but thereafter steered clear of both the lighthouse and the boy.

There were daring and dangerous stunts in the tall towers too, especially among lighthouse children. Dorothy Gaskill recalled antics at the top of Bodie Island Lighthouse when her parents weren't watching: "We used to climb over the railing and walk on the ledge—six or seven inches wide at the most—and lean out." Her brother John frequently climbed onto the cupola and stood on the ventilator ball gripping the lightning rod some 150 feet above the ground.

Jupiter Inlet Lighthouse opened in 1860, a time when applicants for the job of lightkeeper were carefully screened to ensure the best candidate got the job. Retired sea captains were considered reliable. One of Jupiter Inlet Light's early keepers, Captain James Amour, served forty years at the lighthouse. His successor, Captain Charles Seabrook, was commended after his sixteen-year-old son, Franklin Seabrook, turned the lens by hand after a power failure halted its revolutions during the September 1928 hurricane.

By far, the worst deprivation was loneliness. Crews on the waterbound screwpile lighthouses of the Florida Reef kept carrier pigeons in order to communicate with loved ones ashore or send word if an emergency arose. Pets provided companionship and did some of the work. Hardly a lighthouse was without a dog, cat, or both to help with controlling rodents and bugs, or for protection. The Shanahan family at Florida's Sanibel Island Lighthouse had a record number of pets, including a tame deer and a cat they taught to do tricks.

But nothing could replace the contentment and happiness of having a family on station. By the early twentieth century, families were not permitted to live on the offshore screwpile lighthouses, but keepers smuggled them aboard anyway. Wayland Baum, whose father served at several North Carolina sound lights, remembered having to hide in a closet when the inspector came to the lighthouse: "Yes, of course the inspector could see the signs of a wife or children . . . he could tell . . . but the inspector was 'good folks.' He wouldn't say anything if all was in good order."

The unexpected could happen and often was cheered as relief from tedium. In December 1930, keepers T. Gaillard and J. Pinner of Hunting Island Lighthouse watched as an airplane circled the tower, dropped lower and lower, then sputtered and made a dive for the beach. Their families rushed over the dunes expecting to see a crash. But the plane had landed safely; it was simply out of fuel. Everyone was fascinated with the aircraft and its pilot. After a big meal and lots of conversation and questions from the children, Gaillard loaded his kids and the pilot into his old Model T, let some air out of the tires, and proceeded over the sand to the main road into Beaufort, where the pilot bought gasoline. The next morning, the pilot flew off into the wild blue yonder, and monotony returned to Hunting Island Lighthouse.

On some occasions, lightkeepers went above and beyond the call of duty. Many were thrifty and took pleasure in saving money for the government. In 1918, C. A. Sterling, keeper of the screwpile lighthouse at Craney Island, Virginia, did his part for the war effort by buying war bonds and practicing conservation. "During the summer," he told the district superintendent, "I cultivated a garden and produced vegetables enough for home and station use, distributed some among my neighbors who were unfortunate not to have a garden. . . . On account of no coal this winter, I have collected driftwood from the river enough to run me through winter at home; I also have been using driftwood at the station since August."

The government prized such resourcefulness, and most lightkeepers prided themselves on being able to solve their own problems. J. H. Carlin of Brunswick, Georgia, reported repairs he made in 1932 to a post beacon in his care: "Visited the old auto dump grounds and salvaged bolts and clamps from old bumpers, ample to make repairs to St. Andrews Sound Beacon. . . . Had to do a little blacksmithing. . . . cost nothing . . . had my own forge and the coal was salvaged from the waste coal along the railroad track, so we will be out nothing but the little time taken to get the parts together."

When William J. Tate tended the Currituck Sound lights, a string of about forty-two beacons covering sixty-five miles of waterway in North Carolina, he and his wife participated in one of the most famous events in American history. In 1900, Mrs. Addie Tate ran the post office in Kitty Hawk. She received a letter early that year from a Mr. Wilbur Wright inquiring about the weather conditions in the area and the topography of the dunes. Soon after the Tates replied, the Wright Brothers arrived in Kitty Hawk. Of course, as everyone knows, Orville and Wilbur Wright went on to make history with the first-ever flying machine. What's not widely known is how important the Tates were to the Wrights' success. They hosted the men in their home, lent them tools, and assisted in the physical labor of building and launching the gliders. The brothers assembled the first glider on the Tate's front lawn. Mrs. Tate fed the Wrights, did their laundry, and provided moral support and encouragement. She even let them borrow her sewing machine to make fabric wing coverings.

Years after the Wrights left the Outer Banks, William Tate was still thinking of airplanes. Why not learn to fly and inspect his forty-two lights by air? In 1920, he became the first lightkeeper in the nation to do so, flying low and level over the Currituck Sound beacons to affirm they were all working properly. As a result of his pioneering role in aviation, Tate inspired the establishment of the Lighthouse Service Airways Division, which began service in 1926. Remote lights began to be inspected by air, and aviators now had more than 1,500 skeleton tower beacons to guide them. In the meantime, Tate had been asked to unveil a plaque to the Wright Brothers on the site where the first glider was assembled. It was the honor of a lifetime, and Tate helped historians locate the exact spot.

Tate retired in 1939, just as the Coast Guard assumed control of lighthouses. As a lightkeeper he had been cited many times for rescues. In 1917 alone, he received twelve citations for valor. But the greatest accolade accorded William J. Tate came posthumously. In 1999, a 175-foot Coast Guard buoy tender was christened in his honor. The *William J. Tate*, carrying a crew of eighteen and charged with similar duties to those Tate fulfilled as a lightkeeper, is home ported in Philadelphia. William J. Tate joined three other southern lighthouse keepers to be honored in this way.

A helix of spiral stairs is the trademark of almost every lighthouse and the feature most likely to stimulate the imagination. Lightkeepers made at least four trips up and down these stairs each day, often carrying tools or heavy cans of fuel. Echoes were prominent and rapid changes in temperature made stairways screech and groan, spawning stories of ghosts. Kisses were stolen on the stairs and children's games played, but surprisingly there were few falls. At Ponce de Leon Inlet Lighthouse, the great stairway forms a nautilus of 213 individual steps, each one imprinted with footsteps of history.

Windows brought much-needed daylight into the dark interior of a lighthouse, and a cool breeze too. Keepers may have watched for the arrival of visitors or the approach of the dreaded district inspector from the privacy of a window like this one, high on the tower of Ponce de Leon Inlet Lighthouse.

Ponce de Leon Inlet Lighthouse, built in 1887, featured a homespun but functional kitchen (facing page). The head keeper's bedroom at Ponce de Leon Inlet Light (above) had humble furnishings, but served its purpose well.

Keepers in Skirts

The lighthouse women were made of wonderful fiber.
Hans Christian Adamson
Keepers of the Lights, *1955*

Many women have served our nation's lighthouses. Some were officially appointed as "laborers," others as assistant or principle keepers. But given the family nature of the work, it's likely any woman living at a lighthouse—wife, daughter, or sister—knew how to care for the beacon and did just that when needed.

The first woman in America to keep a lighthouse was Hannah Thomas, who tended Plymouth Twin Lights in the Massachusetts Bay Colony in 1776 after her husband marched off to serve in the Revolutionary War. John Thomas fell in battle, and since the lights stood on his land and his wife already knew how to tend them, she was hired as the lightkeeper.

Records for the early years of the lighthouse service are scant, but lists of lighthouse appointments stored in the National Archives show that beginning in 1828, about 125 women were appointed to lighthouse duty in the United States. Most served during the nineteenth century, before lighthouse work became complicated by machinery. Maryland and Michigan, for reasons unknown, had more women serve as lightkeepers than other states. Between 1944 and 1980, there were none, due to the dearth of women in the Coast Guard during these years and the service's reluctance to assign women to lighthouses. In the 1980s, the Coast Guard placed Karen McLean in charge of Maine's Kennebec River Light Station and Jeni Burr took over New Dungeness Lighthouse in Washington.

At least seventeen women tended southern sentinels. All were "lighthouse widows," married to lightkeepers who died while on duty. Two women served in Virginia: Amelia Deweese tended Old Point Comfort Light from 1857 to 1861 and Ella Edwards watched over Nansemond River Light from 1903 to 1906. In Georgia, Mary Maher lit the lamps at Oyster Beds River Beacon and Frances Sickel guarded the Tybee Beacon. No women are listed as having served in the Carolinas.

Florida, possibly because of the high mortality rate of its keepers, had at least thirteen women in charge of lighthouses. Sand Key Light's Rebecca Flaherty was one of the earliest, replacing her husband John after he died from yellow fever in 1830. Michaela Ingraham took over for her husband at Pensacola Light, upon his death in 1840. Several women served as interim assistant keepers, probably until a new assistant was hired, which explains the short tenures of women like Maria Andreau, who served five months at St. Augustine Light during 1859 (the only Hispanic woman ever to serve in the South); Kate Harn, who served at St. Augustine Light for six months during 1889; and Mary Madden, with a ten-month tour at Pensacola Lighthouse during 1869. In fact, Pensacola had six women on duty between 1840 and 1870.

Unquestionably, the belle of southern lighthouses was Barbara Mabrity. She began her life in service of the lights in January 1826, when her husband Michael Mabrity was assigned as the first keeper of the new Key West Lighthouse. Mrs. Mabrity was appointed as his assistant. The Mabritys were active in local government and well-respected in Key West. Early in 1832, they hosted John James Audubon on his visit to Key West. But a few months later Michael Mabrity died of yellow fever. In a time when women seldom nosed out men for jobs, Barbara Mabrity managed to secure the keeper's job at Key West Light. It's possible that the government awarded her the position as propitiation for being a widow with many children. She was fifty years old at the time.

By all reports, Mrs. Mabrity was an excellent lightkeeper and fearless woman. Her attention to the beacon during the great hurricane of September 1835 drew praise from citizens and mariners, and she was commended again during the storms of 1841 and 1842: "Mrs. Mabrity . . . has for a number of years performed the duties of her office with fidelity and to the satisfaction of the Collector of Customs." She also had concern for her family's safety during the Second Seminole War and was grateful for the soldiers on duty outside the lighthouse.

On October 10 and 11, 1846, Barbara Mabrity endured her worst ordeal when a destructive hurricane hit Key West. She remained by the lamps throughout the night as the storm increased. The following morning she was in the lantern cleaning when several people came to the lighthouse seeking refuge. Her six children also joined her in the tower, believing it to be the safest, strongest structure in the town.

Serene amid palm fronds and bright sunshine, Key West Lighthouse gives little hint of its long travail with storms. A devastating hurricane pummeled Key West in 1846 and severely damaged the 1826 tower. Its keeper, Barbara Mabrity, barely escaped with her life. Several of her children perished. The tower was rebuilt a few years later, and increased to its present height of eighty-seven feet in 1895.

Hours later, the old lighthouse walls began to crumble. Barbara led everyone down the stairs but just as she opened the door at the base of the tower, bricks came cascading down. She rushed outside, pulling one child behind her. The other twelve people in the tower died, including her other five children.

The Lighthouse Establishment built a temporary tripod light, and Mrs. Mabrity tended it until they completed the new tower in 1848. She remained the sole keeper until 1854, when the government appointed an assistant for her. With the onset of the Civil War, Barbara Mabrity was forced to sign an oath of allegiance to the Union or lose her job. She signed, but three years later she let slip her southern sympathies and was asked to resign. When she declined, Union officials removed her from her post. The eighty-two-year-old keeper retired to a quiet cottage in Key West, where she died in 1867.

The Coast Guard has not forgotten Barbara Mabrity's years of service. In July 1999, they launched a 175-foot keeper-class U.S. Coast Guard buoy tender bearing her name at Marinette Marine Corporation in Wisconsin. The home port of *Barbara Mabrity* (WLM-559) is Mobile, Alabama.

Large coastal light stations required multiple keepers to attend to the many duties and maintain the tower and its powerful optic. With their family members, the keepers formed a small interdependent community. At Ponce de Leon Inlet Lighthouse, a critical aid for shipping in northeast Florida, a principle keeper and two assistants shared the work. Their comfortable homes faced the entrance to the tower.

EPILOGUE

Lighthouse Redux

THERE ARE TWO WAYS OF SPREADING LIGHT: TO BE THE CANDLE OR THE MIRROR THAT REFLECTS IT.
Edith Wharton (1862–1937)

The whirr and whine of sandblasting machinery eclipses the buzz of insects and rustle of palm fronds on lonely Anclote Keys, Florida. When the wind is right, you can hear the clank of hammers and roar of machinery three miles away in Tarpon Springs. It's noise to which no one objects; there are no calls to the mayor or nasty letters printed in local newspapers. That's because International Chimney Corporation of Buffalo, New York, has begun a much-needed and anticipated $1.25 million restoration of the 1887 Anclote Keys Lighthouse.

Rust and graffiti fall away, revealing the sturdy iron framework of the tower, which was considered a marvel of cheap and durable engineering in its day. The lantern has been removed and parts of it shipped elsewhere for restoration. Warped metal plates on the stair cylinder and twisted braces holding the legs in place are carefully but firmly urged back into shape. New bolts replace century-old ones, and the concrete anchorage is tightened. Spiral stairs feel the rejuvenating footsteps of workers. The tower's entrance door, deformed by vandals who long ago tried to pry it open, is repaired. But first, a tree growing out of the concrete step beneath it is uprooted.

By autumn 2003, the project is nearing completion. Paint has restored a fresh look to the tower's spidery legs and sends a message of renewal to anyone passing by in a boat. The lantern has been replaced and a high intensity quartz beacon is in place, ready for a ceremonious relighting. The state park service has begun building a new dwelling behind the lighthouse. It will serve as a residence for a park ranger—a modern-day lightkeeper of sorts—whose presence alone will discourage vandalism and give the station a lived-in feeling. Connie Wiesehan, the ranger who will live on-site and the only woman ever assigned here as a lightkeeper, has grown to love the old iron tower standing strong and tall amid sabal palms. When the breeze tousles the palms' fronds, she thinks they seem to be whispering their approval of the revitalization project that is saving the disheveled old sentry and giving it a new mission.

"This is a special place for me," says Wiesehan. "When I'm out here and it gets quiet, I can step into any time I want. A lot of different people did this job in years past and they had to eke out a living out on this island. I'll have it easier, but there are still things about living here that will never change, like the responsibility of keeping the light. It may be a modern one that runs on its own, but I'll still check on it just like they did a century ago."

Restorers return the beacon to the tower on September 13, 2003, and dignitaries and members of the various groups that participated in the restoration effort attend a glorious relighting ceremony. Governor Jeb Bush proclaims September 13 as "Florida Lighthouse Day," with a celebration to be held annually on this day. From the beach north of Tarpon Springs, a chorus of excited voices shouts a countdown: "Ten, nine, eight . . . three, two, one, relight the light!" Residents watch through the deepening twilight air as the lighthouse beacon first glimmers, then flashes brightly after twenty years of darkness. A cheer goes up, flags wave, and some even shed tears for a deserving old soldier who has returned to his watch.

"Anclote Keys Lighthouse is back!" cheers Wayne Hawes, president of the Tampa Bay Harbour Lights Collectors Club, one of the groups that has devoted itself to the restoration of the lighthouse. "It was so rundown and vandalized we could hardly imagine it like this, looking new and vital again."

Pat McSparren, who was the first to imagine the lighthouse returned to its former glory, is speechless. One hand gently covers her mouth, quivering, as she pushes back tears of joy. She and her husband, Lary McSparren, spearheaded the restoration effort through a citizens support organization called the Gulf Islands Alliance. They teamed with Hawes' group and were able to secure funding and hurdle numerous political roadblocks.

"I have nightmares about what the lighthouse looked like before restoration," recalls Lary McSparren. "We've given it a thorough overhaul and also renewed its purpose. It's a real lighthouse again."

At this moment, the lighthouse clearly shines as a symbol of humanitarism.

Lighthouses Back on the Beam

"Old lighthouse new again," reads a *St. Petersburg Times* headline about Anclote Keys Light. It's a story heard time and again in recent years in the South and elsewhere in the nation. Lighthouses are experiencing a renaissance unimagined almost a century ago when the Bureau of Lighthouses automated the first lighthouse and began to unman or decommission a corps of aging sentinels. Of the roughly 670 lighthouses still standing in the United States, about half are in public hands as parks, muse-

Anclote Keys Lighthouse has come full-circle. Once a thriving light station that provided a critical service to seamen, it was unmanned in the late 1950s and deteriorated badly before being rescued by the citizens of Tarpon Springs. An aerial view during World War II (bottom) shows the station at its zenith, with civilian lightkeepers and U.S. Coast Guard patrols residing in its quarters (U.S. Coast Guard Archives). The station regained some of its former glory with restoration and relighting in 2003. Florida park ranger Connie Wiesehan, the new lightkeeper (top), now lives on site to deter vandalism and maintain the beacon. (Photograph courtesy of James Stouder)

ums, inns, or other creative conversions. The Coast Guard prompted this shift in ownership in 2000 when it announced it would excess all lighthouses and transfer them to government, civic, and private groups for stewardship. The Department of the Interior conducted the massive transfer program, reviewing applications from interested groups and awarding lighthouses to those best able to care for the towers and interpret them for public use.

Tybee Island Lighthouse was among the first old sentinels to be officially transferred. Cullen Chambers, director of the museum at the lighthouse, has a track record for reviving old sentinels and transforming them into educational facilities. Tybee Island is the site of one of the oldest light stations in the nation and one of the most complete, with all buildings from the late-nineteenth-century era intact and interpreted.

"We have almost 300 years of lighthouse history right here," Chambers says, referring to the 1746 establishment of a navigational aid on Tybee Island. He adds that Tybee Island Lighthouse, and all American lighthouses for that matter, have histories that mirror the growth of the nation. "As we grew as a people and a country, our lighthouse service grew with us. We can learn a lot about American history by studying lighthouses."

Some of the nation's most magnificent museums are found at lighthouses. Neighboring St. Augustine Lighthouse and Ponce de Leon Inlet Lighthouse are remarkably well-preserved and interpreted with extensive exhibits, archives, and educational programs that reprise old lighthouse traditions. St. Augustine's upkeep of the daily logbook is a good example of the vicarious lightkeeping experience practiced at some museums. Ponce Inlet's cat orphanage—a solution to unwanted kittens dropped off at the lighthouse—recalls the many animals that served as companions to the keepers. Both sites also conduct excellent outreach programs for schoolchildren, who study lighthouses as part of their state history curriculum.

The National Park Service offers interpretation and programming at lighthouses in its care at Assateague Island, Cape Hatteras, Bodie Island, Ocracoke, Cape Lookout, Fort Jefferson, and Cockspur Island, to name a few. Private and civic groups have taken the lead in lighthouse preservation as well, often with amazing results. The Coastal Georgia Historical Society saved St. Simons Island Lighthouse and has lovingly restored its interior and grounds, making it the most popular tourist destination on the island. More challenging is the goal of a small group of determined citizens in North Carolina who are replicating the Roanoke River Lighthouse. The Coast Guard sold the original structure in the 1940s and it now stands in the town of Edenton, where it is privately owned. Although the owners weren't willing to sell, local citizens felt it was important to regain this piece of their history, since none of the screwpile lighthouses that once stood in the state still exist. Its reconstruction is a painstaking process, funded by small change and big hearts.

Not all restoration efforts are characterized by such cooperation, nor are all untarnished. The Outer Banks Conservancy restored the beautiful Currituck Beach Lighthouse to its antebellum glory in the 1980s, then fought a tough battle to retain ownership of it in 2003, when the surrounding county tried to wrest it away from the group. "This was a clear-cut case of political maneuvering," says Timothy Harrison, president of the American Lighthouse Foundation. "The county saw a chance to take over a popular and profitable museum. They offered no help to the OBC in its effort to save and restore the lighthouse, but they were willing to take over and reap the rewards when the work was done."

Similarly, the effort to save Cape Hatteras Lighthouse by relocating it 2,900 feet back from the sea's edge had its opponents. The century-old sentinel was in danger of being lost to erosion, and moving it was estimated to cost more than $10 million. Opinion was polarized, with many local residents of Dare County contesting the move as too expensive and unnecessary. They preferred other methods to shore up the tower's foundation, such as groins and seawalls. Those in favor of moving the tower prevailed, however. Lighthouse groups across the nation barraged the National Park Service with letters entreating the agency to save Cape Hatteras Lighthouse, a treasured landmark on the Outer Banks and the tallest lighthouse in the nation.

International Chimney Corporation, which previously relocated three lighthouses in New England, moved the big tower. The media arrived to document the move, giving the project plenty of press. Joe Jakubic, manager for the job, was so confident in the methods used to jack up and roll the tower to its new location, he spent much of his time underneath the tower as crews rolled it over a railway system designed especially for the project. The actual physical move took twenty-three days, but months of planning had made it possible. At the completion of the move, the Outer Banks Lighthouse Society hosted a historic relighting ceremony and later held a reunion of former Cape Hatteras Lighthouse keepers.

At the forefront of American lighthouse museums and the first light station to be officially excessed by the U.S. Coast Guard, St. Augustine Lighthouse has been restored and interpreted by the Junior Service League of St. Augustine. Its keeper's house was completely rebuilt following a devastating fire in the 1980s, and now houses period furnishings, exhibits, meeting rooms, and a gift shop. The tall, boldly painted light tower features a tasteful Victorian entryway (bottom left). Visitors enjoy climbing the 216 steps to the lantern (top) and viewing the magnificent first-order lens (bottom right). The lens was shot out by teenaged vandals in the 1990s, but parents made restitution. The damaged lens panel was repaired for $140,000.

ASSATEAGUE LIGHT HOUSE
LIGHT HOUSE BOARD
ACTS OF CONGRESS

Shedding Light on Tomorrow

Saving old lighthouses and their ancillary buildings is important, but most preservation groups know that an equally vital part of their work is educating the public, namely children, to perpetuate the legacy of lighthouses. Educational programs include in-school programs, on-site activities, and more creative efforts, such as an annual history project sponsored by the Florida Lighthouse Association. The group awards prizes to students who research and write about a lighthouse in the state. St. Augustine Lighthouse has produced "Living and Working at a Lighthouse," an educational curriculum that presents lighthouse history for kids through photographs, narration, and stories, plus a special children's area of the museum.

The vanguard of lighthouse education for youth is the American Lighthouse Foundation, a national society that hosts several children's chapters, holds education conferences, and sponsors "Kids on the Beam," a program that assists schools and youth groups and beguiles children with a loveable mascot called "Lighthouse Kitty." The foundation calls its work "edu-tainment," a commingling of education and entertainment. The ethos is simple: when kids have fun learning about lighthouses and working to save them, they'll want to preserve and care for them as adults. "Saving a lighthouse is one of the best ways to teach kids about citizenship," says foundation president Timothy Harrison.

At risk of sounding trite, it's safe to say the future looks bright for lighthouses. Historic preservation legislation has assured that many will be saved, and not as gift shops, hamburger stands, mini-golf course icons, or shopping mall decorations—conversions that demean their historic integrity and leave little of their important history for the public to appreciate—but as precious artifacts of our maritime heritage. They have become treasured symbols of our everyday life, adorning T-shirts, mugs, lamps, key chains, greeting cards, even a series of stamps issued by the U.S. Postal Service in June 2003. The stamp series featured six notable southern lighthouses—Cape Henry, Cape Lookout, Morris Island, Tybee Island, and Hillsboro Inlet—and joined two other series issued in 1990 and 1995, which paid tribute to lighthouses throughout the nation. "You know something is big when it makes it onto a postal stamp," says Coast Guard historian Dr. Robert Brown.

Lighthouses also have appeared on state license plates, state quarters, and city logos. Their popularity as municipal and commercial symbols is evident in towns all along the southern coast. Cape Henry Light dominates the city seal of Virginia Beach, and St. Marks Lighthouse appears on the logo of St. Marks National Wildlife Refuge. Tybee Island Lighthouse is stitched onto its town's fire department patch, while the Outer Banks' stately lighthouses adorn the labels of the Weeping Radish Brewery and the Duplin Winery, to name just a few.

"Everybody loves lighthouses," says Wayne Wheeler, president of the U.S. Lighthouse Society, another national group devoted to lighthouse education and preservation. "They are cherished symbols of our national identity, like Mom's apple pie, hot dogs, and a white picket fence."

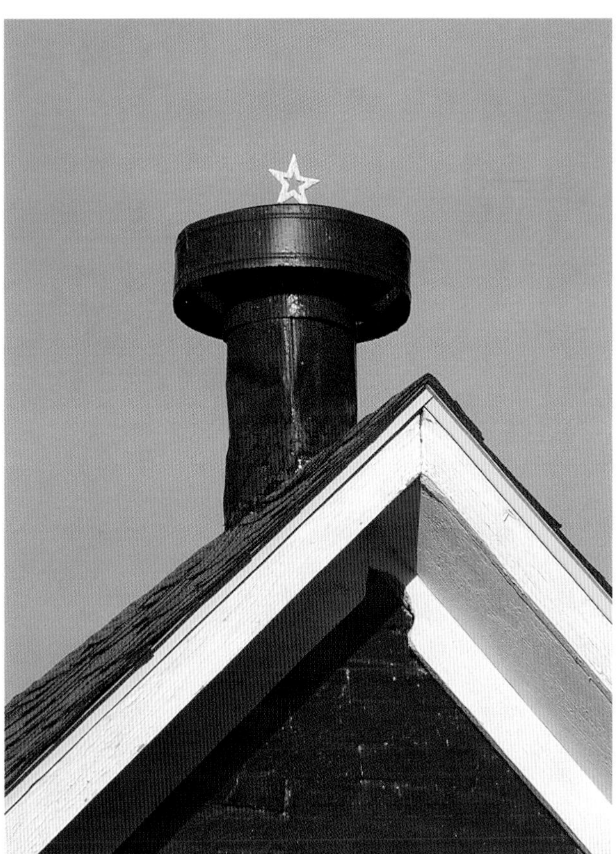

The focal point of Chincoteague National Wildlife Refuge, Assateague Island Lighthouse is a favorite stop for visitors. Its bright daymark makes it easily visible against a backdrop of verdant forest and tide marsh (facing page). The bright-red oil house sports a small star atop its air vent (above).

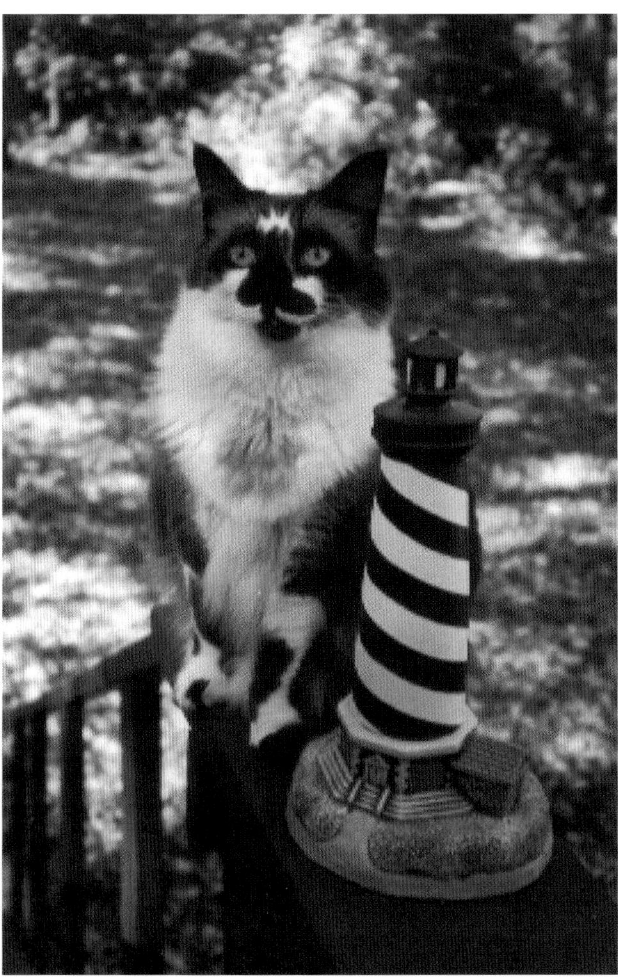

Educating tomorrow's lighthouse preservationists is a major goal of numerous groups and museums in the South. Docents of St. Augustine Lighthouse treat school children to lively in-school programs before students visit the site for an up-close look at an important working relic of Florida's past (facing page). A bit more imaginative is the American Lighthouse Foundation's "Kids on the Beam," an "edu-tainment" youth initiative with a comical cat as mascot that thinks "Lighthouses are purr-fect places to have fun and learn." (Above: Photograph courtesy of the American Lighthouse Foundation)

A Cast of New Keepers

Lighthouses in the traditional sense have lost maritime importance in the past half-century, and will someday be altogether obsolete. Once critical to navigation, they slowly have been upstaged by high-tech gadgetry and hold little importance for seamanship beyond the needs of the small boater. Satellites in geosynchronous orbit above our planet—metallic Global Positioning System sentries sending silent, invisible signals to ships anywhere in the world—are, in a sense, the new sentinels. They lack the majesty of a grand old light tower standing strong on a wave-washed shore. No white-whiskered, furrow-faced keeper is entrusted to look after their signals, but they provide dependable guidance all the same. As conventional lighthouses decline in importance and segue into new roles, they beam a metaphoric message to us about civility, cultural responsibility, and the need to perpetuate the past in the future.

"Who can argue against the importance of saving America's lighthouses for future generations?" asks lighthouse historian and author Robert Trapani, as if the thought of abandoning even one old sentinel—no matter how battered, lackluster, or inaccessible it is—might be unpardonable.

It's an attitude that has become widespread in lighthouse preservation, supported by a multitude of serious advocates. They are the new keepers of the lights, and their mantra is intoned with a heritage-conscious conviction.

As a bumper sticker for the American Lighthouse Foundation asserts: "Lighthouses are worth keeping."

Far in the bosom of the deep
O'er these wild shelves my watch I keep;
A ruddy gleam of changeful light
Bound on the brow of dusky night.
Sir Walter Scott,
Pharos Loquitur, *1814*

Guide to Southern Lighthouses

This appendix lists existing lighthouses in Virginia, North Carolina, South Carolina, Georgia, and Florida. Lights referred to as "active" are currently used as navigational aids and are maintained by the U.S. Coast Guard, often in cooperation with museums, historical and preservation societies, or private owners. Some lighthouses maintain commemorative beacons, but these lights no longer serve as guides for ships and do not fall under the care of the Coast Guard.

A Note to Lighthouse Visitors: Visitors must respect "no trespass" signs posted on or near lighthouses. Such signs are there for the protection of both the visitors and the often-fragile lighthouses. Many of the lights, especially those offshore, are sealed and locked, and the Coast Guard does not allow anyone to dock on them or climb on them. The easiest and probably the most appropriate way to view lighthouses is from a boat. Ferries and lighthouse cruises abound, and lighthouse lovers should have no trouble getting out onto the water to see their favorite beacons. Please enjoy the Southeast's beautiful lighthouses from the water or other unobtrusive public vantage points.

Virginia

Assateague Island Lighthouse
CHINCOTEAGUE

In 1867, a 142-foot brick sentinel with a first-order Fresnel lens replaced the original 1833 tower. The Coast Guard automated the lighthouse in 1965. Celebrated for its handsome red and white daymark, the lighthouse still stands sentry on the Chincoteague National Wildlife Refuge.

Cape Charles Lighthouse
KIPTOPEKE

A sixty-foot masonry tower stood on Smith Island at the northern entrance to the Chesapeake Bay from 1828 until 1864, when a brick tower replaced it. The current 184-foot pile lighthouse was built in 1905, automated in 1963, and shows a white beacon. Its magnificent Fresnel lens is on display at the Mariners Museum in Newport News, Virginia.

Cape Henry Lighthouse, Old
VIRGINIA BEACH

The octagonal stone tower at Cape Henry is the oldest lighthouse on the Chesapeake Bay, marking the bay entrance from 1791 until an iron-plate lighthouse replaced it in 1882. Adopted by the Association for the Preservation of Virginia Antiquities in 1930, it is now a public landmark at Fort Story.

Cape Henry Lighthouse, New
VIRGINIA BEACH

Built in 1882 to replace its aging predecessor, the 157-foot cast-iron tower was manned until 1984. Its white light shines for seventeen miles and a red sector marks dangerous shoals at the entrance to the Chesapeake Bay.

Chesapeake Lighthouse
VIRGINIA BEACH

From 1933 until 1965, when the Coast Guard built the ultra-modern Texas tower Chesapeake Lighthouse, a lightship guided ships approaching Chesapeake Bay. The light is the youngest sentinel in the South and it stands in 177 feet of water, fourteen miles off Cape Henry. The Coast Guard automated it in 1980.

Jones Point Lighthouse
ALEXANDRIA

The oldest existing inland waterway lighthouse in the nation marks sandbars at Jones Point on the Potomac River. Built in 1856, it was automated in 1919 and abandoned in 1926 in favor of a skeleton tower. Although the National Park Service owns it, members of the Mount Vernon chapter of the Daughters of the American Revolution actually care for the lighthouse. The group relit the light in the late 1990s.

The heart of every lighthouse is the brilliant light in its crown. As dusk falls over the eastern shore of Virginia, Assateague Island Lighthouse spills its golden light seaward. The majestic sentinel has been on duty since 1867.

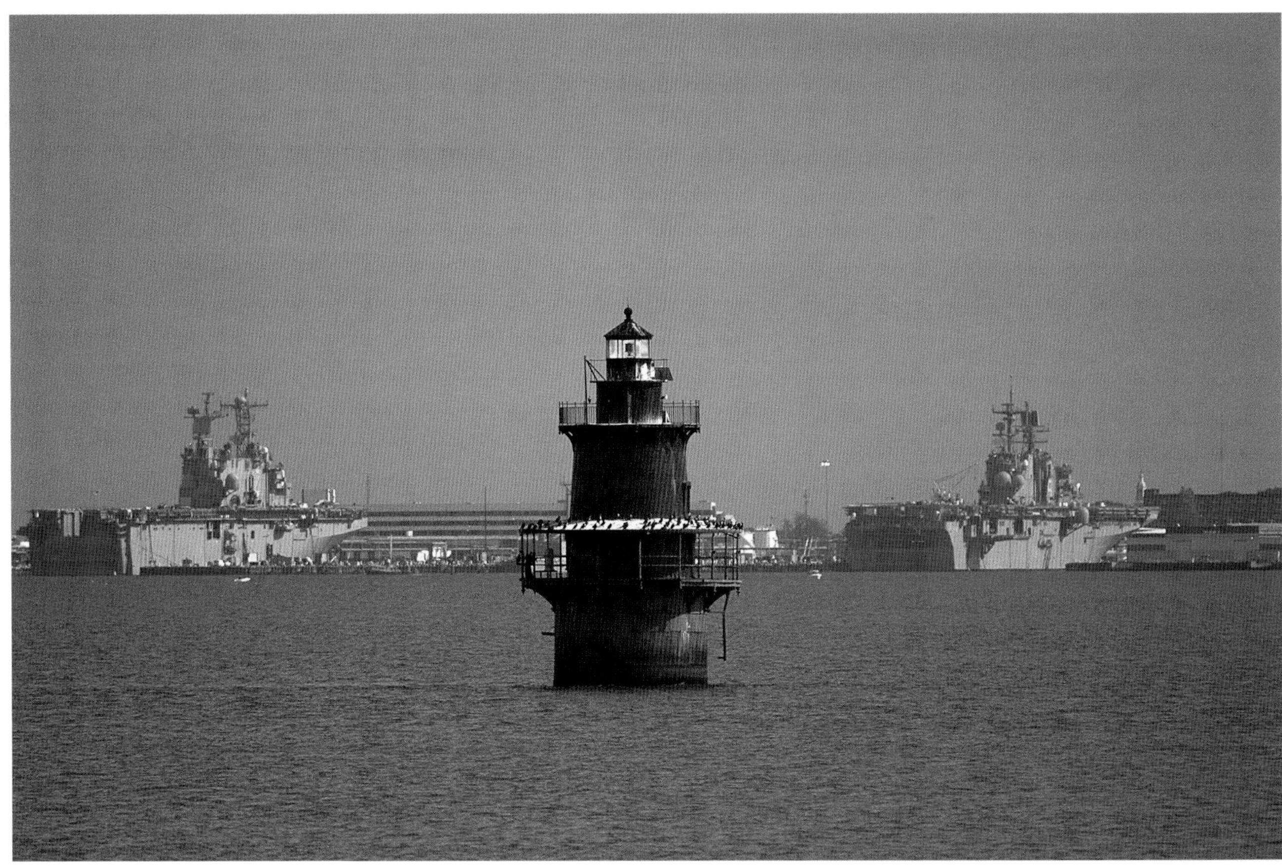

Above: *Caisson technology revolutionized lighthouse construction in the latter nineteenth century and allowed towers to be built on water-bound sites, where they could more easily mark perils. The 1891 Newport News Middle Ground Lighthouse sits atop an iron caisson, warning of shoals and shallows in Hampton Roads. Aircraft carriers at Norfolk's Naval Operating Base are visible in the background.*

Right: *The lightship that marked the entrance to the Rappahannock River in the 1820s was replaced with a screwpile tower in 1870. When an ice floe crushed the second lighthouse in 1893, a caisson sentinel was built. Called Wolf Trap Lighthouse, it takes its name from the HMS* Wolfe, *which stranded on the shoals at the river entrance in 1691.*

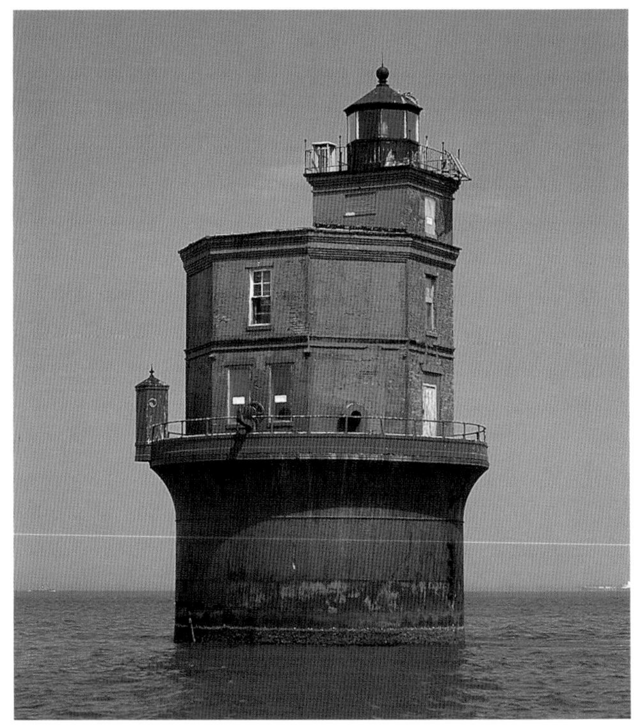

New Point Comfort Lighthouse

Bavon

Pointing the way to Mobjack Bay and the York River, the fifty-eight-foot, octagonal brick tower served from 1804 until erosion threatened it a century and a half later. The Coast Guard abandoned the light in 1963, and vandalism and weather have taken a toll on it in recent years.

Newport News Middle Ground Lighthouse

Newport News

The fifty-two-foot caisson tower that marked Middle Ground Shoal in Hampton Roads began service in 1891, showing a fourth-order lens. Automated in 1954, it was converted to solar power with a modern optic in 1988.

Old Point Comfort Lighthouse

Hampton

The fifty-four-foot stone tower established in 1802 is the second oldest lighthouse on the Chesapeake Bay. It marks the entrance to Hampton Roads, and though automated in 1972, it is still active. It retains its fourth-order Fresnel lens.

Smith Point Lighthouse

Reedville

Since 1802, five light towers and one lightship have marked the point along the southern approach to the Potomac River. The present fifty-two-foot caisson lighthouse was built in 1857 and automated in the 1970s.

Thimble Shoal Lighthouse

Hampton

The original tower was a screwpile structure built in 1872 to warn of shoals near the channel into Hampton Roads. A barge rammed the light in 1909, starting a fire that destroyed it. The Bureau of Lighthouses replaced the light with an iron caisson tower in 1914, and automated it fifty years later.

Wolf Trap Lighthouse

Matthews

First marked by a lightship, the present fifty-two-foot caisson lighthouse was built in 1894 to mark shoals at the entrance to the Rappahannock River. Automated in 1971, it shows a flashing white light.

North Carolina

Bald Head Lighthouse

Southport

The oldest lighthouse in North Carolina, the sentinel marked the Cape Fear River from 1789 to 1930. The original tower was built in 1795 and rebuilt in 1818. Following decommissioning, the 100-foot lighthouse stood empty until the Old Baldy Foundation adopted it and converted it into a museum.

Bodie Island Lighthouse

Nags Head

Built in 1848 and rebuilt in 1872, the 170-foot lighthouse stands at Oregon Inlet. Following automation in 1954, it became part of the Cape Hatteras National Seashore. A museum in the keeper's quarters highlights the tower's long history.

Cape Hatteras Lighthouse

Buxton

The Lighthouse Establishment built the first tower to mark the Diamond Shoals in 1803. It was damaged during the Civil War and rebuilt in 1870. The Coast Guard automated Hatteras Light in 1936, and, in 2000, the National Park Service arranged to have the tower moved back from the eroding shoreline. The tallest lighthouse in the nation, rising 198 feet, Cape Hatteras Light is the centerpiece of Cape Hatteras National Seashore.

Cape Lookout Lighthouse

Beaufort

Known for its distinctive checkerboard daymark, the lighthouse stands guard over Core Banks. The 1812 structure was rebuilt in 1859 following damage from beach erosion. The 169-foot tower was automated in 1983 and stands on the Cape Lookout National Seashore.

Currituck Beach Lighthouse

Corolla

Built in 1875, the 162-foot brick tower was once called Whalehead Light. It marks the northern extremity of the Outer Banks and guides ships approaching or leaving the Chesapeake Bay. The light was automated in 1939 and the Outer Banks Conservancy now operates it as a museum.

Oak Island Lighthouse
Caswell Beach
The tricolor concrete tower, built in 1958, replaced a series of lights that once marked the Cape Fear River entrance. Its modern optic is one of the most powerful beacons in the nation. The tower is 155 feet tall and has been automated. Its keeper's dwelling was destroyed by fire in 2001.

Ocracoke Lighthouse
Ocracoke
Originally called Shell Castle Light, the brick tower was built in 1800. After lightning destroyed the tower, it was rebuilt in 1823. Shell Castle Light has displayed a fourth order lens since 1899 and was automated in 1955. It stands sixty-five feet tall.

Price's Creek Lighthouse
Southport
Only a shell of brick remains of the range lights that once guided shipping along the Cape Fear River north of Southport. Built in 1848 and discontinued during the Civil War, the crumbling twenty-five-foot Price's Creek tower stands on private property at a bend in the river.

Roanoke River Lighthouse
Edenton
The Roanoke River entrance was marked by a lightship from 1835 until 1866, then by a screwpile lighthouse until 1885, when ice destroyed the structure. A new screwpile lighthouse went into service in 1886. The Coast Guard decommissioned the light sometime in the 1940s and later moved it to Edenton, where it is now a private home.

South Carolina

Cape Romain Lighthouse
McClellanville
Located on Lighthouse Island, the station was established in 1827 and served until 1858, when the Lighthouse Bureau built a taller brick tower. It exhibited a first-order beacon from 161 feet high until 1947, when the Board decommissioned the tower after the foundation failed, causing the lighthouse to lean. A portion of the 1827 tower still stands.

Georgetown Lighthouse
Georgetown
Built in 1801 to mark the entrance to Wynah Bay, the tower was seriously damaged during the Civil War and rebuilt in 1867. The eighty-seven-foot-tall light stands on North Island. It was automated in 1986 and is used for youth programs today.

Haig Point Rear Range Lighthouse
Hilton Head
Located on Daufuskie Island, the seventy-foot wooden cottage-style lighthouse was built in 1872 and worked in tandem with a front range light that no longer stands. The Coast Guard deactivated the light in 1934. A private owner restored the tower and keeper's dwelling in 1987 and relighted the beacon.

Harbourtown Lighthouse
Hilton Head Island
Built in 1970, this privately financed lighthouse stands on Sea Pines. Its octagonal shape and bright red-and-white daymark make it a popular tourist attraction. The lighthouse, standing ninety-feet tall, has always operated automatically.

Hilton Head Island Rear Range Lighthouse
Hilton Head Island
The ninety-four-foot straight pile steel tower, built in 1880, worked in tandem with a front range light, now gone, to guide shipping into Beaufort. After the Coast Guard discontinued the light in 1932, it deteriorated badly before a private owner refurbished and relit it in 1985.

Hunting Island Lighthouse
Frogmore
Established in 1859, Hunting Island Light collapsed during the Civil War, due to damage and erosion of its base. The government rebuilt the tower of cast iron in 1873 and relocated it in 1889 after erosion threatened to topple it. The Coast Guard deactivated the 136-foot-tall lighthouse in 1933. A state park surrounds it today.

Morris Island Lighthouse
Charleston
Morris Island, the oldest lighthouse site in South Carolina, received its first lighthouse in 1767. Ruined during the Civil War, the tower was rebuilt in 1876. It was automated in 1938 and decommissioned in 1962, after erosion washed away the island and left the tower standing in water.

Sullivans Island Lighthouse
Charleston
Built in 1962 to replace the obsolete Morris Island Lighthouse, the triangular tower is one of the youngest sentinels in the nation and the only U.S. lighthouse with an elevator. Standing 140 feet tall, it was automated in 1975.

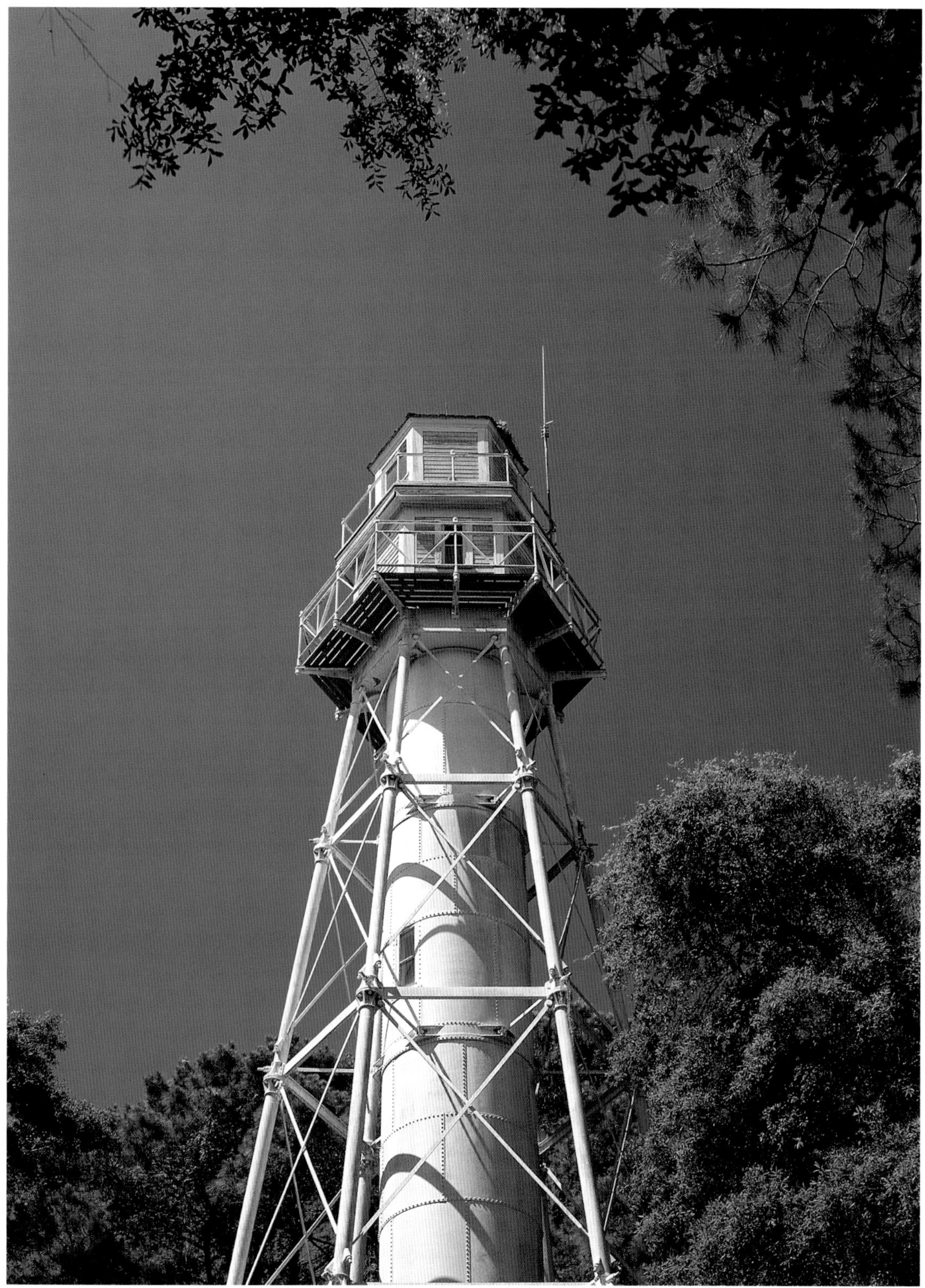

After it was decommissioned in 1932, Hilton Head Rear Range Lighthouse became a rusted hulk and an eyesore. It was refurbished in the late 1980s and now stands in an exclusive development called Palmetto Dunes. Long ago, the 1881 iron pile tower worked in tandem with a smaller front range beacon. In 1898, during a fierce hurricane, its keeper Adam Fripp suffered a heart attack inside the lantern and died. His twenty-year-old daughter Caroline took over her father's duties.

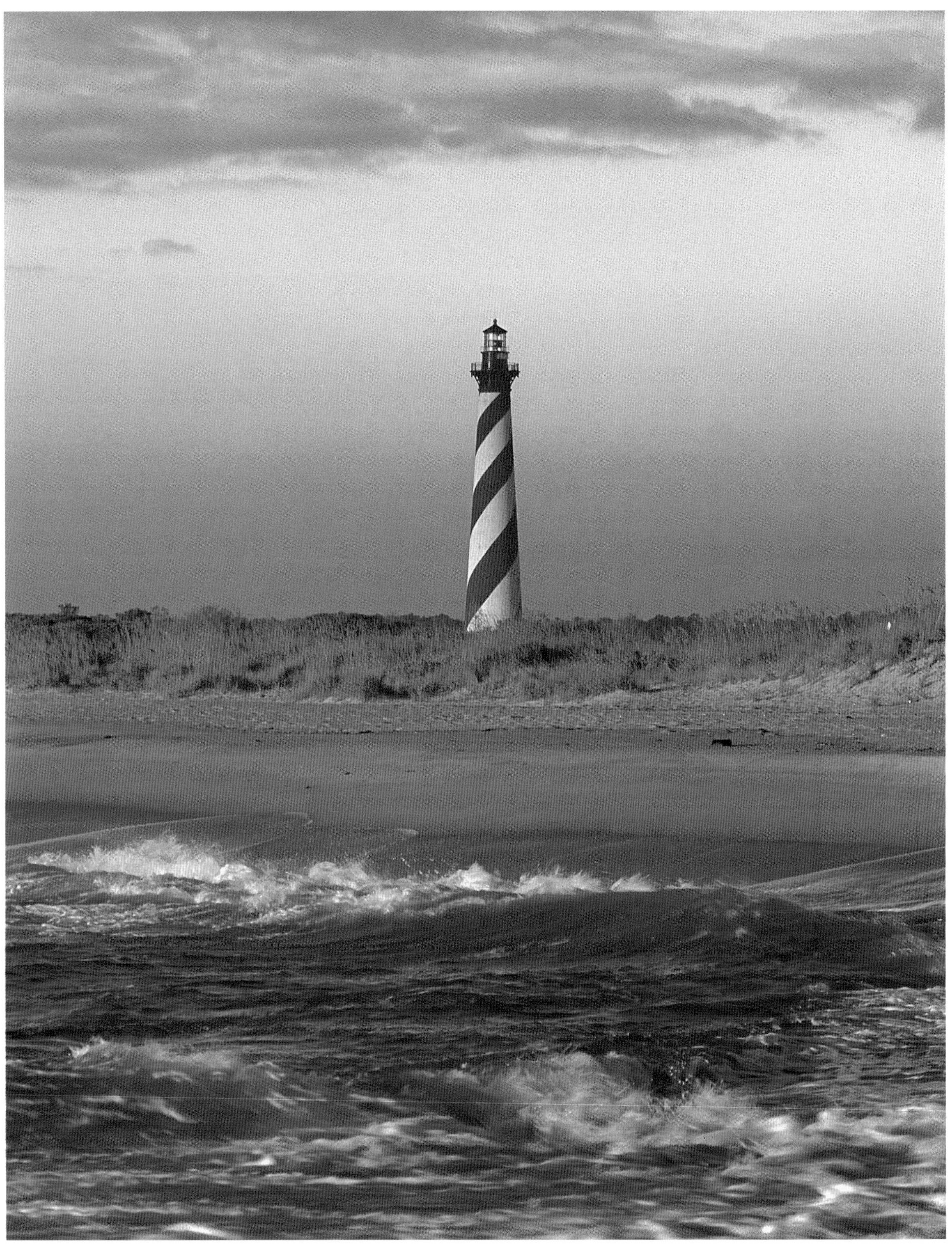

Big brother of all American lighthouses, Cape Hatteras Light reaches skyward 198 feet. It is the tallest lighthouse in the nation and one of the most photographed and visited.

Georgia

Cockspur Island Lighthouse
Tybee Island
Marking the northern approach to the Savannah River, the lighthouse was established in 1848 and rebuilt in 1857 due to deterioration. Constructed of brick on an oyster shell foundation, it stands forty-six feet tall. The light, which was deactivated in 1909, is part of Fort Pulaski National Monument.

Little Cumberland Island Lighthouse
Little Cumberland Island
Built in 1820 on the south end of the island, the fifty-foot lighthouse was a sister sentry to the sentinel on Sapelo Island. In 1839, crews relocated the tower to Fernandina Beach, Florida, and built a new tower on the north end of Little Cumberland Island. It served until it was decommissioned in 1915. A private association adopted the sixty-foot tower in 1967 and has maintained the exterior.

Sapelo Island Lighthouse
Darien
Established in 1820 on a barrier island marking the way to the port of Darien, the brick lighthouse showed a fourth-order lens from 1853 until deactivation in 1899. A steel tower replaced it in 1905 and served until it was dismantled in 1933. The old lighthouse was restored and relighted in 1999.

St. Simons Island Lighthouse
St. Simons Island
Built in 1811 as an octagonal stone tower, the lighthouse served the port of Brunswick. It was dynamited by Confederates during the Civil War and rebuilt in 1872. The 104-foot tower was automated in 1966. Its Victorian keeper's house is now a museum.

Tybee Island Lighthouse
Tybee Island
The oldest sentinel in Georgia, the lighthouse marks the mouth of the Savannah River. Its lower portion was constructed in 1773. It was heightened to 145 feet in 1867. Built of dressed stone, it showed a first-order lens and was automated in 1972. The Tybee Historical Society now operates the station as a museum.

Florida

Alligator Reef Lighthouse
Islamordada
Named Alligator Reef for a schooner that went aground there in 1822, the site received its first lighthouse in 1873. Made of wrought iron, it stands 150 feet tall and is painted black and white. It became automatic in 1963.

Amelia Island Lighthouse
Fernandina Beach
The 107-foot brick lighthouse was moved to its present site from Little Cumberland Island, Georgia, in 1839, to mark the entrance to the St. Mary's River. It has operated automatically since the 1970s and shows a revolving third-order lens. The island takes its name from the daughter of King George II of England.

American Shoal Lighthouse
Sugarloaf Key
Lit in 1880, the tower was the last iron screwpile lighthouse built in the Florida Keys. The 124-foot light was automated in 1963, and in 1990 the U.S. Postal Service featured American Shoal on a series of stamps.

Anclote Keys Lighthouse
Tarpon Springs
Built in 1887, the pile skeleton tower lit the entrance to the Anclote River. The ninety-six-foot tower was automated in 1953 and deactivated in 1985. A preservation group restored and relighted the tower in 2003.

Boca Grande Lighthouse
Gasparilla Island
The 1890 cottage-style lighthouse, which measures forty-four feet tall and stands on iron pilings, once marked the entry to Charlotte Harbor. The Coast Guard added a rear range light nearby in 1927. Although the light was deactivated in 1966, the Barrier Island Parks Society relighted the beacon twenty years later and maintains the site today.

Cape Canaveral Lighthouse
Cape Canaveral
Built of brick in 1848, the first tower was discontinued after the Civil War due to damage and inadequacy. Although a

139-foot cast-iron tower replaced it in 1868, this new tower was disassembled and moved farther inshore in 1894, after erosion threatened to topple it. The Coast Guard automated the light in 1965, removing its magnificent first-order lens to put it on display at Ponce De Leon Inlet Lighthouse.

Cape Florida Lighthouse
KEY BISCAYNE
The bottom sixty-five feet of the lighthouse date to 1825 and show scars of a fire set in 1836 by Seminoles. The Lighthouse Board increased the height to ninety-five feet in 1856, and the taller tower served until 1878, when Fowey Rocks Light replaced it. Restored and relighted by the state in 1996, it is the oldest structure in South Florida.

Cape San Blas Lighthouse
PORT ST. JOE
A brick lighthouse marked the wreck-riddled shore in 1848. Crews replaced the tower twice before building the current 101-foot skeleton tower in 1885. Automated in 1981, it was deactivated in 1996.

Cape St. George Lighthouse
LITTLE ST. GEORGE ISLAND
The present 1852 tower is the third lighthouse on this site. The first, erected in 1833, and its successor, built in 1847, both succumbed to storms. Erosion has plagued the seventy-four-foot tower since its inception. It was deactivated in 1995, and then repaired in 1999 after it began to lean. A private group hopes to preserve and relight it.

Carysfort Reef Lighthouse
KEY LARGO
The cast-iron tower, built in 1852 on the site of the wreck of the HMS *Carysfort*, was the first screwpile lighthouse on the Florida Reef. The tower is 112 feet tall and painted dark brown. It was automated in 1960.

Cedar Keys Lighthouse
SEAHORSE KEY
The small cottage-style sentinel went into service in 1854 as a guide into the Suwannee and Waccasassa Rivers. Standing thirty-three feet tall, it remained active until 1915. Today it serves as exhibit space for the Cedar Keys Historical Society.

Privately built, Harbourtown Lighthouse is widely recognized as a symbol of the lavish seaside golf resort at Hilton Head, South Carolina. It is an official navigational aid, however, albeit an unusual one. Visitors will find a gift shop at the top.

One of the oldest existing lighthouses in Florida, the quaint sentinel on Amelia Island has marked the entrance to the St. Mary's River since 1839. The tower has an unusual hand-hewn-granite spiral stairway.

Crooked River Lighthouse
Carrabelle
The iron-pile square skeleton tower went into service in 1895 to replace the Dog Island Light, which had washed away in a hurricane in 1873. At 115 feet, it is the tallest skeleton lighthouse on Florida's Gulf coast. Automated sometime after 1950, it was deactivated in 1995.

Dry Tortugas Lighthouse
Loggerhead Key
Built in 1858 to replace the aging lighthouse on Garden Key, the conical brick tower stands 151 feet tall. In 1945, an accidental fire destroyed the keeper's dwelling. The lighthouse was automated in 1978 and is now part of the Dry Tortugas National Park. The beacon is still active.

Egmont Key Lighthouse
Tampa
The first lighthouse was erected in 1848 but was destroyed by a hurricane a few years later. Its replacement went into service in 1858. Water damage forced the Coast Guard to remove the lantern in 1944 and reduce the tower's height to seventy-six feet. The Coast Guard automated the light in 1989. The beacon remains operative and the tower stands within Egmont State Park.

Fowey Rocks Lighthouse
Miami
The screwpile lighthouse was constructed just south of Key Biscayne in 1878 and is the northernmost of the reef lights. Nicknamed "The Eye of Miami," it stands 125 feet tall and is painted brown and white. It was automated in 1974.

Gasparilla Rear Range Lighthouse
Gasparilla Island
The pile-design iron skeleton tower on Gasparilla Island served in Lewes, Delaware, until it was discontinued in 1918. Then the Coast Guard dismantled the tower and moved it to the north end of Gasparilla Island to work as a rear range beacon with the Boca Grande Light. The tower is 105 feet tall and has always operated automatically.

Hillsboro Inlet Lighthouse
Hillsboro Beach
Marking Hillsboro Inlet and a dangerous stretch of coast where the Gulf Stream hugs the shore, the pile-design lighthouse was built in 1907. Local residents nicknamed it Big Diamond for the diamond-shaped astragals (window framwork) on its lantern. It stands 136 feet tall and was automated in 1974.

Jupiter Inlet Lighthouse
Jupiter
Built in 1860 to handle shipping headed into Fort Jupiter, the 155-foot tower is painted bright red and stands on a shell midden. Automated in 1965, it operates as an active lighthouse and a museum. The first-order lens had a unique panel repaired after damage during a 1927 hurricane.

Key West Lighthouse
Key West
First lighted in 1826, the lighthouse was severely damaged in an 1846 hurricane. Crews rebuilt the light in 1848 to a height of sixty-seven feet, and added another twenty feet of height in 1895. The beacon was automated in 1915 and the quarters became the home of the superintendent of the Seventh Lighthouse District. Today it is a museum.

Pensacola Lighthouse
Pensacola
The port's first lighthouse was built in 1824, but when the channel shifted, a new light was required. The 150-foot tower was inaugurated in 1859 and is the tallest lighthouse on Florida's Gulf coast. Automated after 1970, it remains an active aid to navigation on the Pensacola Naval Air Station.

Ponce de Leon Inlet Lighthouse
Ponce Inlet
Known as Mosquito Inlet Light when work began on the lighthouse in 1835, a bout of yellow fever halted construction. The brick tower was not completed until 1887. It is the second tallest lighthouse on the Eastern Seaboard, rising 175 feet. Today the Ponce de Leon Inlet Light houses a museum.

Rebecca Shoal Lighthouse
Key West
The last screwpile lighthouse built on the Florida Reef, the beacon was lighted in 1886 at a height of sixty-six feet above the water. Automated in 1925 with acetylene gas, the lighthouse became a target for vandals. The house was removed in 1953 and the beacon was placed on a steel superstructure. The entire station was rebuilt in 1985 to replace the outdated 1953 beacon.

St. Augustine Lighthouse
St. Augustine
The first lighthouse established in Florida went into service in April 1824 on the site of an old Spanish watchtower. Erosion and storms deteriorated the tower, and it was rebuilt to a height of 167 feet in 1874. It shows a first-order beacon. The refurbished keeper's dwelling now serves as a museum.

St. Johns Light Station
Mayport
The newest lighthouse in Florida, the eighty-four-foot concrete, art-deco lighthouse on Mayport Naval Station was built in 1954 to aid vessels approaching the St. Johns River. It exhibits an automatic Vega VRB-25 rotating beacon inside a tiny lantern room. A small museum is housed in its base.

St. Johns River Lighthouse
Mayport
The mouth of the St. Johns River has been guarded by four light towers and one lightship. The first tower went into service in 1830 but was rebuilt five years later. An eighty-foot-tall brick lighthouse replaced it in 1858. The brick tower was deactivated in 1929, and in 1954 the St. Johns Light Station replaced it.

St. Joseph Point Lighthouse
Port St. Joe
The first lighthouse was built in 1839 to mark St. Joseph Bay. It was decommissioned seven years later, but reinstated in 1902 with a forty-one-foot cottage-style sentinel. The light, abandoned in 1955, was transferred to a nearby metal tower. The Coast Guard sold the old lighthouse to a private owner who restored it in 1970.

St. Marks Lighthouse
St. Marks
Built in 1831 on the ruins of an old Spanish fort, the Lighthouse Board tore down the tower in 1842 and rebuilt it. The new masonry lighthouse was automated in 1957 and continues to serve mariners. It stands eighty-two feet tall and is the centerpiece of the St. Marks National Wildlife Refuge.

Sand Key Lighthouse
Key West
A masonry lighthouse stood on Sand Key from 1827 to 1846, when a hurricane toppled it. The replacement, built in 1852, is a 132-foot iron screwpile structure. It was automated in 1982, but caught fire in 1989. After restoration, it was relighted in 1996.

Sanibel Island Lighthouse
Sanibel Island
Built in 1884 to mark the entrance to the harbor at Punta Rassa, the brown pile-design tower stands on Point Ybel. Its kerosene lamp was switched to an automatic gas lamp in 1923, and then electrified in 1962. Since 1949, the U.S. Fish & Wildlife Service has cared for the station.

Sombrero Key Lighthouse
Marathon
The 156-foot screwpile lighthouse was built in 1858 on a key named by the Spanish for its hat shape. It is the tallest of the reef lighthouses and it was the first marine construction to feature galvanized metal. It was unmanned in 1960. The original first-order lens is on display at Key West Lighthouse Museum.

Tortugas Harbor Lighthouse
Garden Key
Built in 1826 on Garden Key, sixty miles west of Key West, the seventy-foot stone tower stood a lonely watch until 1847, when the government built Fort Jefferson around it. The lighting of a new lighthouse in 1858 on Loggerhead Key downgraded the Dry Tortugas Light, but it was still used as a harbor beacon. It was rebuilt in 1874 as a boilerplate tower atop the fort wall. Deactivated in 1921, it is now part of Fort Jefferson National Monument.

One of the oldest structures in the Florida Panhandle, Cape St. George Lighthouse has struggled with the elements throughout its career. It is the third lighthouse to stand on the cape; erosion and hurricanes wiped away its predecessors. The tower was stabilized a few years back by Save the Light, a nonprofit group out of Apalachicola that would like to see the lighthouse moved back from the sea.

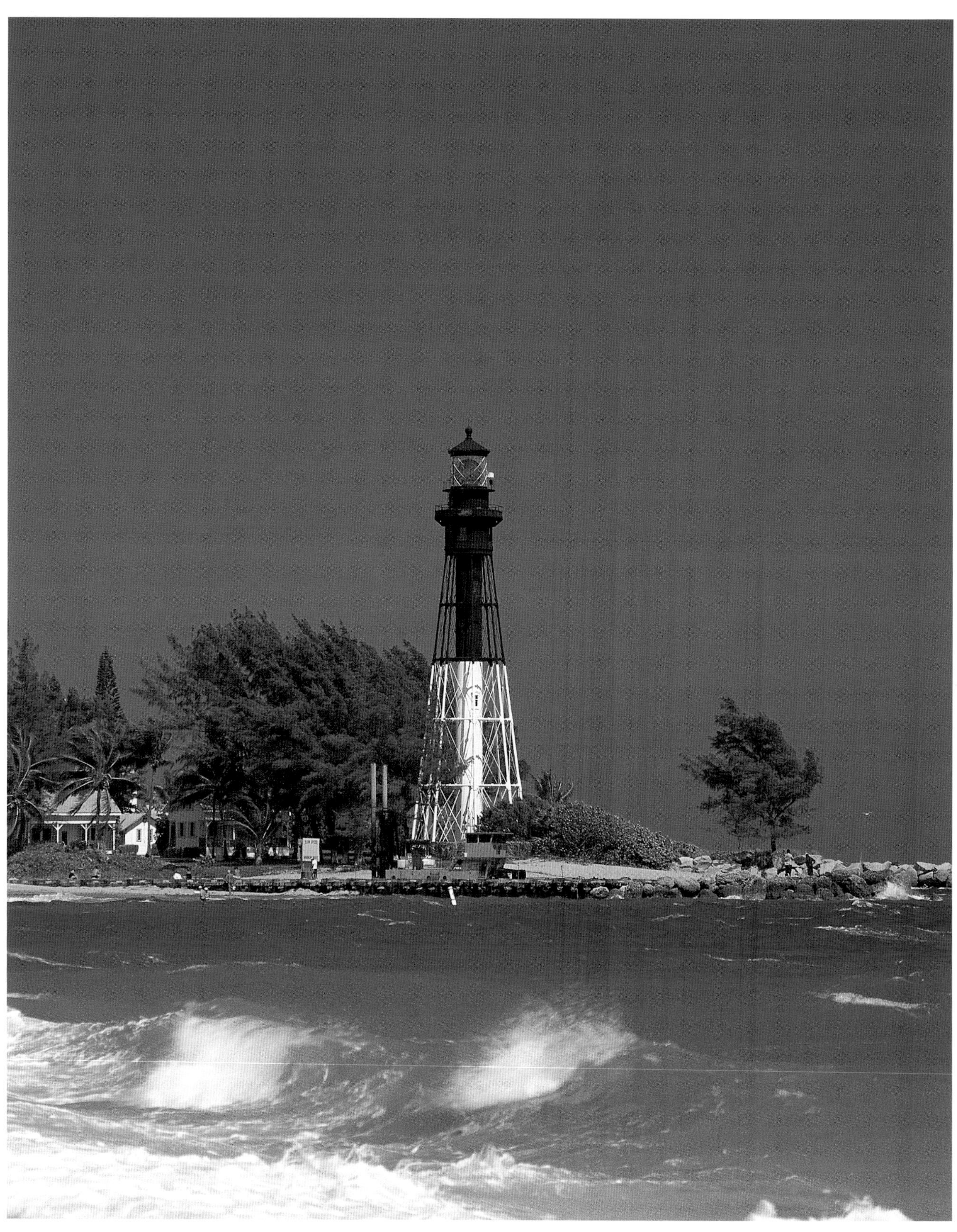

Fabricated in pieces at a Chicago foundry, Hillsboro Inlet Lighthouse was moved by train to Florida and assembled at Pompano Beach to brighten the dark space between Jupiter and Key Biscayne. It went into operation in March 1907 at Hillsboro Inlet. Local residents have nicknamed the tower "Big Diamond" for the diamond-shaped windows in its lantern.

Bibliography

Carr, Dawson. *The Cape Hatteras Lighthouse: Sentinel of the Shoals.* Chapel Hill, NC: University of North Carolina Press, 1991.

Clifford, Mary Louise & J. Candace Clifford. *Women Who Kept the Lights.* Williamsburg, VA: Cypress Communications, 1993.

De Wire, Elinor. *Guardians of the Lights: Stories of U.S. Lighthouse Keepers.* Sarasota, FL: Pineapple Press, 1995.

——. *The Guide to Florida Lighthouses.* Sarasota, FL: Pineapple Press, 1987.

——. *Sentries along the Shore.* Gales Ferry, CT: Sentinel Publications, 1997.

Dean, Love. *Lighthouses of the Florida Keys.* Sarasota, FL: Pineapple Press, 1998.

Duffus, Kevin P. *The Lost Light: The Mystery of the Missing Cape Hatteras Fresnel Lens.* Raleigh, NC: Looking Glass Productions, 2003.

Grant, John, and Ray Jones. *Legendary Lighthouses.* Old Saybrook, CT: Globe Pequot Press, 1998.

Holland, F. Ross. *Great American Lighthouses.* Washington, D.C.: Preservation Press, 1989.

Hurley, Neil. *Lighthouses of the Dry Tortugas.* Aiea, HI: Historic Lighthouse Publishers, 1994.

Jones, Ray. *The Lighthouse Encyclopedia.* Guilford, CT: Globe Pequot Press, 2004.

Kachel, Kenneth. Revised and updated by Jeremy D'Entremont. *America's Atlantic Coastal Lighthouses.* Wells, Maine: Lighthouse Digest, 2000.

McCarthy, Kevin. *Georgia's Lighthouses and Historic Coastal Sites.* Sarasota, FL: Pineapple Press, 1998.

Noble, Dennis L. *Lighthouses and Keepers: The U.S. Lighthouse Service and its Legacy.* Annapolis, MD: Naval Institute Press, 1997.

Roberts, Bruce, and Ray Jones. *Southern Lighthouses.* Old Saybrook, CT: Globe Pequot Press, 1989.

Stick, David. *Lighthouses of North Carolina.* Raleigh, NC: North Carolina Department of Cultural Resources, 1980.

Taylor, Thomas W. *Florida's Territorial Lighthouses 1821–1845.* Allandale, FL: Florida Sesquicentennial Publications, 1995.

Zepke, Terrence. *Lighthouses of the Carolinas.* Sarasota, FL: Pineapple Press, 1998.

Index

About the Author and Photographer

Photograph by Jonathan De Wire.

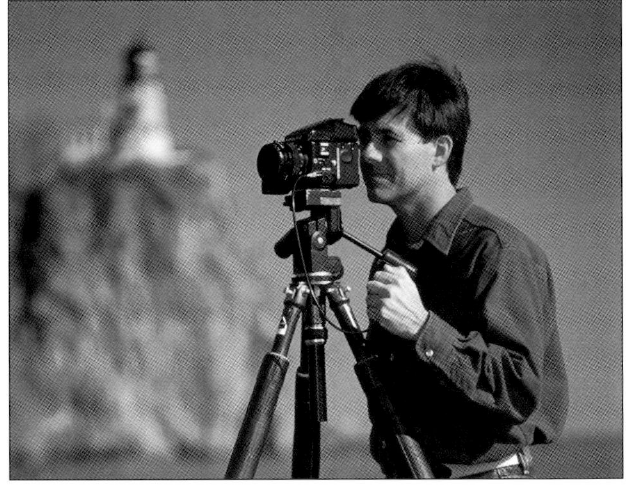

Photograph by Denise Dempster.

Elinor De Wire has been researching lighthouses for more than twenty-five years. She has written eight books and more than seventy articles on the topic. Her travels to more than five hundred lighthouses worldwide are the focus of her lectures and articles. Audiences from Maine to Hawaii have enjoyed her slide presentations on lighthouses, and she has discussed the topic on various radio and television programs throughout the United States. She writes columns for *The Beachcomber* and *Lighthouse Digest*. She also serves in a variety of capacities for several non-profit lighthouse preservation groups and chairs the youth initiative for the American Lighthouse Foundation.

Daniel Dempster has been a professional photographer since 1989, when four of his images were selected for a show at the Kentucky Derby Museum. Since then his beautiful photographs have regularly graced the pages of many calendars, posters, books, and publications. In 1990, Daniel was selected to be official photographer for the Kentucky Derby Festival, a position he held for twelve years, and in 1993, he won two International Festival Association gold awards. His work encompasses all of his many interests, which include travel, wildlife, bird dogs, thoroughbreds, hiking, canoeing, and almost anything involving the great outdoors. Daniel and his wife have had an interest in lighthouses for many years and photograph them any time they are traveling along the varied coastlines of the United States. This is the second book Daniel has published with Voyageur Press. His first, *Lighthouses of the Great Lakes*, was released in September 2002.

Daniel makes his home in the rolling hills of southern Indiana with his wife Denise, his two children Jason and Julia, and their three dogs and three cats.